G000243890

Faces of Your Soul

Rituals in Art, Maskmaking, and Guided Imagery with Ancestors, Spirit Guides, and Totem Animals

Elise Dirlam Ching and Kaleo Ching

Foreword by Matthew Fox

North Atlantic Books
Berkeley, California

Copyright © 2006 by Elise Dirlam Ching and Kaleo Ching. All rights reserved. No portion of this book, except for brief review, may be reproduced, stored in a retrieval system, or transmitted in any form or by any means—electronic, mechanical, photocopying, recording, or otherwise—without the written permission of the publisher. For information contact North Atlantic Books.

Published by
North Atlantic Books
P.O. Box 12327
Berkeley, California 94712

Cover art by Kaleo Ching
Cover design by Suzanne Albertson
Book design by Lyn 'Unihipiliowailelepualu Hilliard

Printed in the United States of America

Distributed to the book trade by Publishers Group West

Faces of Your Soul: Rituals in Art, Maskmaking, and Guided Imagery with Ancestors, Spirit Guides, and Totem Animals is sponsored by the Society for the Study of Native Arts and Sciences, a nonprofit educational corporation whose goals are to develop an educational and cross-cultural perspective linking various scientific, social, and artistic fields; to nurture a holistic view of arts, sciences, humanities, and healing; and to publish and distribute literature on the relationship of mind, body, and nature.

ISBN-13: 978-1-55643-590-4

Faces of Your Soul

To the Divine Spirit in Each of Us

Mahalo

Mahalo nui loa to the Acupressure Institute, California Arts Council and National Endowment for the Arts, California Institute of Integral Studies, Haight Ashbury Free Clinic's Jail Psychiatric Services, Institute of Transpersonal Psychology, John F. Kennedy University, Naropa University-Oakland, New College of California, Oakland Festival at the Lake, San Francisco Bay Area public schools, San Francisco Jail Health Services, San Francisco Sheriff's Department, San Francisco State University, and the University of Creation Spirituality and to the caring staff and faculty of these institutions where we have done much of our work and to the students who have contributed their images and stories that so greatly enhance this book.

To the special people who have been inspirations to us in processes involved in the evolution of this book: Lanakila Brandt, Dane Kaohelani Silva, and Maka'ala Yates for their sharing of *aloha, lomilomi,* and Hawaiian healing arts and culture; Bre Carrington and Sas Colby, artists and educators for the Oakland Festival at the Lake 1,000 Faces Maskmaking Project; Randal Churchill, Marleen Mulder, and the late Ormond McGill of the Hypnotherapy Training Institute; Jackie Clark, Joe Goldenson, Barbara Sutton, and all of Elise's colleagues at San Francisco Jail Health Services; Ruth Cox, holistic health educator; Mardena Creek, the late Frances Mayhew Rippy, and Thomas Thornburg of the Ball State University English Department; Jane DeCuir, our maskmaking model; Sharon Dirlam, sister, and her husband, John McCafferty, advisors; Aileen Donovan and Andy and Mary Franklin, our prayer family; Don Dugal, Jeff Dunn, Murray Turnbull, and Maile Yawata of the University of Hawai'i Art Department; Clarissa Pinkola Estes, Jungian analyst, storyteller, and healer; the Acupressure Institute's mentors of Traditional Chinese Medicine, especially founder Michael Reed Gach, Joseph Carter for his consultation on the acupressure contents of this book, Candace Coar, Alice Hiatt, Sylvia Nachlinger, and Brian O'Dea; the late Ray Gatchalian, peace activist; Deborah Gee and Blair Gershkow of 9 Star Productions; Jose Hobday, Franciscan sister; Jeff Kitzes of the Empty Gate Zen Center; Lynne McCall of WildCare; Ruth Morgan, art activist; Jo Robinson, director of Jail Psychiatric Services; Deborah Schwartz, our cupid; the late John Sommers of the Tamarind Institute and the University of New Mexico; Luisah Teish, priestess of Oshun; the late Michael Tom, artist of Kaimukī; Rodney Yee, yoga teacher; and to our many teachers of Taiji and Qigong.

To Michael Grady, for his enthusiasm, support, and leadership as chair of the Arts and Consciousness Program at John F. Kennedy University, where we have taught for the past fifteen years. To Matthew Fox—author of many books and founder of the University of Creation Spirituality and Naropa University-Oakland, where we taught for nine years—for his support and encouragement so eloquently articulated in his foreword for this book. To Gilles Marin, healer and founder of the Chi Nei Tsang Institute, for introducing us to North Atlantic Books. To everyone at North Atlantic Books who makes the sharing of this book possible and the producing of it a delight, especially publishers Richard Grossinger and Lindy Hough, project editor Anastasia McGhee, art director Paula Morrison, cover designer Suzanne Albertson, and copy editor Adrienne Armstrong.

A very special *mahalo* to Pili (Lyn 'Unihipiliowailelepualu Hilliard) for his abundant *aloha,* for his mastery in designing this book, and for his contributions to this book's Hawaiian language entries.

To our ancestors, our families, and our parents, James and Nancy Ching and Art and Edith Dirlam. To the people of Hawai'i and their spirit of *aloha.* To our guides from the spirit world. To the winged and four-legged creatures, especially our Australian shepherd companion, Teekkona.

Contents

Illustrations

Unless noted, all photographs are by Kaleo Ching

All photographs of Kaleo's masks and paintings are by Lee Fatheree

Additional photographs by Elise Dirlam Ching, Rob Lee, Charlie Lucke,
John McCafferty, John Pearson, Pili, and Rebecca Prongos

Foreword

In this marvelous and practical book, Elise and Kaleo Ching share their many years of deep teaching, deep reflection, and deep practice. Their work, drawing on ancient practices from many spiritual traditions, is now being shared in a very special way so that others can learn and teach themselves and others. A great gift is being given us in this book.

And we need such gifts today. We are hungry for such learning. For it is clear that in our perilous time, institutions of education and of religion are rarely providing the spiritual practices that we need to deepen our journeys and strengthen our souls for the experiences of joy and of darkness that beckon us all. Whether scandals of religion or politics, military or corporation, the shadow sides of our human nature are being exposed on a daily basis from the news broadcasters and from Internet chat circles.

What to do?

Return home. Take care of oneself and in the process reach out to others. Do one's inner work. We have to go "back to the drawing boards," back to purify our own intentions, to deepen our own morality, to get in touch with our own deepest values and beliefs, our own origins. And begin anew.

That is what this book invites us to do. To draw on our deepest capacities for self-reflection and finding inner peace in meditation, in guided imagery, and in journaling in order to expand our creative processes. But such an inner-to-outer journey is by no means a private journey. Though it is personal and often daring in its need for solitude, it is never private. Many are the souls past and present who take the journey with us.

And so Elise and Kaleo instruct us on the presence of spirit guides and how to connect to them, on meeting one's totem animal and how to connect to it (for the animal in each of us is another spirit guide willing and eager to assist us). We have assistance—Westerners call them "angels"—from many sources. Our ancestors also are eager to lend a hand, to open and heal our hearts, to render us strong and full of courage for the journey that accompanies creativity. And this book shows us ways to connect to the ancestors.

This book is special insofar as the authors speak so bluntly in the first person, sharing their stories, their poetry, their encounters. This is not a book of theory; it is a book of practice. This is not a book of ideology or denominationalism; it is a book of universal practices on the path to spiritual, emotional, and creative awareness. It is a book of deep ecumenism in practice. That makes it especially timely for our post-modern times.

Inviting us to connect to our totem animal is one more evidence that we are being led on a path that is deeper than any one spiritual tradition. For what animal ever went to war over a religious ideology? The deeper path offered here is able to serve to awaken our spirit and therefore our traditions. Drawing on ancient Qigong practices, we learn to invoke many animal forms: the eagle, bear, dragon, horse, deer, tiger, dolphin, wolf, crane, snake, cock, monkey. We learn that animals are our ancestors too and they are with us in deep ways. This book guides us to explore the ancient wisdom of Qigong animal awareness, to move as the animal, to write "our animal's story." And always to listen to this wisdom of deep instincts and voices of nature; and in so doing, we strengthen our awareness, grounded-ness, and connectedness as we move along the path of self-discovery.

Maskmaking is about journeying beneath the masks we wear and touching the soul. It is about community. Our ancestors have used masks and the body in ritual, healing, and transformation. The manifestations through maskmaking of inner dimensions of experi-ence take multiple forms ranging from that of warrior to goddess, healer, demon, wounded child, matriarch, totem animal, and others. We are instructed to work with a partner, each making the other's mask. We are maskmaker and we are maskgiver. We also learn to dialogue with our mask.

In our culture, we all wear many masks. But we are free to choose which ones truly suit us, which ones truly tell our inner truth. With the instructions from this book we can arrive at the most authentic of our masks, the deep and true mask, not the outer and superficial mask. A true image of our inner self, that self that expresses the original blessing that each of us embodies, the "image of Divinity" waiting to emerge. What a rich and powerful expe-rience it is for us to massage and sculpt and then to design and play with our masks—and then to listen to them as they tell us of our own, often forgotten, secrets, our own trea-sures of mystery and awe.

Over the nine years that Kaleo and Elise have taught classes in Qigong and Maskmaking at the University of Creation Spirituality (now called Wisdom University), I have seen numerous masks and listened to countless stories from students who have fashioned these masks: always stories of surprise, of magic, of wonder, of healing. Stories that tell how profoundly this process has touched the hearts, souls, and bodies of the students.

And why not? For it is so rare in our culture to be invited inside one's own soul to express what is truly there. The great mystic Meister Eckhart taught us this truth seven centuries ago when he said: "The truth does not come from outside in but from inside out and passes through an inner form." The inner form here is the form derived from entering the "inner sanctum" of our deep selves first and giving birth from inside out.

I am reminded of a story Kaleo told me years ago from his experience of sharing mask-making with maximum security psychiatric inmates in the San Francisco County Jail (the fact that Elise has worked as a Registered Nurse in the County Jail for the past twenty-plus years and Kaleo has chosen to teach in such a setting shows how real their teaching is and how real their spiritual practices are; for real spirituality goes not solely to comfortable retreat centers established in idyllic places of harmony, hot tubs, and happy vistas, but to the trouble spots of the world just as readily). Kaleo said that some of the inmates would come up to him and say, "This is the first time in my life I have ever experienced inner stillness."

Perhaps we have in these epiphanies some concrete evidence of the power of meditation and the practices of this book. Perhaps we have here the real key to "crime prevention," "self-hatred prevention," and "soul-loss prevention." That real key is spelled out in these pages: It has to do with finding stillness and the truth that stillness brings. And then finding the truth about ourselves—about our conditions as human beings in a very imperfect world, about our capacities for creativity, imagination, growth, healing, and making deep choices.

"Nothing in all creation is so like God as stillness," said Meister Eckhart. It is from this stillness that God—by whatever name—is born. And we are born and re-born as well.

The body totem exercises also invite us to make peace and harmony with what may have been a deep injury of a physical as well as emotional or sexual or spiritual rupture. The exercises recommended in this section truly carry out the need to bring together body, mind, and spirit to heal, because when we are injured or abused all elements of our being get abused together. The healing must be as broad as was the injury. Intimacy and joy, awe and gratitude and reverence return when these exercises are practiced.

What does our species need more than these things today? Do we really need more $140 million cathedral buildings? Do we really need more religious propaganda and wars in the names of our various favorite Deities? Do we really need more museum-going and photo ops of religious places reduced to tourist meccas? Do we really need more dogma police and inquisitors to guard over our ever-dwindling religious orthodoxies?

Or do we need the spiritual work, the inner work, that all healthy religion was meant to awaken?

If so, then this book is spot-on and its timing is perfect. For this book truly presents us with theory and practice to care for the inner self in preparation for our outer service. From such care, our "outer work," that is to say our work of service and mending of the world, will find an authentic and a brave grounding. With that, hope and healing can happen.

Matthew Fox, June 2005

Matthew Fox is Founder of the University of Creation Spirituality (now called Wisdom University) and author of twenty-six books including *Original Blessing, The Reinvention of Work, Creativity: Where the Divine and the Human Meet, One River, Many Wells: Wisdom Springing from Global Faiths, A Spirituality Named Compassion*, and his most recent, *A New Reformation!*

Universal Spirit Meditation

Go to a serene place in nature and assume a meditative posture familiar to you. As your eyes gently close, let your mind receive the comfort of your haven. Feel the temperature around you. Let your feet spread over the soft welcoming earth beneath you. Let your spirit enter into the spaciousness of your inner being.

Breathe softly, deeply. Do you smell a fragrance, hear a sound, see a color?

Inhaling, allow your breath to enter your nostrils and glide up into your mind's eye. Listen to the sound, the vibration of your mind. Listen as your breath opens like a blossoming lotus, spreading, expanding, then pressing gently into the inner lining of your cranium and releasing. *Ask the Universal Spirit for clarity and vision on your journey, and let go.*

Let go, and the breath falls like gentle rain, the rain of Hawai'i, *ka ua li'ili'i.* Breath glides into your throat and descends into the spaciousness of your heart. What are the colors, the sounds of gentle rain as it falls in your chest? Breath expands, pressing gently into the cavern walls of your inner ribs, then softly releases. *Ask the Universal Spirit for understanding and compassion on your journey, and let go.*

Let go, and the breath falls like gentle rain, *ka ua li'ili'i,* through your body. What is the sound of rain falling into the ocean in your pelvis? What are the temperatures and textures as it descends deep within? Can you feel the embryo of creativity in the cavern of your pelvis? Hear its breathing? Can you feel your breath as it travels like a wave across the spacious ocean—a wave spreading—and pressing gently into the muscular walls of your pelvis—and then releasing, with kindness? *Ask the Universal Spirit for abundance and creativity on your journey, and let go.*

Breath falls like gentle rain through your legs, washing and cleansing, descending into Gaia, the mother. Can you feel her kindness and love? Pause now and enjoy her embrace.

As you inhale, your breath ascends. What is the fragrance of Gaia as it ascends lightly through your body and into the heavens? Exhaling, allow this fragrance to descend from the heavens. What is the sensation of gentle rain falling from the heavens, entering your body, cleansing and purifying, then flowing into the basin of your pelvis?

Your breath is soft as you inhale. Gratitude travels into every cell in your body. Breathe gently, then release the blessings of your mind, heart, and body into the world.

Introduction

In this book we will be exploring the holistic process combining meditation, acupressure, guided imagery, journaling, art, and maskmaking. Some of the introductory and exploratory material also appears in our upcoming book on Qigong and the creative process.

- **Meditation** (lying, sitting, standing) guides us into a quiet and centered relationship with our interior wilderness.

- **Acupressure** is the mindfulness of meditation applied to acupressure points. Acupressure points are portals to the energetic and physical body and also to the subconscious realms.

- **Guided Imagery** brings us in contact with guides from the spirit world and images from the hidden caverns of the subconscious.

- **Journaling** helps give voice and definition to the randomness of thoughts, the world of dreams and fantasies, the myriad dimensions of the psyche. It creates dialogue with creativity. Its voice may transform into painting, mask, myth, story, poem, or song, as we follow our inner paths.

- **Creative Process** (art, maskmaking, story) offers sensory exploration of the terrains, figures, and symbols inhabiting our inner world.

All guide us as we explore more deeply the universe within.

Explore the emotional layers and the subconscious depths of your inner world. Let them speak through the language of guided imagery, writing, and art. Dance your dreams and stories. Discover the embryos in your body and spirit waiting to be born.

Meditate in greater stillness. Share the wisdom and blessings of your ancestors, totem animals, and spirit guides.

Ultimately the journey along these inner paths is about relationship: to self—body, mind, and spirit—and to others. As you work through the experiences, answer the questions, and explore new territory and old territory in new ways, keep this question with you: *What are you learning about your outer journey—your relationship with other sentient beings, with the living earth, with your community, your culture, your work in the world?*

Meditation

What is meditation? It is the inner dimension of spiritual practice, done lying, sitting, or standing, with focus on a chosen object for meditation, such as breath, mantra, divine image, or sound. Each form is useful at different times for summoning various attributes of mind, body, and spirit. Meditation may encompass contemplative prayer, which addresses a higher spiritual source.

Lying Meditation

Lying meditation is the best preparation for trance work, for going into the subconscious, for preparing yourself for a journey to the places akin to the dream world, although you may prefer to sit if you find yourself prone to lapsing into sleep when lying down. Lying meditation is restorative. It is deeply relaxing. It is an opening posture, with the back of your body fully supported by the earth, the front of your body fully open to the heavens. It allows for the maximum degree of surrender. It allows you to begin to develop breath awareness without strain to the rest of your body or mind.

Find a quiet place with a smooth floor. You may lie on a rug or a blanket, but the surface should be firm. If you become chilled, have a blanket to pull over you. Wear loose clothes. Remove shoes and eyeglasses. Lie on your back.

Notice if your chin or your nose is pointed toward the heavens. If it is your chin, lengthen the back of your neck so that the occipital ridge in the back of your skull slides away from your upper (cervical) spine. If your nose instead of your chin still does not face the heavens, you may need a folded towel under your head or a rolled towel under your neck. If you use a neck roll, the back of your head should still rest comfortably on the floor.

Bend your knees and bring your feet in closer to your buttocks with both feet flat against the floor. Now lift your buttocks and move them toward your feet. This will elongate the lower (lumbar) spine. Gently flatten your lower back against the rug on the floor. You will feel it release. Now let your legs slide down on the floor while keeping your back flat. If you have discomfort in your lower back, you can lie with a blanket roll under your knees so that they stay gently flexed. If discomfort persists, bend your knees and let your feet be parallel and flat on the floor about hips' distance apart, so that your knees fall naturally in and rest against each other.

Now lift one shoulder at a time and slide each shoulder blade down your back toward your waist so that it flattens against the floor. Then allow your arms to rest on the floor, slightly out from your sides, with palms facing upward, if you are feeling open and receptive. If you are feeling vulnerable or introspective, you may flex your elbows and fold your hands over your belly, but keep your shoulder blades flattened against the floor as described above. Try both positions of your arms at first to see which feels most emotionally comfortable.

So much effort for such a passive position? But well worth the effort. Once you have found your own way to aligned comfort in this posture, it is easy to set up next time. In yoga this posture is called *savasana*, corpse pose. As the laying out of a corpse is something to be done with care, sensitivity, and reverent attentiveness, in the awareness that this is a posture that should remain peaceful for a very long time, so is the preparation for lying meditation a worthy and even sacred one.

For the revitalizing benefits of this posture, unobstructed circulation of the life force, the Qi, is necessary. Let the breath, a vehicle of Qi, come to your awareness.

As you inhale, let your belly soften and rise, as it invites the major respiratory muscle, the diaphragm, to descend and the air to enter the bottom, then middle, then top of your lungs. Once your inspiration is full, the air then exits the top, then middle, then bottom of the lungs as the abdomen falls and the diaphragm returns to its resting position at the bottom of the exhalation. When you pass into deep relaxation, allow your breath to find its natural rhythm as you keep your belly soft and your whole body relaxed.

This posture may be used as a preparation and position for a guided imagery that you have selected and memorized or taped. It will help you let go of distractions and attend to concerns of your creative spirit.

Sitting Meditation

Sitting meditation is perhaps the best form to use for long periods of meditation. If done with proper alignment and props, it allows for maximum comfort combined with alertness. It is perhaps the most ubiquitous form of meditation.

Perhaps the favorite and most practiced posture through the ages of humanity's spiritual search is the lotus posture. However, as elegant, ancient, and traditional as it may be, for many inhabitants of the modern world, who have often acquired tight hips from sitting in chairs or knee injuries from competitive sports, a more accessible posture is a simple cross-legged position.

Sit cross-legged close to the edge of a cushion on the floor. Your cushion should be high enough that your hips are higher than your knees and you have your natural lordosis (concave curve) in your lumbar spine. If you are experiencing difficulty with your knee(s), put a cushion(s) under your knee for support. Have something warm (blanket or rug) under your legs. You may place your hands in your lap, cupping the back of one hand in the palm of the other with the thumb-tips touching, or you may rest your hands on your knees. Then bow your chin slightly so that your eyes look at the floor in front of you with a soft gaze. Some people prefer to close their eyes, which is fine if you stay alert. Remember that the main thing is to be comfortable and on the edge between being alert and very relaxed.

If you experience discomfort in back or knees in this position, sitting upright in a chair (not using the back rest), with feet planted evenly on the ground hips' width apart and with the natural alignment of your spine, is a fine alternative. Try to align the joints to create 90 degree angles at the ankles, knees, hips, and elbows.

Standing Meditation

Standing meditation in Qigong, Zhan Zhuang, means to stand like a stake or a tree. It develops body strength. It allows you most readily to feel the current of Qi, life's vital force, flowing between heaven and earth through your body. It helps you to adjust ingrained imbalances in your posture (body alignment). For more guidance in standing meditation, see our upcoming book on Qigong and the creative process.

Acupressure

Acupressure is meditation in interaction. Based on use of acupuncture points, it comes from awareness of the patterns of energy (Qi) flow in the body developed over the 5,000-year history of Traditional Chinese Medicine.

"The Journey" by Kaleo (mixed media lithograph, 28″h x 20″w)

Guided Imagery

Guided imagery is magical. It is a technique combining principles of hypnotherapy and shamanic journeying to access wisdom, images, and messages from subconscious and meta-conscious realms.

It is like dreamwork. Everyone has images waiting to surface from the subconscious, just as everyone has dreams. You only need to give them an outlet and work with them in order to bring their meanings into your life.

Not everyone, however, has an easy time evoking images, just as not everyone has an easy time recalling dreams. If you find yourself having difficulty with the guided imagery, try to spend extra time with the exercises described in this book. Also, perhaps your preferred perceptual mode is not visual, but instead is auditory or kinesthetic (sight vs. sound or feeling modes). If so, you might want to pay more attention to images that arise in your preferred mode. Is your spirit guide speaking, chanting, or dancing when you encounter it in the realm of the subconscious? What sensations, temperatures, and textures does the environment embody? You are unique and will experience guided imagery in your own unique way.

Each one of your trillions of cells has DNA (deoxyribonucleic acid), genetic material, in its nucleus. We believe your DNA contains biological blueprints of your ancestors with messages and wisdom from your entire ancestral line. Fresh blood, oxygen, and nutrients feed every cell in your body. So does the bioelectric current of Qi. Thus past and present meet. Let your ancestors share their wisdom with you, as they have shared life itself.

Guidelines for Guided Imagery

You can have someone read your guided imagery smoothly and soothingly to you; you can make a recording of it yourself, then play it back. You can read it over several times yourself, then commit to memory the steps as outlined, so that you can follow the journey on your own without an external guide. You can also use the numbered steps provided as a quick visual reference if you're in the middle of a journey and forget what to do next. A quick cue may guide you further without totally disrupting your journey-mind.

- *To practice a guided imagery exercise, you should be in a comfortable meditative position, standing, sitting, or lying.*

- *The numbered steps of each guided imagery process are provided as an outline, a sketch, of the upcoming journey.* They may help prepare you before you go, prompt you during your journey, and remind you where you have been when it is over.

- *Remember that guided imagery provides a structure, a path for you.* Listen to your own inner voice, your own knowing. You are empowered to step off the path, come back to the path, take another side trip, and create your own journey whenever you desire.

- *Your imagery process may evolve step by step.* Let each journey take you a little deeper.

- *A series of journeys may have a similar theme, guide, or territory.* Notice how they link together, chapters of a story. Or journeys may have very different components and seem entirely unrelated. If this is so, how do they interface with the rest of your life?

- *Set your intention for your journey before you begin.* What is your issue, your concern, your question for this journey? Write it down; then *let it go* to the back of your awareness. Look at it later and see how your journey addressed this intention.

- *Start from a safe and serene place in your inner landscape.* If you encounter terrain that seems too difficult at any time in your journey, you can always return to this safe place.

- *Make sure your inner guides have your best interests at heart.* If one is not both wise and caring, then you can turn it away. If you feel it has some important lessons for you, you can bring in a more auspicious guide who is both wise and caring to help you work with it. Or you can ask it to go away and return only after it has evolved these essential qualities in itself.

- *Use your breath as a guide.* Allow your breath to be full and long, nurturing and relaxing. If you find your journey getting to be too intense, use your breath to center you by slowing it down and bringing the inhalation down into the bottom of your lungs while stretching out the exhalation.

- *Be aware that the inner journey may not always be easy.* There may be tests. You may be called upon to apply inner resources you weren't even aware you had. You may learn many new things about yourself in this process. Usually if difficult issues surface, it is because your subconscious feels you are ready to face them. But if you feel overwhelmed by them, call upon your external resources—trustworthy friends, support people, counselors, spiritual teachers.

- *If a journey has brought up a lot of inner "stuff," give yourself an appropriate outlet afterward to bring balance into your being.* If you are feeling energy surging, you might want to do something physical like walking in the park or doing Qigong. If you are feeling inspired, engage in creative process: art, writing, dancing, whatever moves your spirit.

- *Keep in touch with your guides.* Sing their songs. Dialogue with them. Do art about them. Invite them with you in your waking and dreaming life journeys. Surround yourself with images of them. Acknowledge where they reside in your body and honor their presence with supportive care. Thank them for their presence in your life.

Journaling

Your journal is your mirror. Look into it, dialogue with it, and observe what it reveals. Ask how you can make better choices for yourself. Ask for guidance toward greater clarity, understanding, and wisdom. Let your journal be your intimate friend.

Feel free to keep your journal private, so that you can be as honest and thorough as possible. This is your own personal journal process. Explore, create, experiment, take risks—whatever feels comfortable at this time in your life. Do your innermost work in it. Give voice to whatever wants to surface. *Do not deny your voice!*

Use alchemical processes to transform it: Melt it; rip it to pieces; burn it to release its smoke and scatter its ashes; bury it in your garden; hide it in a river bed; lose it in the desert, mountains, jungle; create a collage painting with it; keep it under your pillow; place it on your personal altar; store it in your mask or totem; share parts with others or keep it forever private.

Keep your journal in your own unique way. Some people use tattered and doodled spiral notebooks; others use elegant designer diaries. We have seen a journal scribbled on torn cafe napkins, smeared with lipstick and coffee stains, but ultimately bound into a timeless treasure. Some people use multi-colored pens and pencils, others pastels and collage, others black only. Some write in total privacy. Others love the stimulation of a crowded cafe. Whatever you choose, start by asking your journal why you picked this place, this writing instrument, this receptacle for recording. Spelling, punctuation, and grammar are not important here. What matters is that you come from the Qi of your body, mind, and spirit!

Realize that the questions included herein for your journaling process are intended as catalysts. Journaling is an experiment. If you are having difficulties with any parts of the process, your journal is also a good place to explore these. Our struggles are our teachers.

Use the questions as far as they inspire you, but most important is your relationship to the words and images flowing through you. The pen, pencil, or paintbrush becomes an extension of your body. It is like the Taiji sword—a channel through which your Qi glides, spirals, or stabs—this time onto the spaciousness of the pages in your journal.

Try to write in your journal daily. Record anything—imagery, prayers, sketches, ideas, letters to friends, major or minor complaints, things to do, secret desires, random thoughts, gut feelings, opinions, impressions, even grocery lists. Keep it, along with pen and flashlight, by your bed and upon waking record your dreams.

You may begin your journal recalling a journal from your childhood. Do you still have it? What is its cover like? What are its contents? Do you recognize the person writing it? What is the relationship between this early self and the self you know now?

Creative Process

Creativity conjures mystery, fascination, intimidation, envy, longing, liberation. Creativity is about the relationship of the self to the Self—of the embodied ego, who moves through the daily world earning a paycheck, pushing a grocery cart, grooming the dog, or mulching the garden, to the higher Self, that person in harmony with spirit. Creative self-expression is a tool for the process of what C. G. Jung calls individuation.

Creativity from your body, mind, and spirit gives form to abstraction, voice to the inner dialogue. It is a vehicle for greater self-knowledge.

Creativity gives you the opportunity to release fear ("I might make a mistake!") and embrace self-discovery ("Anything is possible and the journey is mine!").

Creativity is about the joy of discovering the inner body, inner spirit. Sometimes the adventure leads us into darkness or into luminosity. It is Qigong, the balance of opposites: the integration of structure and freedom, body and breath, dragon and tiger.

Creativity expresses the relationship between positive and negative forces and experiences in one's life. Through warm yellows and reds and cool blues and greens, between settings of night and noon, in themes of sadness and joy, polarities do their metaphorical dance. In one word or color, you might express a mood of exhilaration, a place and time of light, where darkness has shrunken to the black eye of yin in the white body of yang; in another you might express harmony and balance, like the complete circle with yin tail in mouth of yang, yang in yin.

Creativity is a goddess who must be nurtured, seduced, respected, appeased. She is like the sparrow in the Taiji movement "grasp sparrow's tail." The metaphorical sparrow lands on your outstretched hand but cannot be grabbed and captured, for she will feel your intention and the contraction in your arm muscles and will be disturbed into flight. To embrace her you must keep your arm still and, instead, shift the weight of your body onto your back leg to bring her close to you. Then the sparrow, as the muse, will perch quietly and alertly, ready for your relationship to unfold.

Creativity is the language of dreams, the little known, the unknown, the subconscious. Its vocabulary consists of word, movement, color, space, line, shape, density, and energy, which can take you to the heights or depths of your soul at a pace safe for you. It is a language by which your ancestors, your sacred source, and your inner being send you messages.

The following principles derive from long hours of our experience teaching, creating, practicing. They are based on the premise that creativity nurtures understanding, healing, and compassion for self and others.

- **Study the Lessons**

  Inspiration has a hard time expressing itself without some training. To write creatively, it is helpful to learn writing techniques; to make art, it is helpful to learn about art materials and techniques; but these processes can happen joyfully together. It helps to read writers and study artists whom you like, identify techniques, styles, subject matter, then try the craft yourself. You want to have a variety of tools in your tool box, a variety of spices in your kitchen. The same principles apply to massage, martial, verbal, or performing arts.

- **Let Go of the Lessons**

  The shadow side of the craft of creativity is the trap of conformity. Writers and artists do and should learn from each other, even imitate each other as practice. But creative principles as dogma can produce a generic form of creativity, recognizable and ultimately boring. Creating originally and well means honoring the wisdom trained and honed within.

  Letting go of the rules and advice does not mean throwing them out but transcending them; using them but not being controlled by them; developing the trust in yourself that comes from caring practice. Letting go can be both frightening and freeing. At some point fear recedes and faith in self becomes firm. This is the point where creative process and personal growth commune. The work of art leads its creator deeper on the inner journey. Whose opinion matters when the final authority lies deep within?

- **Self and Others**

  Who is your audience? Is your creative process for yourself only, or do you intend to share it with others? Ultimately creating for yourself is something to be shared, if only indirectly through your increasing insight. Ultimately creating for others is personal, as the subject matter, symbols, metaphors, forms, themes, and images come from personal observation and experience, even when disguised behind third person voice or hidden in abstract expressionism.

- Yin and Yang of Creativity

  Yin and yang dance through creativity. The relationship of creative inspiration, which is predominantly a right brain process, to craftsmanship, which is more of a left brain function, can take on adversarial tones very quickly. This battle may manifest in creative blocks. It may show in such attitudes as "I'm not creative—this drawing is lousy" or "How can I edit this when it comes from my heart?" How can a drawing be lousy if it is an embodiment of your truth; how can the work of the heart be prepared for sharing? The beauty of art is that it is your soul revealed; the challenge is that it is a form of communication. The key to this relationship between right and left brain processes is separation of yin and yang, understanding them, working with them, and bringing them back into dialogue in a cohesive whole.

  The right brain process often seems more exciting—exploring new wild crevices of imagination, discovering, receiving wafts of inspiration, giving them voice or form, putting them together. The left brain task perhaps feels more tedious, yet it commands respect and helps you to decide what to keep and what to omit.

  Creativity is a cycle of yin and yang. Try separating inspiration and reworking by an incubation period. Many times a lapse of a few days, between the flash of creativity and reworking the creation, helps hone the piece more smoothly.

  Try sharing your piece with a friend. You will discover the yin and yang of subjectivity and objectivity. Not only will the observer see flaws you missed, but share new epiphanies about your creative piece. But remember, as you keep open and take in new lessons and awarenesses, the work of art is yours, and you are its ultimate creator and guardian; moreover, the real work of art is the process of growth within yourself and between yourself and others.

- Yin and Yang of Emotions

  Many, perhaps all, of the spiritual paths of the world emphasize compassion for self and others. One of the steps of the Buddhist Eightfold Path is right conduct. Applied to creativity, this means being mindful of the effects of creative process on self and others. Sometimes creativity brings up joy and celebration. Sometimes it brings up pain and rage. How can you portray the light and dark, the heights and depths, the illumination and despair, of your experience with honesty and compassion?

- Honor Your Sources

  What are your origins—of body, mind, emotions, spirit? Who came before you? Who taught you? Who fed your spirit? How can your creative process honor the complex layers of its origins, of your origins?

- Creativity as Prayer

  When you portray something creatively, it becomes part of your spiritual family. Nurture the company of guides. Keep the spirits present and the relationship of body-life and spirit-life active. Poems and stories and works of art are allies from the spirit world, friends from a wider reality.

• **Take Risks**

Creativity is about relationship: of self to subject matter, writer or artist to audience, self to materials, parts of self to whole. Like any relationship, it is dynamic. It involves taking risks—of one's own choosing and pace, with self-responsibility. Creativity is like Qigong, in which you move ever more deeply, expanding, growing, then assimilating the wisdom into the body.

Transformation becomes deeper with time, practice, and commitment. It is like a relationship with a 14,000 foot peak, requiring new ways of seeing, listening, walking, breathing, adapting to sun, wind, storm, the moods of the mountain. The risk is internal, for one is climbing the inner mountain, but the experience is just as challenging, just as rewarding. Creativity demands openness to change. Not only will you as creator change words into poem or paint and canvas into art. You will be changed by them.

CLIMBING CASTLE PEAK
by Elise

Scratching up an old melted mountain
bending to wind like low twisted whitebark pine
heads tucked like mountain hemlocks
hair flattened against faces like dead needles
you and I persist

So many to follow:
flesh scoured down to dirt caked bone
small mystery trails in three inch dust
crumbly porous rocks rising and falling
a skinny path, a scary place to squat
no room for error, only exhilaration
wood turned stone from millenniums of seasons
stars hidden in a blue cape waiting for us to lose our way
to show themselves remote, numerous, laughing

You stop to scratch in dirt your own private glyphs
choose a bone for your pack, a stone for your pocket
a smell of coyote mint for curious nose
stop to drink stout tea
eat bread crusted by nine thousand foot wind
pluck burs from a paw sore dusty dog
roll ritual tobacco
crouch in a grotto of stone

For the moment we give ourselves to climbing
red brown old cooled andesite neck of rock

With you here I am safe to feel myself slipping
along my just dead mother's bones
that close I feel here to home

Exploring the Creative Process

Creating Sacred Space

Your creative process is sacred. Before you begin, how do you create sacred time and space?

Kaleo: Door to Creativity

The day begins in nature with the ancient practice of Qigong. I am the fragrance of jasmine, the breath of dense bamboo, the medley of birds, as I stand in Zhan Zhuang meditation. My feet sink into the Mother, Gaia, my final destination.

Thank you, Pele, goddess of raging fire, for your abundance. *Ē Pele ē, ke akua o ke ahi ʻenaʻena, mahalo nui loa iā ʻoe i kāu hoʻonuʻa ʻana.*

E hoʻomākaukau!

In my studio I light sage. My subconscious spirals with the fragrance. Pele, my muse, is aroused by the lure of fire.

Exploration: Your Ritual

What is your ritual for creating sacred time and space? In meditation, invite images to emerge: a setting in nature, an altar in your home, the lighting of a candle, the burning of sage.

Do you chant, move, or sing? Do you summon your muse or an ancestor?

How do you set your intention before you begin? How do you end?

Then you may want to sketch your ritual or create it with your body. Journal about it. Create an altar for your practice area. If your practice space is also used for more mundane purposes, you might want to purify it, using energy work or burning incense or herbs to change the atmosphere from secular to sacred.

The Creative Journey

As a child were you encouraged to create, to listen to and trust your inner journey, or were you discouraged? Were you taught to respect fact and left brain knowing more than intuition and the mystery of the muse? What creative processes did you experience in your childhood? Did you take ballet classes, study art in school, write stories, or perform plays? What things did you try with your voice, words, hands, or body that represent creativity? Describe in your journal how your relationship to creativity has evolved. Describe positives and negatives, wonders and disappointments. Identify experiences that have discouraged your confidence in your creativity. Identify sources of creative energy and joy.

Exploration: The Creative Journey

The Child's World

1 In meditation go back to the time when you were a child. What age are you?

2 How is it to explore the world with the eyes, ears, nose, tongue, fingertips, and sixth sense of a child?

3 How do you perceive the world at this age? The inner world? The outer world?

4 How do you play—with others and alone?

5 As this child, write, collage, and draw your experience of your inner and outer worlds.

Seventh-grade students at Albany Middle School

The Adult's World

1   Return to your adult awareness. Observe your inner child's creative expression. What are the boundaries between the inner and outer worlds? Are they distinct or nebulous or do the worlds flow in and out of each other?

2   What kind of child is revealed through creativity? Is it a wounded child, a rebellious child, an adapted child, a hidden child, a happy child?

3   How does your child's creative expression ask to enter into your adult's creative process? Does it want healing? Does it want you to make a new collage with your child-self at the center?

4   What lessons does the child bring to the adult? What support, caring, and healing does the adult bring to the child's world?

5   Write, collage, draw in your journal this interaction between child and adult.

Dialogues on Your Creative Journey

Creativity is a dialogue between yang and yin, between you and your muse, between your intention and your trust in the process.

Exploration: Dialogue with Image

Have before you a large selection of photo-rich magazines, a large sheet of paper (18″ x 24″), glue, and drawing supplies.

Sit in meditation. Invite the delight of your child-self to join your adult awareness. Ask your muse for an intention for your creative journey.

Pick a magazine. Give yourself only thirty seconds to flip through the pages. An image calls to you. You feel a response to it in your body, in your intuition. Quickly, tear out this image and place it somewhere in relation to the paper.

Now look at the image. How do you respond to it emotionally, physically, spiritually, mentally? Where did you place it? What is the relationship between the image and its location? Dialogue with the image. Why did it call to you? What does it mean to you? Close your eyes and let the image take you on a journey.

Then let the image, along with lines, colors, shapes, words, join with the paper.

Journal about this experience. How did the message from your muse influence your creative process?

Exploration: Dialogue with Collage of Images

Have before you a large selection of photo-rich magazines, a large sheet of paper (18″ x 24″), glue, and drawing supplies.

Sit in meditation. Summon your muse and ask her for an intention for this collage. Then, remembering that creativity is a dialogue between you and your muse, between your intention and your trust in the process, let the intention recede to the back of your mind.

For ten minutes tear a stack of images from the magazines. Work quickly, allowing the images to call out to you, to choose you.

Then for twenty minutes, let your intuition, your instinct, your body move images, words, colors and shapes onto the paper.

Now look carefully at your finished collage. Allow it to speak to you. What do the images say? Did you tear, bundle, fold, or cut the images? How did you position the images on the paper—carefully, randomly, horizontally, in a spiral? How did you layer the images? *What does your creative process reveal about you?*

In meditation observe: Where does the collage reside in your body? What is the sound in this part of your body? Release the sound with your exhalation. Let the sound move your body. Sing it, shout it, dance it.

Now journal about your experience.

The journey continues. What lies behind the door to the temple, the gate to the garden, the eye of the elder in your collage? Create from a deeper layer.

Circle of Self

Your self-concept directs your creative process. Perhaps it compels you to create. Perhaps it fosters creative blocks. This exploration encourages the dialogue between who you believe you are and how you create.

Spontaneous Writing

Take ten minutes to write nonstop in your journal in response to this question: Who do I believe myself to be? What comes up? Do not judge or edit—just keep writing. Put pen to paper and keep the ink flowing.

The Circle

Have a large sheet of paper (18″ x 24″). Draw a circle.

On the *inside* of that circle, write:

- what you are grateful for
- what brings you joy
- what is sacred for you

- what your strengths are

- your goals in life (personal, spiritual, family, health, career)

- moments of triumph in your life

- mentors, friends, allies, guides, guardians

- what you want to develop and maintain

Open a box of oil or chalk pastels. These are energy sticks, wands of emotion. What colors, what emotional energies, entice you? Let your emotions, your energies, your physical body select the colors. How does your body move to color your inner circle with energy that protects, nurtures, and heals you?

Now on the *outside* of the circle, write:

- what you resent in your life

- what brings you distress

- what is hurtful to you

- what are your weaknesses

- what hinders you (personal, spiritual, family, health, career)

- moments of loss and failure

- negative influences in your life

- what you would like to change or let go of

From your box of oil or chalk pastels, let your body and emotions choose the colors. Allow your body to splash, scrape, push the colors of your outer circle with the energy that hinders you.

Incubation

Tape this sheet on a wall at home. Allow it to speak to you. Write its messages and your responses in your journal.

Integration

After a week place the sheet with your circle of positives and negatives in front of you. Sit in meditation. Observe the circle with non-judgment. Observe the dance of yang and yin.

Then on a new sheet allow the positives and negatives to come together, yang and yin in an integrated symbol of yourself at this time.

Confronting the Inner Critic

Elise: Judgment in Jail

Judgment will slap me in the face if I carry it into the jail. It is easier to have judgment from a distance. But behind bars morality is not so black and white as it seems reading about crimes in the newspaper.

There was a man I will call Ben. He had already done time for one murder, and I had known him when he was in jail going through the court process the first time around. It had been murder over something petty, an argument over $40. Now he was back, charged with another murder. This time he would never know life beyond bars—not just because of the sentence he was facing, but his failing heart would give out before he even had a chance to receive his verdict again. Mostly he was very polite to me, to the staff. But when he became depressed, I could see him go into a very deep dark place, a place none of us could reach, a place, perhaps, where the violence ignited. We all knew instinctively to keep our distance then, to care for him, to listen when he was ready to ask, but not to push. There was no room for outsiders in his dark arena.

Ben emerged once again from his dark place. I looked in his eyes and wondered where he had been. What was in his past and in the secret corners of his mind? The end seemed very near. His breath did not come easily anymore. Who was I to judge his soul? Criticism had no answers. At that moment he was simply a person in need of help.

There is also nothing harder on one's creative process than the inner critic. What is behind this face?

Meditation: The Inner Critic

Sit in meditation. Breathe deeply into your pelvis, into the dan tian of the body, and feel your groundedness. Let your breath become regular and calm. Then bring your attention up to your heart. Feel the lightness and openness of your heart as the breath passes by on the way in and out of your lungs. Then bring your attention up to your mind. Feel the strength of your mind as it pulses with your breath. This is where your inner critic resides.

Allow this critic to assume a face. Is it familiar? Have you met before? Is it male or female? What expression does it have? What colors and lines form this face? What is the look in its eyes? How do you feel here, now, face to face?

Bring to mind a time when you know the critic has gotten in your way, adversely affected your relationship with someone or your relationship with yourself—your creativity, self-confidence, willingness to take a risk.

Ask the critic, why the interference? From what was it trying to protect you? Why does it feel the need to try to help you in a way that ultimately hurts you?

Ask it, what is its history that makes it so contrary? Then listen as it tells you how it got to be this way. Listen to its story.

And when it is finished, both of you breathe deeply. Ask each other, is there some role for the critic that could be more helpful to you?

Give it a new name to honor the process of change. The inner critic has shifted into: _____.

Then inhale deeply and on the exhalation let the face of your new ally on the creative journey fade into the realms of your subconscious.

Journaling and Art: Transforming the Inner Critic

The critic as an inner figure may have the power to stop you in your tracks, but it also has the capacity to transform and become a genuine servant to you, to your process of art and writing, and to the larger creative process of your life's journey.

Write, draw, paint, collage, and sculpt the story of your inner critic.

As it reveals its history, how do you come to understand it better? Art and writing create space and awareness for change. Your creative dialogue spins a thread of new colors and textures and purpose. Who has the inner critic become now? How can it serve you?

What can you do to support this crucial metamorphosis? What steps in your outer reality, your daily life, can you take to give this new voice strength and meaning?

Receiving the Mystery

Exploration: Heaven and Earth

Go with thick blanket, flashlight, and journal on a clear night to a hill with a wide view away from city lights. Spread your blanket. Lie prone, your body embracing the earth mother. Absorb her fragrance. Then turn over and lie supine facing the night sky. Are there familiar cairns for you there in the heavens? Identify familiar patterns; then let them go. Contemplate what surrounds you: infinity of stars, infinity of space among them. Imagine that the stars are lights of compassion and the space among them is the void. Both are parts of the Great Mystery of the universe. Hold the night sky in your heart: Receive compassionate light; enter endless darkness. As earth holds your body's weight from below, let the night sky hold the wonder of your spirit from above.

Writing: Night Sky

As you practiced this meditation of the night, how did your sense of time and space shift? Realizing that you have shared in an experience as old as consciousness itself, begin a poem or story by imagining you are another person hundreds or thousands of years ago. Your poem might be a chant or a ballad. It might be so brief as to be timeless, able to travel across centuries on the indelible lines of a haiku.

Art: Night Sky

Paint your inner and outer experience of the night sky. Notice the temperatures and textures of both inner and outer dimensions. What most pulled you on the path: darkness above, darkness below, darkness within? How did you orient yourself? Did the heavens serve you as a guide? As you lay beneath the night sky, what most attracted you: shimmering stars or the thick space among them, heavenly bodies or heavenly void? Notice the emotions that come up as you paint the light and paint the darkness.

Intimacy with the Night: Vesta

II

Spirit Guides

Journey to the Lower World

The path of this journey, a descent through an opening in the earth to the lower world, is ancient and cross-cultural. You may find it useful and also comforting to use for many explorations, including the upcoming guided imageries for encountering guides from the spirit world, for the earth is a nurturing, supportive, yin element, and the lower world is a welcoming abode.

Preparation: Earth and Internal Alchemy

According to Traditional Chinese Medicine, earth is associated with the organs of the spleen (yin) and stomach (yang). The spleen organ and meridian are about nurturance, meditation, and grounding. Their tissue is muscle. Earth is associated with the sense organ of the mouth and its taste is sweet. The element of earth is yin: surrender, receptivity, the great lap of Gaia.

On this journey, we'd like to invite you to explore the element earth.

Lie down on the floor or ground. Feel the element earth supporting you. With your palm, feel your spleen, located on the left side of your abdomen. It lies protected, nestled in your large cavernous rib cage. It curls around to the front near your stomach.

Inhale and allow your breath to enter into the left side of your abdomen into the spleen and stomach. Breathing gently, feel how these organs expand, pressing gently against the inner lining of your ribs, then contract. What is the color of your breath as it fills these organs? Enter this field of color. As you move through it, how does it feel on your skin? What are its temperatures and textures? Feel how they induce comfort. As you relax, notice an opening in the distance. It calls to you. Approach it, enter it, notice the shifts in your body as you move through this portal.

You find yourself in an inner landscape. Look around. Where are you? What is the terrain? Is it mountain, desert, or jungle?

Notice the vegetation in this terrain. There are plants, herbs, flowers, and fruit. Go up to one of the flowers and inhale its fragrance. Choose a fruited plant. What kind is it? Pluck one of its fruit. Close your eyes. Smell the fruit, open your mouth, and bite down. The tip of your tongue responds to the pleasure and transmits the juice throughout your body. Feel the fruit's texture as it slides into the cavern of your throat and down the tunnel into your stomach. Enjoy the sensations of this fruit in your body.

When you are ready, be aware of your breath. Has it changed in any way? Now just allow the rhythm of your breath to bring you gently back to conscious awareness.

Guided Imagery: Descent to the Lower World

Steps

1 Walk down the wilderness trail.

2 Enter the cave.

3 Descend the tunnel and approach the light.

4 Enter the landscape of the lower world.

5 Explore the landscape with all your senses.

6 Find your power circle.

7 Return as you came.

Process

Breathe softly and taste the sweetness of breath as it ebbs and flows. Feel its rhythm as it enters and gently expands into the walls of your throat, then releases and empties into the tunnel of your throat. What is the sound of its release? Follow it. It leads you down a trail in the wilderness, into the wilderness within. Where are you? Listen. The sound gets louder. It guides you to the mouth of the earth, to the entrance of a cave. Observe the opening and your surroundings.

Enter the cave. As your eyes adjust to the darkness, they find a tunnel leading into the earth. The tunnel is a powerful passageway. Travel into this tunnel and notice its colors and temperatures. What do you smell? Reach out and touch the walls. Notice their moisture and texture. Perhaps you find them covered with copious roots or a matrix of webs or ridges of sediment. If you encounter any obstacles, acknowledge them, and realize you are empowered to move on by. You descend deeper and deeper into the tunnel. What changes do you notice?

Finally, you see a light, very faint but gradually getting brighter, as you descend the tunnel. As you approach the light, notice its color and intensity. You feel safe and comfortable and the light welcomes you. It invites you to enter. Do you hear sounds from the other side? What does it feel like as you pass through and emerge in another world?

Where are you? What does this new setting look like? Do you find yourself in forest, mountains, ocean, jungle, desert? Explore this place with all your senses, watching, listening, smelling, tasting. Touch and feel with your fingertips, the soles of your feet, your protective covering of skin, your intuition.

Notice a certain spot that attracts you. As you enter its circle of energy, you feel safe and empowered. What vibration do you feel inside the circle? What sound do you hear? What color is the energetic field of the inner circle? Absorb the energy. Sit in awareness in this circle, taking in all that surrounds you.

Eventually you realize it is time to go. Leave the circle and return to the entrance to the tunnel. Inhaling, allow yourself to return up the tunnel. Do you notice any changes as you ascend? Exhaling, you find yourself emerging through the opening in the earth, and you return along the trail through the wilderness the same way you came.

Inhale and feel the comfort and strength of your breath as it fills the chamber of your throat. Exhale and emerge along the current of breath into your familiar world.

Journaling: The Lower World

Was the path through the wilderness familiar or strange?

What was it like descending the tunnel? The tunnel has many symbolic associations: the birth canal, the tunnel to the underworld of the dead, a corridor to the unknown. What emotions came up for you in response to this powerful passageway?

What was the terrain of the lower world like? Did you feel strange or at home there? Where did you find your circle of power and safety?

Art: Circle of Empowerment

Gather drawing materials and magazines full of visual images for collage. Then sit before a large sheet of paper and feel the emptiness of its terrain inviting you to create.

Close your eyes and recall yourself sitting in the circle of power and safety in the lower world. What besides yourself fills your inner circle? Observe what accompanies you in this haven. What emotions and sensations fill you in this place?

Open your eyes and, staying with the emotions and sensations you experienced inside the circle, gather images from the magazines.

When you are done, close your eyes again and recall your circle. Now observe what lies beyond the circle, what surrounds it. What emotions and sensations surface as you observe beyond the circle's boundary?

Open your eyes again and, staying with the emotions and sensations you experienced looking beyond the circle, gather images from the magazines.

Then begin your drawing of your circle of empowerment. Use your collage images and drawing tools to re-create your experience of the inner and outer circle.

Encountering Your Spirit Guide

Spirit guides are helpers from the spirit world. We all have such helpers. They may take many forms. They may be the totem animals or ancestors of the following chapters, or real or mythic beings of human form from story, religious tradition, myth, or imagination. The purpose of the following guided imagery is to introduce you to or deepen your relationship with your main spiritual guide from your inner world. This will be someone who has your best interests at heart, as well as wisdom to share with you. We hope that this chapter will help you to dialogue with your guides and help you in your life's journey. Be open and receptive. You may be surprised who shows up.

Guided Imagery: Spirit Guide

Steps

1   Follow the steps for "Guided Imagery: Descent to the Lower World" on page 10.

2   A figure approaches: Who is it and does it have your best interests at heart? If not, send it back and ask for your true guide.

3   Observe each other.

4   Interact and receive guidance.

5   Receive the gift.

6   Take your leave.

7   Return as you came.

Process

Follow the guidelines in "Guided Imagery: Descent to the Lower World" on page 10. Travel down the wild trail to the earth opening, down the tunnel, and enter the lower world. Return to your circle of power and safety and be seated. Notice how centered and comfortable you become. Now observe your surroundings.

In the distance a figure is coming toward you. You understand that it is a guide from the spirit world. As it approaches, its form takes a clearer shape for you. Who is this being? Ask it if it has your best interests at heart. If not, send it back and ask for your true guide to emerge.

As this figure approaches you, notice how it moves. What color is its aura? What is it wearing? It comes and stands before you. Look into its face. What is its expression? What do you see when you look in its eyes? Welcome one another, touch each other. What does your guide's skin feel like?

Your spirit guide now circles you, and you enter into relationship with it through conversation, dance, song, or silence. Pay careful attention. It is revealing something of significance that will *ground, focus, and direct you* in your life's journey. The dialogue may not be verbal; it assumes a form that is most meaningful for you to understand and for your guide to communicate—words, movement, visual images. It may also lead you on a further journey.

In time your interaction returns you to your power circle and you are ready to leave. Your spirit guide has a gift for you—an amulet. What is it? Receive this object of protection, hold it, and examine it carefully. This is a special gift for you from the spirit world.

Then you and your guide embrace, knowing that you will continue to travel together on your life's path. *All you need to do is nourish the relationship.*

You return to the entrance of the tunnel. Exhale and cross the threshold into the darkness. Inhale and ascend the tunnel the same way you came. You see a glow at the end of the tunnel, which is the mouth of the cave you first entered.

Exhale and allow yourself to pass through the darkness and into the orifice of the cave. Inhale and your throat fills with moist breath. Exhale and your breath glides from your throat, over your tongue, into the familiarity of the world around you. Listen, for you may have received a gift of voice.

Journaling: Spirit Guide

In your journal describe your experience of meeting your spirit guide in the lower world. The more detailed you are, the more alive this experience will be, revealing more personally meaningful symbols. What was it like to reenter the landscape of the lower world and your power circle? What being did you encounter? Describe it in detail. What were its colors, textures, smells, sounds? What was it wearing? What was your sensory experience? What was your relationship with your guide like: your interaction, your journey, your feelings? Did metaphors or symbols present themselves to you? What did your spirit guide reveal to you? Or you to it? What did you learn about grounding, focus, and direction in your life?

What was the amulet the spirit guide gave you? An amulet is a protective charm to ward off evil or bring blessings. How will this amulet help you at this time in your life?

Art: Tunnel, Amulet, Spirit Guide

The Tunnel

Select your media (painting, drawing, or collage materials). Go back to the walls of the tunnel. Allow your paper or canvas to be the walls of the tunnel. Spread your chosen medium on the walls. How do you produce the textures? Are there words or symbols carved or drawn on the walls? Draw, paint, collage, or etch them into the surface before you.

The Amulet

Recall the amulet your spirit guide gave you and sketch or draw it. Make your amulet. Do you hang it around your neck? Or sew a pouch for carrying it?

You and Your Spirit Guide

Before you, arrange tools (paper, pens, graphite, pastels, brushes). Sit in meditation. On the inhalation draw the Qi up from the earth; on the exhalation allow the Qi to release back into the earth. Enter the tunnel, go to the lower world, and get in touch with your spirit guide. Look at your guide closely and deeply. Then look inside your own body. Where does your spirit guide reside in your body? Open your eyes and allow your spirit guide to choose tools and colors. Allow your guide to release words, images, rhythms, and synchronicities onto paper.

Our Journeys with Spirit Guides

The following excerpts from Kaleo's and Elise's journals include lessons and discoveries from their own explorations with one of their spirit guides, Pele, goddess of fire. Let the following stories, guided imageries, and creative explorations with spirit guides be catalysts for your own journey. Blessings!

Kaleo's Journal: Pele, Goddess of Fire

6/15/98

While driving on the way to teach my Qigong and Creative Process class at Matthew Fox's Naropa University-Oakland, I hear the radio announcer. "There've been more shootings and killings in our public schools." Something inside of me snaps, and I find myself weeping for the youth, for their suffering, for their future. Something inside me just died. What's happening to our country? Where is the God I once knew but know no more? In the evening during our faculty meeting at Naropa, I share my sorrow. I remember the deep red soul in the dark corner: the crimson dress of Clarissa Pinkola Estes, Jungian analyst and powerful storyteller of *Women Who Run With the Wolves*. I hear her voice: "Kaleo, you need a ritual of cleansing. Meet me in the Cave tomorrow morning."

6/16/98

I enter the Sacred Cave of the Goddess. It is totally dark except for the light from two candles. It's humid within, cool. There's a quivering of energy above the drone and rhythm of soft breathing. Anticipation. The Cave is filled with many women and some men. It feels like a womb. Incense and burning wax fill the air. Clarissa's energy feels solid, grounded. Her presence is very strong as she lays me on my back. She begins chanting and shaking a rattle, while dancing a raw egg over my heart. A river of vibrations floats above me.

Whoosh! My wings spread open. I am flying over the Ka'ū desert of Hawai'i, birthplace of my mother. Hot wind and the smell of sulfur and ocean fill the air. I kite over ocean waves crashing on furious lava. Pele, goddess of fire, and Nāmakaokaha'i, goddess of the sea, do battle again. There she is! Pele, the crone, in white dress, long white hair whipping in the wailing wind. Her eyes are molten lava. She beckons to me. I follow her over the fresh skin of black encrusted lava fields pulsing with subsurface fire. At Halemaʻumaʻu, at the crater's edge, I peer in. She looks up at me and opens her arms. *E komo mai.* Just for a second I hesitate, then jump in. She cackles and laughs triumphantly and grasps me to her hungrily. She kisses me. Her tongue parts my lips, darts in, and enters my mouth. I gasp and am forced to swallow. My rib cage becomes cavernous, glowing molten rock! *Pōhaku ʻenaʻena.* Sounds of fire sweep across this inner landscape.

"Pele's Lair" by Kaleo (mixed media acrylic painting, 36″h x 28″w)

Clarissa's rattle sweeps over my left lung and heart. She chants: "Release! Release! Before bitterness consumes you."

Thick beds of heavy black *pāhoehoe* lava have long layered my heart. But a fissure opens. Steam and sulfur, *uahi ʻawa* and *kūkaepele,* escape. I see the glowing red beneath. As my heart opens, I weep. The source of my tears is ancient.

6/20/98

Ē Pele ē.
Cavern of my dan tian sucks
your steam, wind, sulfur.
Molten liquid from your belly
fills my soul.

The last three days and nights have been tumultuous. Within me, fire throbs. Steam condenses into rivers of tears. At night I call out to her! My dreams are sometimes sexual, sometimes frightening and violent.

6/21/98

The brutality so rampant in the world continues to disturb me deeply. Here it rages again, this time in a village in Chiapas, Mexico, where soldiers raid a church, mercilessly, pointlessly killing many. In my art studio, I spread the crimson-blackness, dirty blood, gushing from the humid body of Gaia over the white canvas. It is the blood of injustice birthing an inferno: someone's sacrum, a liver, a hand, a bloody hook, a child's body parts, a crucifix, the ravaged church. I hear screams, the scurrying of children, the weeping of women and elders, the stomping of pursuing leather boots, the cracks of gunfire, the bashing of skulls, the tearing of skin and flesh, the raping. Hysteria. Hundreds of jungle birds scream and take flight. Fifty people died that day in Chiapas, Mexico. My breath shortens. I am angry and afraid. This crimson-black blood is the piss and bile of Pele. She is furious. *Ē Pele ē, ke akua o ke ahi ʻenaʻena*—goddess of raging fire.

6/25/98

Today I talked with Franciscan Sister Jose Hobday and Oshun Priestess Luisah Teish, both wise mentors and friends. They warn, "Don't analyze your encounter with Pele. The mind is tricky. Trust your body and heart; they do not lie. Also, be careful what you ask for. You might get it."

6/29/98

Timing is pivotal. For twenty years I've been preparing the vessel of my body through Qigong, meditation, and creativity. Now is the time of testing. How will this vessel endure?

7/8/98

Pele summons white tiger. Seven hundred pounds of tiger stalking the inner terrain of my body. I can hear his breath, feel his weight, his sinuous movements. He knows where to go. He claws and scrapes adhesions from my inner body. He leaps onto the bed of my diaphragm, sits on his haunches, and licks my lungs to cleanse and strengthen them. He rubs his musky fur along my inner rib cage, organs, and glands, stimulating them. His powerful paws scoop warm meat fresh in my belly. He drinks my blood and wanders through the long tunnel of sulfuric gases and lava in my intestinal tract. He descends into my rectum and defecates. He returns to den in my body to sleep long hours, building strength for life's next encounter.

"Embracing the Tiger" by Kaleo (mixed media drawing, 40″h x 30″w)

7/12/98

White tiger roams in a field of fresh crusted *pāhoehoe* lava. At my heart, he finds a wound. *Kupukupu* fern sprouts in the crack. Clawing and gnawing, tiger scrapes away dried blood and adhesions, opening the wound. A warm glow emerges, brightening as more scab is peeled off. He licks and cleanses the wound. It quivers and pulses. The healing begins.

Guided Imagery: Exploring the Layers

What physical and psychic wounds lodge within your body? How are they affecting you, blocking you, teaching you?

Inhale gently, softly, enjoying the warmth of your breath as it fills your body. Exhale and feel the protective field as your breath presses against the membrane of energy that surrounds you. Notice your body swaying within this field of energy. What colors wrap around you? What emotions? Observe. Then whenever you're ready, on an exhalation, let go.

On an inhalation, encourage your breath to enter through your skin. How thin is the layer of fascia? What are its temperatures and textures? Do you find areas of pain, tension, inconsistency? What emotions do you feel right beneath your skin? Observe. Then whenever you're ready, on an exhalation, let go.

On an inhalation, allow your breath to move deeper and spread into muscles and tissues. Do you find them to be fatty or toned, taut or loose? Are there blockages, spasms, adhesions lodged within? What colors, sounds, emotions do you find? Observe. Then whenever you're ready, on an exhalation, let go.

On an inhalation, allow your breath to enter deeper still into the organs of your body. What is there? Are there imbalances in the organs? What organs feel too dry or too damp, too warm or too cool? What organs feel strong and healthy; what organs feel weak or undernourished? What emotions do you notice? Observe. Then whenever you're ready, on an exhalation, let go.

On an inhalation, allow your breath to enter into your core. What do you encounter deep within? Listen to the rhythm, the pulse, the sound. Observe. Then whenever you're ready, on an exhalation, let go and enter into the deep inner stillness free of all sensations.

7/14/98

During the night, from deep within, Pele whispers, "To please me, embrace yourself. Enter the tunnel into the crater's depth; explore the dark, fathomless well within. Understand your ancient sorrow and grief. They have wisdom for you."

7/18/98

Night Prayer: *Ē Pele ē.* I welcome you into the ceremony of my dreams. Dance with me. Sing to me. Bring me *hō'ailona.* Confront the waters of my subconscious with the fires of your pit.

Morning Prayer: *Ē Pele ē.* As the sun climbs over the crater's rim, I feel your fire in my heart. Beneath my feet, I feel your strength and perseverance that formed this earth. I breathe the air and drink the water you released from Gaia's bowels. Divine breath inspires your wild actions. I will share with others the gifts of Spirit that you have shared with me. May my actions this day honor you and *Ke Akua* (God).

Koaʻe kea, the white-tailed tropicbird, circles in the wind on the wings of my prayer.

Morning prayer at Halemaʻumaʻu crater

Guided Imagery: Invoking Your Spirit Guide

Who are your guides from the spirit world? Who is the being who helps you most in your efforts to bridge heaven and earth? Is it factual or legendary, an ancestor, power animal, a loved one who has died? Is it Kali, Quan Yin, Buddha, Christ?

Enter your body by opening the crown chakra and the perineum (1st chakra). Notice your center. Find the silk thread that runs through your core, connecting heaven and earth. What is the vibration of this ethereal thread? Allow the vibration of this energetic axis of your body to diminish, to quiet, to calm.

Bask in the stillness radiating throughout your entire body. Then let the invocation to your spirit guide emerge from this still place and resonate along the silk thread. What are the words, tones, sounds of this invocation? When you are finished, sit down with your journal and allow the invocation to transform into your morning and night prayers.

7/21/98

I've been very sick for days in bed with high fever and chills into the bones, coughing up toxic green stuff. I've had diarrhea and vomiting. My body is in perpetual turmoil, and my fascia and joints are inflamed. At times I lie here doing Qigong healing for the infected left lung. Suddenly I realize that this is where Clarissa cleansed my rage—my heart and left lung. I am being reminded how important forgiveness is for healing. Forgiveness, purging, release.

7/29/98

A week has gone by. During my illness, Pele is very active and contrary and won't let me rest. I become desperate and ask for help. Suddenly, I feel new presences enter my body! A golden, laughing Buddha strolls into my heart. Then I feel a brilliance in the center of my brain and my third eye opens onto the Christ. White light radiates from the hearts of his palms. I am shocked! I was a devout Catholic up until my teens; however, during the late '60s, after becoming aware of the horrific injustices committed in the name of Christ, I rejected Christianity. I wonder: What is this white light? Is my rage at Christianity shifting? Softening? Perhaps Pele and Buddha bring balance.

8/1/98

Christ is white light: clarity, intellect, love, but also self-righteous moralism, guilt, and shame.

Buddha is golden light in the chambers of my heart: laughter, nurturing, and compassion, but also self-indulgence, worry, and procrastination.

Pele is crimson red, black, in the crater of my pelvis. She is the sweat of passion, adventure, wildness, creativity, but also rage, stubbornness, narcissism, destruction.

They speak to me:

Pele: Kaleo, I create, tend your gardens, and weave leis with ʻōhiʻa lehua. I nurture your pelvis. With fire I purge all obstacles from your body. I am keeper of your lower dan tian, near which reside your kidneys, urinary and reproductive systems, and intestinal tract.

Buddha: I cook sumptuous meals, am patient, and love to laugh. I am keeper of your middle dan tian, near which reside your heart and lungs, your cardiovascular and respiratory systems.

Christ: I heal with Light. I am keeper of your upper dan tian, near which reside your brain, pituitary gland, your eyes, ears, nose, and mouth, your endocrine and nervous systems.

8/2/98

Last night: Buddha, Pele, and Christ dine together in Buddha's cave located in my heart.

Buddha layers the floor of his cave with fragrant *'awapuhi* blossoms. He has prepared a nine course banquet—designed to nourish and integrate the dan tians of pelvis (body), heart (spirit), head (mind). Each course is designed to open specific chakras. Each course fuels the alchemical processes of body and soul—metal (lungs), water (kidneys), wood (liver), fire (heart), earth (spleen).

Pele brings a *kukui* "torch" lei and an eternal flame for illumination, ritual, creativity, protection, and purification. *Ua ola loko mālamalama.* This flame nurtures the body, heart, and mind.

Christ brings meditation and prayer, spaces between the tangible blessings and sensory delights offered by Pele and the laughing Buddha.

As dinner begins, the mood of Pele shifts from anticipation to fury. Her fire burns wildly, whipped by the changing wind inside Buddha's cave. A portal to the outer world opens in response to a gust of her breath. Myriad smells of incense and offerings pour into the cave. Many sounds and voices flow of prayers from many religions. The fervor is palpable and mounting. It gets louder! Now there are images of centuries of hypocrisy, savage violence, greed, corruption, and genocide in the name of God.

Buddha says, "I understand, Pele. I left wealth, power, and Nirvana itself to confront the suffering in the world. Listen to my mantra. I chant to bring the jewel of enlightenment into the lotus of the world, even as the lotus shrivels, even as there is no end in sight to the suffering."

Christ says, "I, too, understand, Pele. I suffer deeply. They crucified me, and now they commit atrocities in my name."

8/3/98

The *pāhoehoe* lava crust still covers my heart. Within me, Pele, Buddha, and Christ continue their conversation. Dialogue, understanding, forgiveness are important, and I find my anger transforming into healing energy, an energy I can channel into my sacred work in the world.

9/20/04 Six Years Later

I come from Hawai'i. From my mother, who was born and raised in Pāhala, a sugar cane plantation in Ka'ū, near Kīlauea volcano on the Big Island, I learned to sing old Hawaiian songs. I learned the importance of *'ohana* (family). From the people of the islands, I learned the spirit of *aloha* (loving kindness) and *kōkua* (helping others).

And now, I close my eyes and listen. I hear the *kāhea* (invocation chant) far off in the distance and find myself going back, traveling through time and space. It's such a beautiful day! It's 1966 and I'm 18 years old and body surfing at Makapu'u. The waves are huge! Amazing to be immersed totally in the power of the sea! Suddenly, I'm caught in a strong current. It's pulling me out to sea! Everything's receding—the bobbing heads of the body surfers, the shoreline, the Ko'olau mountains. How I love the Ko'olaus, so ancient, raw, and enduring, standing tall. I always feel their presence.

It all feels like a dream and I recall another day—I'm just a kid, having spent the day surfing at Queen's. I'm looking at the drowned surfer lying on the sand after being hauled out of the ocean by the lifeguard—his body is purple, bloated, fluids leaking from his nostrils and mouth. I also see a childhood friend, Stephen, who borrowed my surfboard one day—they found his body tucked under the coral reefs at Diamond Head three days later.

The powerful current drags me farther out to sea. Will my body ever be found? I'm cold, helpless, exhausted. Fear grips me, squeezes my lungs. I feel so heavy. I tell myself to breathe, relax, but I'm so tired. I call for help, but feel resigned. Who can hear me at this distance? Suddenly I hear something. Just four words. "Eh Bruddah, hang on." A *Kanaka Maoli* (Native Hawaiian) man on his surfboard paddles alongside me. I grab the edge of his board and catch my breath as he tows me back into the breakers, where I ride a wave into shore.

It all feels like a dream as I lie on the sand, tasting the salt on my lips, hearing the waves pounding the beach. The sun massages me; the calm strength of the Ko'olaus reassures me.

As my body absorbs the healing of the *'āina* (land), I'm reminded of the other Hawaiian who helped me just a few years ago. I was board surfing and broke a couple of ribs when I got pounded into the coral reef. I would not be here today if it had not been for the *kōkua* of those two *Kānaka Maoli* surfers.

And now, Pele calls me home. Home to my roots. She reminds me about honor, love, and respect for *Ke Akua* (the Divine), *nā 'aumākua* (the ancestors), *ka 'āina* (the land), and *nā po'e kānaka o Hawai'i* (the people of Hawai'i). And I give thanks through *pule* (prayer), through tithing to Hawaiian educational and cultural associations, and by sharing the spirit of *aloha*. To share *aloha*, I teach integrative processes of Qigong, art for healing, and acu-lomi (integrating the traditional arts of acupressure and *lomilomi* massage). Elise and I also share this book as an expression of our *aloha*.

For the past six years, Elise and I have made pilgrimages to the Big Island. We always spend time at Volcanoes National Park and do *pule* (prayer) at Halema'uma'u Crater. This place is also sacred for me ancestrally because my mother and grandparents lived only about twenty miles away in Pāhala. Every year I attend the Hawaiian Lomilomi Conference and have been embraced by the presence and wisdom of venerable healers such as

Alva Andrews, Ikaika Dombrigues, Aunty Mary Fragas, Desmon Haumea, Haunani Hopkins, Kai and Linda Kaholokai, Uncle Robert Keliʻihoʻomalu, Papa Kepelino, Aunty Margaret Machado, and my *kumu* (teachers) *lomilomi*, Dane Kaohelani Silva and Makaʻala Yates.

Kumu Dane Kaohelani Silva, Big Island of Hawaiʻi

Life is prayer. *Mahalo* to Buddha, Christ, and Pele. My Qigong practice is ancient mantra, my body chanting in honor of my Asian ancestors: "On, Ch'ung, Mal-li, Chae-ha, Haeju Choi." My Catholic schooling provided me a religious and educational structure. My Hawaiian *lomilomi* practice embodies *aloha* and *pule*.

PULE A KA HAKU (THE LORD'S PRAYER)

E kō mākou makua i loko o ka lani
E hoʻāno ʻia kou inoa.

E hiki mai kou aupuni
E mālama ʻia kou makemake ma ka honua nei
E like me ia i mālama ʻia ma ka lani lā.

E hāʻawi mai iā mākou i kēia lā, i ʻai na mākou no nēia lā.

E kala mai hoʻi iā mākou i kā mākou lawehala ʻana
Me mākou e kala nei i ka poʻe i lawehala iā mākou.

Mai hoʻokuʻu ʻoe iā mākou i ka hoʻowalewale ʻia mai
E hoʻopakele no naʻe iā mākou i ka ʻino.

No ka mea, nou ke aupuni, ā me ka mana.

Ā me ka hoʻonani ʻia ā mau loa aku.

ʻAmene.

1/22/05 Elise and Kaleo's Journey

It is the one year anniversary of my mother's death. I'm writing this to give you an understanding of origins, in this case of how Elise's and my integrative process evolved over the years.

I keep learning during this lifetime how important it is to keep my relationships with myself and others sacred. We are what we ingest, through our eyes, ears, mouth, nose, mind, and intuition. For me, fulfillment comes from feeding and nurturing the Divine within and sharing with others. We hope our story inspires you in your sacred work in the world.

And now, I close my eyes and listen. I hear the *kāhea* (invocation chant) far off in the distance, and I find myself eagerly going back, traveling through time and space.

It's 1989 and Elise and my relationship is in gestation; it's about nine months old. We are newly in love, happy and comfortable. In our world, all goes well. We're living off Piedmont Avenue in Oakland in a green fourplex. Our upstairs apartment overlooks the parking lot of Fenton's Creamery. From our living room window, I love to watch the eager ice cream connoisseurs coming and going, while I work at my artist's easel. In our dining nook, Elise types away on one of many papers for her Transpersonal Psychology degree at JFKU.

Then we hear the news on the radio. We are stunned, and turn on the TV. The image is etched in our minds: in China, one young man in a white shirt standing up to stop advancing tanks. Days later we watch the Chinese Army's response as it storms through Tian'anmen Square squelching the student protests. Many protesters are killed, wounded, imprisoned. There is shock around the world.

Our Peet's coffee, usually luscious, tastes bitter now as we watch the images flash across the screen. So much violence! So much blood, again, being shed in the land of my ancestors.

The brutality is oppressive. I recognize it: the void, the humid darkness, the viscosity of fear, the dripping of pthalos, the screams of crimsons and reds. They're in my body. "Get out! Out of my heart, out of my body!" They fly from my fingers onto the white expectant canvas. In this whiteness, colors, shapes, images, emotions emerge. The violent acts, the crushing of souls, the shattering of bodies—a ritual of darkness. The spreading of textures, the interactive colors, the splashing of paint—a ritual of light.

My ancestors speak. Cosmic Qi fills my body. Qi gushes forth in an alchemical fusion of the ancient with the present, of the elements of nature, of human souls. Qi flows through the rivers of meridians, through forearms, fingers, paint brush, onto canvas. It's all Qigong.

I can feel Elise's eyes on me. When I'm done, she quietly hands me a poem she just wrote, "Wrath of the Dragon." This is the first time she's shown me her poetry. I'll never forget this moment. After reading her poem, I understand the depth of her compassion, her commitment to Spirit. Anyone who can paint with words like this must have the gift to access other realms, must have the sensitivity, humility, and wisdom to harvest from these realms. This moment is the birth of our collaboration of art and poetry.

Again, I hear the *kāhea* (invocation chant) and find myself traveling though time and space. It's a year later, and we're in the sanctuary of the redwoods. We've just left a prayer bundle of herbs in a secret cache by the stream. As we turn, we notice the cave. It's inviting and we enter and journey into the tunnel down into the underworld. Elise has been here before; she knows the way and guides me with her voice and drum. I trust her and I sink deeper into the spongy earth. The fragrance is redwood. The wind, so warm and soft, carries the voices of the ancient ones. They reassure me and I sink even deeper. The tunnel, the gurgling of the stream, the pulse of the drum, the pulse of my heart, the blood in my veins—I'm being swept into the mystery, until I emerge into the soft quiet of a clearing in the rainforest at dusk. Suddenly white tiger approaches. I tremble, but as I look into his eyes, deep blue as the late afternoon sky peeking through the canopy of leaves, fear gives way to curiosity, then to trust. He shares with me skills of quiet watching, of looking to the source within. He shares with me the courage to create and the desire to live with passion. He shares with me Tiger's Breath Qigong movements. When it is time for me to leave, he teaches me a *kāhea* that will always guide me back to this realm, to his territory. This journey is the beginning of Elise's and my integration of her guided imagery with my art and maskmaking.

Again, I hear the *kāhea* and find myself traveling through time and space. It's the early '90s. A door of thick glass and steel slams shut! I jump nervously! Someone's screaming! Lungs bursting! Rage! I find myself enclosed by cement and steel reinforced walls that imprison. Solid glass cages house inmates in County Jail orange garb. I'm on the upper tier, in the Jail Psychiatric Unit, teaching Qigong, meditation, and maskmaking to maximum security inmates. In this moment in class, we're all seated and I'm guiding them into the inner realm, into a world of freedom and serenity. We are traveling through the tunnel to meet our totem animals, my voice and drum guiding them safely on their odyssey. As we emerge into the landscape of the other world, I open my eyes softly and peer down onto the bottom tier. There's Elise. She's working as a Registered Nurse with her inmate patients. She wears a white lab coat—a stroke of white in a sea of orange. I close my eyes and the soft breathing of the inmates brings me back to the landscape of the other world. I love teaching in the County Jail! In here, there's such an edge. I learn difficult but intimate lessons about the human condition. And my students here are so full of gratitude for the experiences and lessons we share.

Again, I hear the *kāhea*. This time, Elise and I are at the Piedmont Yoga Studio standing with careful alignment and attentive surrender in Virabhadrasana II, a yoga warrior pose. Rodney Yee is demonstrating the subtleties of the pose, the balancing of yin and yang. What an inspirational and brilliant teacher you are, Rodney! I'm grateful for your wisdom. And how our friendship and creativity blossom as you, Elise, and I teach our annual workshops that integrate your yoga, Elise's guided imagery, and my maskmaking process.

Again, I hear the *kāhea* and I find myself traveling through time and space to the present day. Our *'ohana* (family) grows as Elise and I teach integrative art as healing classes at educational and healing institutions. Over the past fifteen years we've developed and honed about ten different classes that have evolved from our spiritual and creative practices.

Our classes integrate Qigong, guided imagery, journaling, art, and maskmaking. Qigong is body ritual. Elise's guided imagery encourages risking, trusting, opening to the journey into the mystery. The journaling, art, and maskmaking embody the discoveries.

The Qigong, acupressure, and massage classes I teach and my private bodywork practice are also about integration—about entering into the layers of the body and the realms of the subconscious and dialoguing with meridians, flesh, blood, and bones—about connecting with the Universal Spirit and dialoguing with the client's body, psyche, and soul.

We love our work. We see our students transform as they trust, discover and express their truths. We see them growing, moving toward healing, integration, and empowerment.

Our students and clients grace us with their stories. We've always wanted to keep their inspiring stories alive, to share them with others, to spread their lessons in wisdom and compassion.

About eleven years ago, in 1994, Elise showed me a short story she had written. I was totally impressed by her writing skills, now in prose as well as poetry! This moment began our collaboration in writing our books: this book, and our book in progress on Qigong for creativity.

It's been quite a long haul of writing—eleven years of expanding, reworking, adding explorations and stories as our own experiences expand. Sometimes the writing has been a flood of ideas and images, as when Pele's tumultuous but powerful creative energy surged through us and we wrote wildly for months in a storm of discovery and inspiration. Sometimes the writing has been a careful collaboration of honing the words we share. Both parts are a labor of love: the challenge of balancing the excitement of creative process and the discipline of refinement. We hope these pages bring more understanding, love, and light into your lives and into the world. We hope they inspire the joy of creativity, the grace of prayer and meditation, the awe of the mystery.

'Okika Kea (White Orchid)

Elise's Journal

6/19/99 First Pilgrimage to the Big Island

One year after Kaleo's healing with Clarissa, we make a pilgrimage to the Big Island of Hawai'i to honor Pele. Kaleo's mother was born and raised on the sugar plantation in Pāhala, just miles from Pele's lair at Halema'uma'u crater. There we meet a childhood friend of hers, Beneficio, now in his 80s, sitting on his *lānai* across from the home where she grew up. He "talks story" with us about the old days, about the work in the fields, *kani ka pila* (playing music), playing cards, and boxing with Kaleo's uncles, around 65 or 70 years ago. This was before Kaleo's parents met and moved to O'ahu. Later, Kaleo and I visit his grandfather's grave nearby, a link to a lineage traced back 1,000 and more years.

The interconnectedness of people with the land impresses me. You cannot live in the shadow of an active volcano and think human beings dominate nature. You cannot live at the southernmost tip of an island chain and not be penetrated by the power of wind and sea. You cannot live inhaling sulfur and take for granted the air you breathe.

Elise heading over *pāhoehoe* to the Pu'u 'Ō'ō lava flow

The land here is vital, animate, fire making earth, releasing water and air from the bowels of earth, fire exploding from a crater high above our view to pour down as lava. It sends an orange glow at night, as Pele and her sister, Nāmakaokaha'i, goddess of the sea, do steamy battle.

9/2000 Second Pilgrimage to the Big Island

Kaleo and I return to the Big Island. We receive many *hō'ailona,* many signs.

Four *nēnē* geese welcome us and fly just above us beyond our reach as we do ritual and prayer at dawn at Halema'uma'u crater. A rainbow, *he ānuenue,* comes and spans the mile-wide crater's rim, then sinks into the pit, where it nestles for over one-half hour, arcing from the crater floor. However, the volcanic eruption has been elusive, nothing for a visitor to witness for over a month now. Yet our second to last evening, we learn the flow has made its way over the *pali,* the cliff, into view and is heading toward the sea once again.

Nēnē (Hawaiian geese) at Halema'uma'u crater

We drive to the end of Chain of Craters Road where the asphalt ends and Pele's wide path begins. The hike is tedious.

The *pāhoehoe* is rough, rolling, and vast. It's hard to keep our sights on the smoke of our destination five miles away and on our footing at the same time. And falls embed little shards of volcanic glass in our arms and legs. But the smoke intensifies until finally we arrive at the flowing lava's edge. The wind laughs heat at us over the flow. Our faces flush. Our eyes sting. Our throats burn with dragon's breath. The lava's gray mass blanketing the orange glowing body of fire oozes toward us. As it stalks, it sets the scruffy vegetation aflame. Its movement seems reptilian: slow, deliberate, patient, stubborn, elegant.

We scramble a bit up the hillside and find ourselves perched in a foolish position just beneath a skylight where lava peeks through a *piko,* a navel, in the lava tube that channels it down the slope. Kaleo says, "Let's get out of here!" We descend to where the flow is more gentle, if ever lava can be gentle. And don't ever imagine that it is predictable. Visitors to the flow do not die daily, yet enough ghosts haunt the edges of this new land to fill a nighttime of campfire stories about their too intimate and final encounters with the great wild goddess of fire.

Fresh lava flowing from Puʻu ʻŌʻō

We trudge back over the *pāhoehoe.* It is dusk now. Behind us, a loud explosion. We turn. The entire hillside is on fire and the *piko* has ruptured into three red lava rivers raging down the slope where we had been standing. The power and passion of Pele are not to be taken lightly. This *hōʻailona* is unnervingly grand.

9/2001 Third Pilgrimage to the Big Island

It is September 11th at six a.m. As I am walking to Halemaʻumaʻu crater, I recall a weird dream about two *nēnē* geese in the road, one flattened, one crossing. I arrive at the crater, receive its acerbic greeting. I send *pule,* prayers, across the churlish mouth. The crater's edge is eerily bare of offerings, none of the usual fruit, flowers, and fresh pork bundles. And no *nēnē.* But around the rim beyond the well-used path, I spot two sulfur-frosted coconuts, perched precariously three years now between deep cracks at the very rim, offerings shriveled, homely, but long lasting. Then Kaleo arrives: "Terrorists have hijacked planes and destroyed the World Trade Center and crashed into the Pentagon! Thousands may be dead!" I am stunned. The crater, holy and uncomforting, still gasps acrid breath.

We mourn along with other stranded visitors at the lodge. We return to the crater the next morning, offer prayers for the dead, the survivors, the leaders, the perpetrators, to *Ke Akua* to lift darkness from our hearts. I shed tears, feel muzzy and confused. Then Kaleo exclaims in wonder, "*Hōʻailona*, a sign!" I step back. There, at my foot, a *koaʻe kea* feather lodges between crusty chunks of *ʻaʻā* lava, as the lovely white birds themselves wing above their home in the inhospitable crater.

9/2002 Fourth Pilgrimage to the Big Island

This year, it's Kaleo's second *lomilomi* (traditional Hawaiian massage) conference in rainy Hilo, followed by a maskmaking/*lomilomi* retreat led by *kumu* Dane Kaohelani Silva, Kaleo, and others. The retreatants are practitioners of the Hawaiian healing arts, especially *lomilomi* massage and *lāʻau lapaʻau* (healing herbs). We laugh together as the rafters drip our constant companion rain. We carve *lāʻau lomi* (bodywork sticks) from forked guava branches. We stroll the writhing shoreline and tremble in the *mana* of deep, remote, misty, and mysterious Waipiʻo Valley.

Kaleo and I teach maskmaking and guided imagery. The masks created by the healing arts practitioners evoke the inner healer. The process of setting the intention, forming the mask mold on a partner's face, and connecting through touch is like doing massage. It asks for focused alignment of mind, body, and spirit. Then through paint and adornment, the finished masks emerge from the depths of the maskmakers' creative pools. They embody bits of the *mana* of the Big Island: flower leis and *lau kī* (ti leaves), fertile green of tropical rainforest, black and red with metallic sheen of volcano, blues and grays of shifting warm skies and mirroring ocean, images of warrior, lover, healer, dancer, worshipper at the shrine of *Ke Akua* where the island dips beneath the sea.

Kaleo and I return to Halemaʻumaʻu crater one last time before leaving the Big Island. We meet Malulani, whom we've met here before. We help her clean up cigarette butts and trash along the trail near this sacred site.

We finish our work and get ready to leave the crater's realm. Suddenly, out of the mist a double rainbow emerges, spanning the road beyond us, then begins coming closer. Finally it is right around us, encircling us in its luminous hoop and caressing us with its layered light. "It's embracing us! We must have strong *mana*!" exclaims Malulani. Then the rainbow recedes back up the road and into the mist.

Mahalo Ke Akua mau loa, aloha nō.

9/2005

Each year Kaleo and I return to the Big Island. While Kaleo reconnects with the Hawaiian *lomilomi* community, I use this time to let the raw landscape of the land feed me creatively, personally, spiritually. Each year we visit the land where Pele destroys and creates in her perpetual cycle of death and birth.

Each year I too die a little, am born a little. There is so much to let go of, so much to surrender. There is so much to learn, to deepen, to practice, to share. Returning to Halemaʻumaʻu crater is a gauge. How does it feel to be here this time? What has gone, what has come in my life, in my being in the past year? What coals of wisdom from the crater's edge can I take with me to stoke the cauldron of inner alchemy in the upcoming year?

Elise doing Qigong *ma ka ʻae kai*

Guided Imagery: Retreat with Your Spirit Guide

Your spirit guide is nudging you. It is time for you to go on a retreat. This is a chance to combine the inner and the outer journey in one. Your guide, of course, will accompany you, as it always does. Ordinary reality has its demands, so you and your guide must work together to make this retreat a reality. In your journal, reflect on the following questions.

- What is your intention for your journey? This is an important aspect of your preparation. In what area of your life do you want clarity and insight? How do you hope to change as a result of this journey?

- When will you go and for how long?

- Where will you go: a sanctuary in your home, a campground an hour away, the mountains, the ocean, the Arctic, Nepal?

- Will you go on an organized outing, such as a yoga or Qigong retreat, a vision quest, a pilgrimage to sacred sites, a Zen *sesshin*? Or will your retreat be self-led?

- Where will you stay: retreat center, monastery, motel, tent?

- Will it be only you and your spirit guide, or will you invite anyone else to accompany you?

- How will you travel: by bicycle, car, train, plane?

- What clothes and gear will you take? What process materials will you bring: journal, writing tools, art supplies, collage materials?

- What rules will you follow on your retreat as far as talking and silence, schedules, times for inner exploration and outer exploration, amount and kinds of food you will eat?

Now close your eyes. Your spirit guide is ready to lead you on a rehearsal run of your journey, just as you have planned it.

Your Spirit Guide Meets the Shadow

NOTE: If you suffer from clinical emotional symptoms, please consult a specialist. These exercises are not offered as substitutes for psychotherapy or psychiatry.

The shadow. It is the darkness within that rides our backs and claws the walls of our hearts. It drags us down by the hair and smothers us with its slimy skin. It sucks our energy, mists our minds, and tricks our wills. But creative process can help to confront and transform the dark figures of the inner journey.

The shadow comes by many names: depression, despair, addiction, fear, doubt, failure, abandonment, and many more. It contains the stuff from our subconscious that is obscured to our awareness. Bringing a part of the shadow into the light of awareness is the first step toward transformation. What shadow figures do you feel ready and willing to confront and transform? Keep track of your waking and sleeping dreams and their inhabitants. Record what you recall. Then find a quiet space to dialogue with them. Ask the dark figures you encounter who they are, what they want from you, what purpose they serve. Ask them what they are trying to show you about your life in ordinary reality. Ask them how you can help them to transform.

Always remember, you are in control and you can invoke your spirit guide to help you at any time. You decide if and how to engage the figures from the shadow. You can end the dialogue, like closing the door, at any time. You can summon your spirit guide and your own inner strengths, enter into the darkness, and change it from within. In one Qigong meditation that we lead, your spirit guide shines a light through the lens of your third eye, where it reflects into the recesses of the shadow to reveal the yin and yang of the wisdom and challenge that the shadow harbors. You can step back, see what is positive and negative, and learn from the lessons to bring more health and wholeness into your life.

One theory of dreams proposes that dream characters are all aspects of oneself. This perspective can help confront the disagreeable ones with more understanding. From facing the shadow can come acceptance and forgiveness, in your own time, your own way.

A strong guide, a flashlight, and a map make a big difference in a dark forest. They make a difficult journey possible.

Elise: Confronting Violence

What is the relationship between weapon and spirit? When I spin my wooden Taiji staff, my blows are fighting only the demon of fear within. Without fear, there is no enemy, not even death.

Working as a Registered Nurse in the County Jail (for twenty-three years!) is Taiji/Qigong practice. It requires focused intention and groundedness. There is a lot to be afraid of in jail, but not always what one might expect. The threat is as likely to be a lawsuit as a shank. A weapon could be a toothbrush handle, a sharp pencil, an open wound, teeth, bloody saliva, smeared feces. The danger is not always visible. It can also come in the form of tuberculosis, hepatitis, or AIDS.

It is difficult to sustain empathy in the face of constant demands. How badly do I want to give that man special care when I learn he just handcuffed and tortured his wife last night? What are the boundaries of compassion?

But on a deeper level the question is a very personal one: that of identity. The barriers begin to break down. The professional role is just a costume to create distance. Take it off and there is no more "I" and "they." What has kept me from becoming a prostitute, a heroin addict, a murderer? The faces and bodies on the other side of the bars, beneath the gunshot and stab wound scars, the tattoos of gang identity, the needle tracks, simply represent a different set of life experiences, a surface difference.

During my first year of work, a man who was in jail for accusations of cannibalism had sliced open his arm. When we nurses responded to the "man-down" call, we found him lying in an expanding pool of spurting crimson arterial blood. As I knelt over him, I thought, if one has gone as far as cannibalism, what could be left, except to cannibalize oneself?

As we wheeled him on the gurney back to the medical office, a voice pressed against the inside of my brain: "There but for the grace of God go I." I was not a particularly religious person, but the words shook me up. The jail bars seemed thin barriers. I knew what really bugged me was, being human, not only was I also capable of being that person on the gurney; on a deeper level, I was that person: There go I. There are no heroes here. Only *namaste* matters: The sacred in me bows to the sacred in you. Yin and yang stay close together, spiraling. The conviction that we are all related, all one, encompasses the societal Shadow.

Art and Writing: Voice of the Shadow

All the systems of the body work synchronistically to cleanse, nurture, maintain, and heal. The soul does this through creativity. We approach creativity with the intention of healing. During years of teaching the creative process, we have often found students contact and express their pain first, then move on to healing and transformation.

Sit in meditation. Quiet your breath, your body, your mind. Call on your spirit guide for guidance, support, and inspiration.

Bring into your attention a face from the shadow. Where do you experience awareness of this face in your body? Where does it reside? What is the feeling it evokes inside?

You want to bring the face into neutral territory. In order to do this, create a safe place where you can perceive it objectively. Where do you place this face so that it can talk to you in a way that feels safe to you? You can put it on a stage or on a movie screen where you can close the curtain whenever you want. You can listen to it through a protective glass wall. You can place it ten feet away from you with your spirit guide between you.

Now allow this face of shadow to express itself. Who is it? How old is it? What does it have to say? What does it do?

Your spirit guide is there to support you. Just listen. Just observe. When you're ready, you can ask this face to be still and leave.

Now put your experience into images on paper through drawing, painting, and collage. Let your body scratch, tear, dig, rub, pummel energies of colors, lines, forms. Your body will let you know when the creative process is done.

Your spirit guide invites you to engage your art piece in some way. Do you burn, bury, tear, baptize, forgive, or bless your art form? Listen to the voice of your guide in your inner body. Release the sound of your guide through your hands, your body, your voice.

Now, in your journal, write about your creative process. What happened as you listened to the face from the shadow? Then how did your spirit guide move you to create? Where are you now in your process of healing? Where do you go from here?

Kaleo: Maximum Security, Jail Psychiatric Unit

My body moves sluggishly through the pungent air, thick with despair, anger, madness. I'm in the Jail Psychiatric Unit, teaching Qigong, meditation, and maskmaking.

Tom. The voices and phantoms in your head are quieted now by the prescribed medications. A few years ago in a drug-induced violent rage, you murdered several of your family members. Yesterday your mother and sister came to visit you. I'll never forget your mother's eyes—such sorrow, love, and fear. She feels your illness, your pain. Every Sunday at Mass, she prays for your soul. I see you phoning her almost daily and wonder what your conversation is like. Your body is so heavy with remorse, your longing to die, your fear of death. You say you must do penance for your sins and it's better to do it here on earth than in eternity. Today is your birthday. I brought you some special food from your homeland. Your eyes reveal gratitude, but I can feel your tears falling. We both cry inwardly so no one can hear or see.

Robby. During Qigong practice today, as I touched your arm to open the meridian flow, I almost recoiled. Four years ago when we first met, you were tanned, athletic, and muscular. Now an odd-colored flesh hangs on your body. The smell is putrid. It's flesh deprived of sun, fresh air, and nature. It's the flesh of jail food, artificial lights, cement walls. It's the gray of the cell you live in. Muscle has surrendered to hopelessness, knowing it's in for life.

"Randy"

I feel each of you, your despair. I feel your violence, your rape, your murder. I feel your remorse, confusion, grief. I feel the self-inflicted razor slices covering your body. I feel you, your screaming, your banshee wailing, your body slamming itself against the walls of your padded cell. Bam! Bam! Bam! Oh God, is this the human condition?

At night, violent dreams stalk me. Talking to therapists is not enough. My body and soul crave release. I make a mask of an inmate with whom I have worked closely. Then, in the sanctuary of my studio, I ask for guidance from Pele and the Divine.

I cut six inches of my hair and tie it with pig gut to the mask. I add deer fur, rib bone, hide, incense, Chinese joss paper, and candles.

The mask demands fire: purging, drying out, purifying, burning out the old, turning what is black to ashen white. The odor of burning wax, fur, hide, hair, and bone reveals death in life, life in death. My chant accompanies the smoke into the heavens.

What's left of the mask I bury in the soft, fragrant, wet earth. The violent nightmares dissolve, never to return.

Guided Imagery and Art: Forgiveness

Steps

1   Have an abundance of art supplies ready.

2   Sit in meditation, meet your spirit guide, and enter your circle of protection.

3   Someone who has caused you hurt approaches.

4   Feel your reaction.

5   Embody your response in art.

6   Go back to your circle and encounter this person.

7   This person asks for forgiveness and you respond.

8   Embody your response in art.

9   Journal in response to your drawing.

10   What is the next step in your healing process?

Process

Before you begin, have in front of you an abundance of art supplies that manifest a variety of emotions, textures, colors, and densities.

Sit in meditation, allowing your breath to be natural and soft. Each breath allows your body and mind to rest. Each breath brings you deeper into relaxation. Each breath brings you deeper into yourself until you feel the presence of your spirit guide approaching. How safe you feel as your guide leads you into a circle, a sacred circle within your inner terrain. Where are you? What is the color of the circle you're in? Feel how protected you are. Understand that no one is permitted to enter this circle except by your invitation.

Then notice in the distance a diaphanous being waiting in its own field of color. It is the presence of someone you dislike or with whom you are angry. It could be a parent, a friend, an adversary, someone who has died, or even your own past self. How have you been hurt by this presence? Feel your reaction to it. Invite it to come closer. Look at your pain. Where does it lie in your body? What is its shape, color, texture? How does it affect your breath, your facial expression, the sensations along your skin and in your organs?

Then come back to your breath. Notice its rhythm and pulse. Leave the presence of the person where it is and turn your attention to your immediate outer world. From the art supplies laid out before you, let your spirit guide inspire you and your instincts move your body. Choose colors, textures, and tools and gather them into your palms; then exhale your warm, moist breath onto them. Now allow your reactions to the person's presence to draw themselves.

When you're ready, pause in your creative process. Close your eyes. Become aware of your breath, and allow it to take you back into the sacred circle. Notice how comfortable and safe you feel within this circle. Feel the presence of your spirit guide supporting you. Then notice the presence of the person you are dialoguing with standing just outside of this sacred circle. Listen as it asks you for forgiveness. Is it sincere? How does your body, your gut, react? Accept your honest response and tell this presence what you need to say. Is it time for you to reject or forgive? Observe closely—what are your reactions to each other? When you're ready, allow this presence to dissolve into the distance, sending with it any final word or intention.

"Alchemy" by Kaleo (mixed media mask, 18″h x 12″w x 7″d)

Again, turn your attention back to the outer world. Allow words, symbols, sounds, new colors to enter the drawing: colors and shapes of rejection, forgiveness, or healing. Allow the pulse to move from your organs, bones, connective tissues. Feel the emotions run through the flesh of your drawing. Perhaps you feel drawn to delve beneath the fascia or create layers on top of your drawing's skin.

In your intimate space, at your altar, bless the drawing. You may want to leave it for a few days then look at it and see what the lessons are. As you confront your drawing, ask your spirit guide, what is the next step toward wholeness for you? What needs to be done to resolve, heal, move on?

You may feel moved to burn the piece. What do you feel emotionally as it transforms into ash and smoke? Gather the ashes, mix them with liquid to make a salve, and paint the shape of what needs to be released onto your body wherever it is lodged. Using meditation, spiral deeper into your body—into that place. Use the rest of the salve to mix with paint or gel medium. Paint the shapes of your emotions on canvas. Allow colors and shapes to shift, transform, and heal. Observe the shifts, transformations, and healing that occur in your body, mind, and spirit as you paint.

Observe how you shift over time. Sometimes, when you resolve dark issues that have been holding you back, you will notice that you have more energy to move forward in the world. You may notice yourself becoming clearer about your sacred life's purpose.

Thank your spirit guide for accompanying and supporting you on your ongoing journey.

Sacred Purpose

Your *sacred purpose* gives focus, direction, and structure to your life's journey in the world.

For us, the goddess Pele is one source of inspiration and guidance from our inner worlds. Your relationship with your spirit guide can deepen your responses to your life's big questions. This process involves first looking within, recognizing and accepting your gifts, then realizing how you share them in daily life and identifying how you can share them more fully and surely. It also involves knowing your audience, with whom or what you want to work. To enhance your sacred purpose means to embrace your own life, to enter into a conscious and meaningful relationship with the world through giving and receiving. It means to give and receive with a sense of the sacred.

Writing: Autobiography of Work

Elise: Sacred Purpose in the World

Twenty some years ago, I was bored with teaching freshman composition in a Midwestern university and headed west. I found myself tutoring Arapaho children on the Wind River Reservation in Wyoming and moonlighting as a bartender in a wild oil-rig and ranching town.

Little did I know then that I would end up several long roads and sharp curves later as a nurse in the San Francisco County Jail.

Jail nursing is a soup of experiences. Cut wrists, tearful faces, bodies wasted from AIDS and tuberculosis, bodies scarred with needle tracks, drowned with booze. Accidents happen; fights happen; those with violent inclinations will find creative ways to hurt themselves or others, from sharpened toothbrush handles to dismantled blades of disposable razors. One time we nurses responded to a "man-down" call, to find a corpse hanging from his sheet in his private cell, too many moments dead to respond to CPR. We must perform it anyway, until someone qualified to pronounce death arrives. I wonder if anyone can help feeling a sense of failure when staring suicide in the face. If only...?

I remember feeling funky at work one day, feeling like I was just a slender spoke in a gigantic wheel, spinning along on the journey to nowhere. The same faces, same bodies, return to jail over and over—more stab wounds, bullet holes, needle tracks. And who knows what happens to the ones we never see again? A few successes—those who never come back because they are leading happy and healthy lives free of crime. But how many are far away behind bars for the best part of their lives? And how many are dead, from the bullet that found its way home, the heroin that was too pure, the noose strung just long and tight enough?

Jail health care seems anything but the holistic path I had envisioned for myself as a nurse. Healing is a holistic and transpersonal process, involving body, mind, emotions, spirit, interconnectedness. The times working in jail where I feel part of that process are rare.

Yet making a difference happens day to day. To think otherwise is to miss the road. The trail of my sacred life's purpose began in the mists of childhood longings and disappears around tomorrow's bend. And in the present it is a path of intertwining parts, all feeding, supporting, challenging, enriching each other. My practice of Qigong helps ground and center me on the path. This book Kaleo and I are writing is a chronicle of that road. Our relationship is the earth beneath my feet and the sky above the crown of my head. Teaching together the integrative process of guided imagery, Qigong, and art, each class, workshop, or retreat going deeper, is a rich, solid stretch of the road. Leading others on guided imagery journeys for self-discovery and empowerment honors and explores the mystery of that path. And being a nurse in the jails is part of the road as well, in its continuity, perspective, and raw form of service.

Write your autobiography of work. It may be half a page long; it may be ten pages long. In it consider the following:

- What was your first inkling of a life's purpose and when did you feel it?

- How has your relationship to purpose evolved over time?

- How would you define your sacred life's purpose at this time?

- What are your gifts; what are you good at; what do you love to do?

- Who or what is your audience in relationship to your purpose?

- How does your work support and fulfill your purpose?

- How are your choices affected by your body/mind/spirit practices?

- Are you at a crossroads in your life's journey now?

- What steps have brought you where you are and what steps are before you?

- How can your relationship with your spirit guide help you in relationship to your sacred purpose?

Guidelines for Sacred Purpose: The Ongoing Journey

The following are some guidelines for keeping your relationship to your sacred life's purpose an active, integrated, and focused part of your life.

- *Dedicate your sacred purpose to your spiritual Source.* Talk to your spirit guide. Surrender to its wisdom and timing, as well as to the wisdom and timing of the universe. At the same time, take an active and responsible part in your journey.

- *Begin with a Sacred Purpose Journal.* What kind of journal do you choose for this work? Do you choose a large artist's sketchbook, so that your process can be varied and expansive? Or do you choose a small notebook that you can carry everywhere with you in your pocket? In your journal, keep track of how your life's purpose is evolving and manifesting. You may want to include collage, drawing, wisdom from your spirit guide, and photographs of mentors. You may want to record your dreams.

- *Are you vague about the form your sacred purpose is to take?* If so, ask your spirit guide what it wants and expects of you. Ask it what passions remain hidden within you. Ask it what you can do to arouse your energy and to illuminate your path. What qualities does your spirit guide possess that are ready to be cultivated in you?

- *Take action to bring about insight and discoveries.* Talk to people who practice the endeavors that interest you. Be present in the environments where you might want to manifest your intention, around people with similar visions.

- *If you already know what your sacred purpose is, how can you bring it to life?* What can you *do* to give it breath and movement? Do you need to resurrect buried skills? Create a community? Do volunteer work to give you experience?

- *List goals and timelines for your sacred purpose endeavors.* Be specific. Do you need to get training? If so, where? How long will your education take, and how much will it cost? How will it affect your family, home, and life-style? Do you need to get experience? If so, how and where and with whom? Will sharing your sacred purpose be a career or an avocation? If a career, how much money do you need to make, and are your income expectations compatible with the possibilities for manifesting your sacred purpose? If not, which part will compromise and how?

- *Take one step at a time.* How do you go about achieving your sacred purpose, at the same time maintaining your other commitments? What is your first step? Taking an evening class? Volunteering once a week? Involving your family and enlisting their support in your transition?

- *Do art about your sacred purpose.* Look at the Fool card in the Tarot deck. The fool, representing not foolishness, but innocence, creativity, and openness to adventure, is beginning a journey, a quest. He faces many choices. He carries a staff dangling a bag over his shoulder. One way of looking at this picture is that the staff is the yang and the pouch is the yin support for his journey. The staff can assist him over rough places. The pouch carries elements to help him on his journey. You might want to make your own sacred purpose staff and pouch. What are they made of, what do they carry, and how will they be of help to you on your own quest?

- *Keep in mind: The messages from your spirit guide, the symbols from your dreams, the clues in your art speak the language of the subconscious.* They may be cryptic, contradictory, mysterious. They may require action before their meanings gain clarity. This is where ongoing work with them has its rewards. Often the messages that seem vague or paradoxical at first become clearer as you relate to them over time. Also a single message may be ambiguous, but when you put many messages together, a pattern of meaning may emerge.

- *Ask yourself: How can you share your sacred purpose with your community—your family, friends, coworkers, or the globe itself?* Look to your spirit guide for wisdom: What is its community, and how does it give and receive support? What people support you in your quest? How will your quest benefit them and how might it place demands on them? How do your relationships need to change? Are there relationships or activities you need to let go of to make room for your sacred purpose? How can you facilitate these changes with understanding and consideration, combined with clarity and self-assurance?

- *Find a trusted friend and share your sacred purpose process with each other.* Compare journaling, art, dreams, goals, and progress with each other. And honor the confidentiality of your sharing.

Guided Imagery: First Journey to the Snowcapped Mountains

Preparation: Packing and Making a Prayer Bundle for Your Inner Journey

You are about to go on a day trip. It is a journey to help you deepen your relationship with your sacred life's purpose. You know a few things about this trip: It involves flight; it takes you into the terrain of the snowcapped mountains; you will encounter beings and messages from the unknown.

Write in your journal: What do you choose for your satchel or backpack? What is it made of? What color is it? How many compartments does it have? How will you carry it?

Then list the items you will pack in your bag, all the things you feel are essential for this day trip. What clothing will you take? What food and drink? What else is important for you to bring? Notice what you consider, what you include, what you leave out.

Then on paper or in your journal, do a collage of packing your bag.

One last item to include in your bag is a prayer bundle. This bundle contains your commitment to deepening your connection to your sacred life's purpose.

Out of what do you make the pouch for your prayer bundle? Cloth bag, fur, hide? How do you decorate it? How do you fasten it shut?

What are the contents? Gemstones or healing herbs? A gift from someone who inspires you? Items from your altar or secret chest? How are your choices related to your life's purpose?

Then gather the materials you need for the pouch and contents of your prayer bundle.

Write your intention on paper. Create the pouch; then place all the contents, including your written intention, into it, and with a blessing, close your finished prayer bundle.

Steps

1   In meditation, enter the terrain of your mind.

2   Find yourself, with pack and prayer bundle, in the vast open plain.

3   A winged creature arrives and escorts you to the snowcapped mountains.

4   Fly over the home of the oracle.

5   Drop your prayer bundle before the oracle.

6   Return as you came.

Process

Sit in meditation and close your eyes. Inhaling softly, feel your breath entering your nostrils and gliding up the passage into your forehead. What temperatures and textures are you aware of? Exhaling, feel your mind entering deeper and deeper into relaxation.

Allow yourself, then, to enter the spaciousness at the core of your mind. This spaciousness is a vast plain, and your breath is the wind sweeping across this plain.

You carry with you your travel bag packed just as you planned. In it is also your prayer bundle, reminding you of the intention of your journey.

Thus prepared, you gaze out over the wide plain then up to the open sky. At first it seems there is nothing there but clear vast blue. But you spot a dark speck. It's moving toward you. As it draws closer, you realize it is a winged creature. It soars toward you, spiraling downward on the wind currents, until it comes to land in front of you. What is it?

You can tell by the look in the eyes of the winged one that it does not intend to make a meal of you, but rather has come to help you. It offers to fly you over the snowcapped mountains, a realm where sacred intentions are brought to gain perspective, wisdom, and clarity. It motions you to join it in flight. Are you to ride its back, or curl within its talons, or spread your own wings and follow its lead? You thrill at the prospect of flying. Fear gives way to trust and excitement as you grab your pack and prepare yourself for flight.

The winged creature and you begin to spiral upward until you are flying high above the plain. What is the feel of the wonderful wings beating around you, the sound of feathers shaping the wind, the sensation of moving air past your skin? You look off in the distance and see snowcapped mountains. They loom larger and larger as you approach. Finally you are flying among the peaks.

The tallest peak houses the site of the oracle, where sacred intentions are offered and advice sought. The winged one flies over and you take the prayer bundle out of your pack and drop it in front of the oracle. The oracle will consider your case and have wisdom to share with you when you return.

But for now you and the winged one fly back together, out among the peaks into the open sky above the vast plain. The sky is beginning to redden, to darken, and as you land, the first stars are beginning to show in the indigo twilight.

You say good-bye to your winged friend, who ascends into the darkness. As its silhouette disappears, you look up to see its shape outlined among the stars.

Guided Imagery and Art: Return Journey to the Snowcapped Mountains

Steps

1   In meditation, enter the terrain of your mind.

2   Find yourself, with your pack, in the vast open plain.

3   The winged creature arrives and escorts you to the snowcapped mountains.

4   Arrive at the oracle.

5   Receive your answered prayer bundle with a map.

6   Study the map of your life's intentions.

7   Return as you came.

Process

Sit in meditation and close your eyes. Inhaling softly, feel your breath entering your nostrils and gliding up the passage into your forehead. What temperatures and textures are you aware of? Exhaling, feel your mind entering deeper and deeper into relaxation.

Allow yourself, then, to enter the spaciousness at the core of your mind. Once again you find yourself in the vast plain, and your breath is the wind sweeping across this plain.

You carry with you your travel bag. Have you packed any differently for this return journey to the snowcapped mountains? You realize your prayer bundle is still at the oracle, and you are anxious to retrieve it.

Once again, you gaze out over the wide plain then up to the open sky. There it is! The dark speck of the winged creature is moving toward you. Watch as it spirals downward on the wind currents to land in front of you.

You and the winged one greet each other happily, and then you grab your pack and prepare for flight.

Together you fly to the snowcapped mountains and find the tallest peak, home of the oracle. The winged one cruises down and lands there. You come to your feet and look around. What do you discover besides peak and snow? What is the setting of the oracle?

The oracle has responded to the contents and intention of your prayer bundle. You find its response. Your prayer bundle lies right where you dropped it, and tied to it is a folded paper.

You open the paper and find a map through time and space, revealing the course of your life's intentions, from backward, early on in your personal history, to forward, into the uncharted future.

Where and when does it begin? What is the very first intention retrieved from your childhood? And as your journey moves through the months and years, how does one intention evolve into the next? What landmarks do you perceive along the trail? What scenery? What important stops? What obstacles do you recognize? What support has come your way?

What is the landscape of the future? The trail's direction may be very vague, but there may be hints about what lies ahead: sounds or scents riding the wind from afar, messages brought to you in response to your hopes and dreams for the future, cairns marking the trail into the distance. What is the shape of the trail as it recedes into the unknown: winding or straight, narrow or wide, steep or flat, rough or smooth, barren or lush?

This map is yours to take back with you, to contemplate in order to move forward with your sacred life's purpose.

Thank the oracle for its sharing, knowing you may return in the future to seek more of its wisdom. Then take your pack, prayer bundle, and map, and fly with your winged friend, out among the peaks and back into the open sky above the vast plain. The sky is darkening, and as you land, the first stars are showing.

Say good-bye to your winged friend, who now ascends into the darkness. Once again you see its shape outlined among the stars.

Sacred Purpose Journey: Cynthia

Art: The Map

Bring out your drawing tools: paper, pastels, pens, pencils, graphite, charcoal, magazines for collage, glue. You may want to include textural or three-dimensional items in your map: dirt, sand, herbs, twigs, pebbles, beads, feathers, moss, glitter, yarn, and more.

You might begin by sketching your map, a rough outline, an overview. Or you might want to divide your map into segments, or quadrangles, one for each phase of your life, because it covers so much territory, and you want to draw it in as much detail as possible. To what scale are you creating your map? Perhaps you need a legend for your map to define symbols.

Before you begin your map, sit in meditation in front of the blank sheet. Recall the intention encased in your prayer bundle. When you are ready, begin: you, the cartographer of your own life.

Guided Imagery: Working with Obstacles

To feel the passion for life's purpose in you and the power flowing through you, you may need to identify the obstacles impeding it. The obstacles may be exterior: time, money, others' expectations.

This exploration will address inner obstacles, inner resistance. This means identifying how the resistance manifests in your emotions and behavior and confronting its sources. You may notice that confronting and transforming inner obstacles help make the external ones more manageable.

Resistance in its nature seems static, something that blocks your path. But it also has a mutable quality, a slippery underbelly to its stuck appearance, that allows it to change guises.

Resistance can be like *kupua*, a protean entity of Hawaiian tradition that can assume the form of human or beast, like Kamapua'a, the pig-god of O'ahu. In one form he was an adored chief, in another a destructive beast. Pele first encountered him in his human form and found him irresistible. However, he soon revealed his other less attractive side, and his destructive powers almost proved her undoing. He was lord of water; she was goddess of fire. He nearly drowned her before she sent him scuttling to the steaming waters where her lava seethed into the sea. There he assumed another of his forms, a thick-skinned hog-nosed fish, and escaped.

Before you begin your guided imagery, write in your journal:

- How do you experience resistance in relationship to your sacred purpose? Does it take the form of irrational fear, self-doubt, inconsistency, lack of commitment, fatigue? What is obvious? What tricks you into believing it is something else?

- If resistance were to assume an identity, what would it be? What are its name, gender, temperament?

- If the part of you that wants to realize your sacred life's purpose, your inspiration, were to assume an identity, what would it be? What are its name, gender, temperament?

- Once these two conflicting parts have revealed themselves to you, let them meet and dialogue in the following guided imagery.

Steps

1 Invoke your spirit guide.

2 Find a convergence of paths in the woods where inspiration and resistance meet.

3 Where is resistance coming from; where is inspiration going to?

4 Your spirit guide mediates dialogue between resistance and inspiration.

5 The agreement.

Process

Enter meditation. Quiet your breath. Now let your body, your mind, and your emotions be still.

Invite the presence of your spirit guide to watch over this journey and to mediate when the dialogue between the parts becomes difficult.

You find yourself in the inner terrain along a wide path in the woods. Listen to the sounds and smell the fragrances of the woods. Journey deeper into the woods until you come to a place in the path where two branches converge.

You observe two entities, inspiration and resistance, who have come down different branches to this convergence. Perhaps they have distaste for meeting each other, but the path comes together now and narrows, winding into hidden terrain in the distance. It is the place where the map ends and the unknown unfolds.

The path that goes forward is the path of your sacred purpose. Inspiration wants to proceed, but resistance blocks the path and perhaps has strategies for preventing movement. The parts begin to dialogue.

Inspiration questions the background of resistance to discover the origins of this stubbornness. What are its sources, its lessons? What function does resistance serve? What does it require to transform into an ally on the path?

And resistance questions if inspiration has something interesting to say, something worth listening to, because so far inspiration has been a threat. As resistance questions the path inspiration is taking forward into the realm of your sacred purpose, what enticement and reassurance can inspiration offer to resistance?

Their dialogue unfolds. Your spirit guide is ready to help at any time, listening, watching, sensing. And you are their witness. The goal of their interaction is to reach an agreement, so that your resistance can transform into a more supportive role and your inspiration can move toward fulfillment.

When their dialogue feels complete, what agreement have they reached? Do they feel ready to proceed together along the path into the future, a path of cooperation in relation to your sacred purpose?

Is there anything you need to do to facilitate the transformation of resistance into an ally?

When the process feels complete, you watch the two entities getting ready to proceed together along the path into the future. Thank your spirit guide for its assistance. Now return to the present time and place, and in your journal, transcribe this encounter.

Art for Incubating Your Sacred Purpose: Gestation Vessel

Once you have formulated an intention related to your sacred life's purpose, it is helpful to manifest that intention in concrete actions. One way to do this is to write down your intention and then place it in a sacred place, as with the prayer bundle.

You can make an incubator for your intention to place on your altar or in your studio. Think of the gestation vessel as a cave, a womb, where your intention can grow and develop symbolically, paralleling its development in your outer life. Over time, you can take out your intention, see how it has manifested, rework it as needed, and replace it in the vessel for further growth.

The Vessel: *Pua Mohala*

Find or create a vessel with shape and size that appeal to you. Is it made out of twigs and branches, wood, metal, or cardboard? Gather art supplies: paints, drawing tools, scissors, glue, collage materials, fabric, beads, sticks, feathers, yarn.

Then close your eyes, summon your spirit guide, and ask it to inspire you as you create a home for your intention. Let not your mind but your guide choose how you shape, color, decorate this container.

When you are finished, realize that your gestation vessel may change over time, as your intention evolves.

What is your ceremony for placing your intention in your gestation vessel? What sacred tools do you employ: sage, incense, candles? What sacred actions do you perform: mudra, dance, prayer? Your gestures are invitations to the spirit world to bless and support you in your sacred life's purpose.

Continuing Journeys with Your Spirit Guide

As you dialogue with your spirit guide through journey, art, journaling, and caring attention, realize that some revelations will be dramatic, some subtle, some taking months to incubate. But trust in the process. Most importantly, keep the dialogue going.

Ē Pele ē, ke akua o ke ahi ʻenaʻena
Ka Wahine ʻai lehua

Ka pākaʻawili, ke koaʻe kea
I loko o kou aʻa, ke kikowaena

He kūkae Pele, he ahi e ke koko
Ka ʻikuā lā, i ka pilipuka

E hoʻomohala ʻoe, e loaʻa ʻoe i mōhai aʻu
Ka ʻawapuhi me ka lehua, ke ʻala o ke aloha

ʻĀmama, ua noa!

Pele, goddess of fire
Who consumes the lehua

White-tailed tropicbird
Spiraling into your womb

Sulfur your dung, fire your blood
Divine elemental voice before dawn

Receive my offerings
Of ginger and lehua, the fragrance of aloha

The prayer is ended, the taboo released!

Prayer by Kaleo
Hawaiian version by Pili

III

Totem Animal

Meeting Your Totem Animal

To Native Americans an animal ally is not just a representation of a single animal. It embodies the power of the whole animal species. It can be a source of great strength, wisdom, guidance, caring, and insight. When you meet an animal ally in your inner work, you might want to investigate the traditional sacred and symbolic meanings such a creature has had to other people from other cultures in different times and contexts. For example, what lessons would the wolf model for the Oglala Sioux? What have been the symbolic qualities of the tiger in India or China? What stories have the Egyptians told about the ibis? Many times such investigation will show you things about yourself in relationship to this being that are useful and meaningful to you in how you live your life.

For the purposes of this book, we use the terms *animal ally, power animal,* and *totem animal* interchangeably. You may find you have one ally that accompanies you for a very long time. You may have secondary animal allies or ones that come and go. You may find you have different animals for different phases of your life. As with any guide from the spirit world, it is important to nurture and honor the relationship and its transformations. Kaleo's main ally is the white tiger, who has been at his side for many years. Elise's is the white wolf, who has stayed with her for more than a decade. Do you already know who yours is to be?

Qigong Movement

Meditative movement can be a way to discover and befriend your power animal.

Our Qigong practice invokes many animal forms: the eagle, bear, dragon, horse, deer, tiger, dolphin, wolf, crane, snake, rooster, monkey.

We prepare students for encounters with animal allies by exploring the ancient wisdom of Qigong animal awareness. The students learn our "Eight Animal Qigong" form and move like the animals to feel the uniqueness of the animals in their bodies. Our arms spread like wings of eagle; then arms embrace our hearts with the strength of bear; our sacrum descends into the power of the celestial dragon; our legs thunder like the powerful horse running with the wind; our hearts are still, listening, as deer to the rain in the forest; our feet land heel-to-toe quietly as tiger; as dolphin, we swim with courage into the depths of ocean; we are wolves whose songs echo in the moonlit mountains. Moving in Qigong like animals prepares our bodies, minds, and spirits for meeting our animal allies face to face through guided imagery.

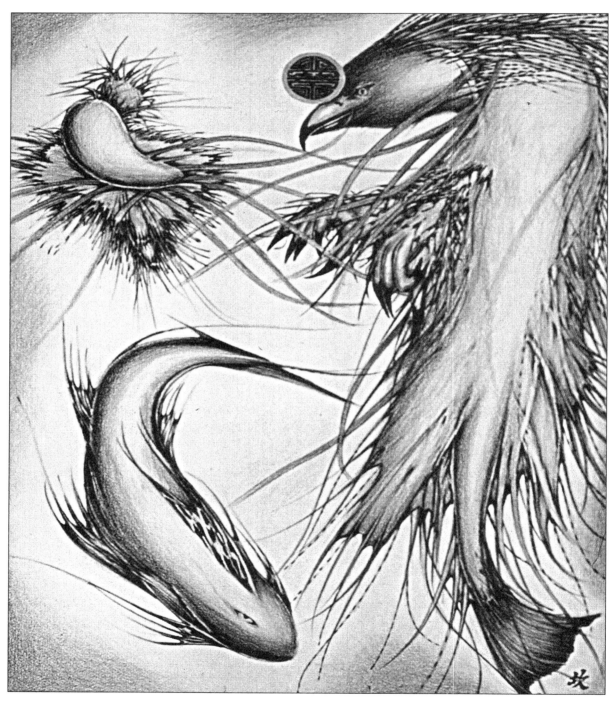

"Raptor" by Kaleo (mixed media drawing, 30″h x 22″w)

Guided Imagery: Meeting Your Totem Animal

Steps

1   Journey to the lower world.

2   Find the trail, observe the landscape.

3   Note traces of the animal(s).

4   Your animal ally approaches and you meet.

5   Receive a token of remembrance.

6   Receive signals for communication.

7   Take your leave and return as you came.

Process

Close your eyes and enter meditation. Your breath is natural, soft, fluid. It carries you gently into the lower world. (*See* "Journey to the Lower World" on page 9.) You find yourself walking on a trail in the wilderness. It guides you to the entrance of a cave. Observe the opening of this cave and your surroundings. Enter the cave and notice its interior. You discover the tunnel leading into the earth. It feels safe and inviting and you descend into this tunnel. As you go deeper, be aware of your breath. Each breath takes you deeper down this passage. What does it smell like? The fragrance brings you deeper still, until you see a light at the end of this tunnel. Approach it and move into the light. As you emerge into the terrain of the lower world, feel your consciousness shift.

What is the setting in which you find yourself? You see a trail leading off into hiding. Does it move through the underbrush, around rocks, through sand dunes or mounds of snow, into the deep forest, between mountains? Where does it disappear? Follow it.

Along the trail, you find animal traces. Are they feathers, fur, or scales? Do you see pellets or scat? Do you smell the aroma of some animal's urine or rank animal body? Do you hear hooting or growling, sighing or screeching, purring or slithering? You see tracks. Are they the bear's—long, almost humanoid, but with the piercings of sharp claws? Are they the wolf's—doglike but so large and with front toes parallel? Are they the heart-shaped tracks of the deer, the webbed tracks of the river otter, or the winding traces of a snake? Follow these tracks.

In this world of the wilderness, your whole body and all your instincts are alive. You stop, sensing a movement in the distance. Do you freeze and watch silently like a deer or crouch down like a canine in anticipation?

The creature you have been following is coming toward you. As it nears, notice what sort of animal it is. Is it covered in fur, scales, feathers, or bare skin? Watch it carefully. See how it moves as it comes even closer. You can tell by the way it approaches that it is friendly. Feel its breath as you come face to face. Look deeply into its eyes. What do you see?

You understand that this animal is an ally. What attributes and powers does this ally have? It also has its own language, its own way of expression. How does it communicate to you—through movements, sounds, eye contact? What shifts do you feel as you bond with this ally?

You feel your ally's sense of loyalty and caring. It gives you a token of remembrance. What is it?

Ask your ally what signals you can use to summon each other. Perhaps it offers a certain sound to let you know it is near. Perhaps you have a name or song by which to summon it.

Thank your power animal and take your leave, knowing you will be in close contact.

Return through the tunnel, ascending the same way you came. Reenter the cave. You might want to etch your communication symbols on the wall of the cave. Emerge through the opening in the earth. Return along the trail through the wilderness until you come back into the room.

Journaling: Totem Animal

Journal about your experiences with your totem animal. Was its identity a surprise? What associations do you have with this animal? What special abilities are carried by its species? What are its animal ways that can help you with your own life? What are its obvious meanings and lessons? What are its secrets? What are the nuances of your relationship that make it an extremely personal one for you? How can you nurture your relationship? What were your token of remembrance and your signals for summoning each other?

Art: Totem Animal's Appearance

Now that you have met your animal ally, it's time to get to know it better. Take time during the following few days to draw or sketch it. Try different techniques.

You may want to draw the semblance of your ally. Draw it from imagination and memory or from a lifelike representation, such as a photograph. If your animal ally is accessible, go to a place where you can observe it—owls by night or early morning, elks at the refuge, reptiles at the vivarium, sea otters at the shoreline, big cats at the zoo, native wild animals at the local wildlife sanctuary.

As you dialogue with the animal through art, notice how this close-up relationship changes your awareness. Drawing a bald eagle—the arrangement of individual tail feathers, the slope of shoulders and breadth of chest, the talons in the feet holding a warm dead mouse, the curve of yellow beak, the stretch of narrow tongue, the shadows around the golden eye—allows an intimate entrance into the animal's life. Expressing through color, shape, and form its wild cry, the spreading of its wings, the joy of gliding on air currents, its wide view from above brings you closer to its world. Unless you have been very closely acquainted with this animal before, once you have experienced this intimate interaction, your relationship will reach a new level of understanding and appreciation. This interaction nurtures a deeper appreciation: of the animal as an individual representative of its species; of the wild nature of the living earth; of the wilderness of your own inner being.

Art: Totem Animal's Energy

Another way to get to know your animal better is to explore through art its energetic being.

With an array of art materials before you, begin your process. You may want to express the energy, sound, textures of your ally.

Feel your totem animal. Do you want to bond with its power, its focus, its wild instinct? Do you want to express its fierce roar, its agility, or its speed? What colors, shapes, forms are inspired as the falcon veers and dives at 200 mph. for its prey, as the tiger pounces and plays with its cubs, as the wolf howls, as the otter swims? How would you convey the heat and danger of the fire-breathing dragon, or the galloping sounds of the unicorn, or the power of the talons of the owl as it crushes its prey, or the cuteness of the bunny?

Look at the wonderful art materials before you. These are vibrant sticks of energy. The sienna dusty chalk pastel may feel like the desert wind that the golden eagle rides. The charcoal flakes and powder may feel like ashes that birth the phoenix. The watery *Caran d'Ache* crayons may feel like the slippery skin of the playful seal in water. The greasy, thick oil pastels may feel like the walls of the den of an animal. Mix them with massage oil and they feel like a slick pup emerging from its mother's womb.

You can put your hand into these textures of colors and energies and express the nature and instinct of your animal ally. Your hand playing with chalk, charcoal, or oil crayon will arouse your own animal instincts and allow you to bond more deeply with the animal.

Merging with Your Totem Animal: Through Human Eyes

Kaleo's Journal: Tiger's Breath

Nostrils flare. Breath enters, slithers, hugging the cavern of my throat, gliding into the cool, moist darkness of the tunnel, descending down into my dan tian. Tiger's breath, low and guttural, reverberates and sends its power into Heaven and Earth.

Preparation

Have ready body paints and brush, a bowl of water, and a mirror. Wear shorts and tank top to leave plenty of exposed flesh.

Guided Imagery: Merging, Painting, Voice, Movement, and Your Totem Animal Within

Steps

1   Meet an animal in your inner landscape.

2   Observe its movement.

3   Inhale and invite the animal into your body.

4   Your animal inspires the painting of your body.

5   It inspires you in movement and dance.

6   Exhale and the animal leaves your body.

Process

Sit in meditation. Allow your breath to bring you gently back into the inner landscape. It feels so comfortable here, as you find yourself entering the wilderness within.

Your animal ally awaits you and you greet each other. Your eyes connect. You become acutely aware of how it moves as you circle one another. How beautiful it is! Notice its colors, shape and textures. Is it striped, spotted, or patterned in a special way? Observe its grace, the undulations of its flesh, the contracting and relaxing of its muscles, the suppleness of its joints, how its mind and body are one.

Feline: Julie

What do you say? How do you invite your animal to join with you today, to enter into your body and to breathe as one with you, to move your body as it moves, to give you its voice?

As you inhale, you sense the anticipation of merging. Then, you feel your ally entering you. Feel its awareness within you. Sense how it explores and perceives your inner landscape: colors of the inner jungle, depth of the sea, heat of the volcano, clarity of the lofty mountains—the wondrous composition of your inner being.

Observe your breath. Each breath you take brings you deeper into this process, bonding you more and more with the animal.

And you begin to feel animal breath filling your lungs. The sound of your breathing changes. You feel animal sinews tensing and stretching, long supple animal spine uncoiling. You may even feel animal wings spreading from your own shoulder blades, animal fur rubbing beneath your skin, animal fins swimming your arms, or animal legs crouching beneath you.

And now you rise. Feel the synchronicity of your animal within you. Its body is your body. Move to the feast of art materials and paints. Allow your animal to see the colors through your eyes, to feel the texture of the paint with your hands and fingers. Allow your animal to reach out and choose the warmth of reds, the coolness of blues, the clarity of white.

Your animal ally understands that your skin is its canvas. It may be necessary to camouflage it with the cool green darkness of rainforest. It may want to wear long sharp quills or raised stripes of black and white. It may be necessary for your animal to exhibit the teeth and eyes of a ferocious snarl. It may be time for your animal to lower its tail and eyes and show the pink vulnerability of its belly. It may desire to paint brilliant winged patterns of courting and mating. Or it may be time for your animal to choose colors and patterns to adjust its body to the lofty snowcapped mountains or the heat of the volcano.

Permission. Allow your animal to paint your skin with colors, shapes, textures of its environment, its experience, and its choosing.

When your animal is finished painting, you will know. You can hear completion in its breathing. Return to the rhythm of breathing that allowed you to merge. Its breath is your breath, its sound is your sound, its spirit whispers with your spirit.

Now listen to the sounds. They may be the sounds of moving through jungle, slithering over desert floor, gliding in the wind. *You are one.* Your body moves to the rhythm.

Trust and permission. Allow the animal within to be free. Allow it to move. Your fingers may transform into talons or claws. Your nose may grow long and pointed with a moist tip. Your arms may sprout wings, thighs may develop scales. Your neck may triple in length. You may leap into the air or drop on all fours or slither on your belly. Your skin may change colors. You may stalk with the fearless vigilance of a predator. You may feel the heart of a tiger pumping in your chest. You may see with the vision and clarity of an eagle, hear with the asymmetrical ears of an owl, breathe fire like a dragon.

Trust and permission. As your animal body moves, what sounds does it make? What sounds do you release?

Your animal ally will let you know when it is time to rest. Come to a place of stillness. Listen to your heartbeat, your inner pulse. What emotions do you experience? Thank your ally for its presence, for this communion. When you're ready, exhale the animal out of your body. Your bodies separate fully, and you return to your accustomed awareness.

Journaling: Your Totem Animal Merges with You

What was the experience of merging with your animal? Of being one? Of having your animal explore your inner landscape and then paint you?

What colors and shapes spread over your body as your animal designed, painted, camouflaged, adorned itself?

What was the feeling of the animal moving? What sounds did it make as it galloped, stalked, killed, mated, gave birth, lazed around? What moods, emotions, characteristics and personality did you as animal experience? How did you transform?

What was the sound of your animal's voice? Was it a flirtatious whistle? A lonely wail? A joyful song? An angry hiss? A breath that slithers along the earth's floor? What emerged from the animal's throat?

How can you give voice and movement to your animal ally in your personal practice or creative self-expression? Let the sound of your animal inspire you to move, write, draw, and paint.

Merging with Your Totem Animal: Through Animal Eyes

Guided Imagery: Your Totem Animal's Body and Being

Steps

1   Go to the lower world and meet your animal.

2   Enter its body on the inhalation.

3   Experience the world through the animal's senses and actions.

4   Separate on the exhalation.

5   Return as you came.

Process

Sit in meditation and allow your body to rest and relax. Feel the waves of your breath, and enter into the quiet of your inner body. Become one with your breath as it flows and ebbs, enters and releases. On the next inhalation, allow your soft breath to glide through the portal of your mind's eye. It carries you gently back into the inner landscape, each breath taking you deeper, until you find yourself entering the wilderness within.

Ah, yes! There it is! Your animal ally awaits you. You greet each other. Feel its presence next to you as it peers closely into your face. How does its breath feel on your face? Is it silky or rough? Cool, warm, or hot? What does it smell like? Is it fragrant like berries or mint, earthlike like roots, or does it smell like flesh and blood? Smell it and allow your breath to pace with that of your animal's, each breath bringing you closer to one another. Each breath brings comfort and ease.

Your eyes meet and you feel the trust. Look into its eyes and notice their shapes and colors. How inviting they are! You feel so safe. Look deeper into its eyes. On the next exhalation, your breath leaves your body. On the next inhalation, enter into your animal. Your breath flows as one.

How wondrous! You are in its body, experiencing the inner being of your animal, perceiving with its senses.

Look. What is it like to see through your animal's eyes? Listen. What is it like to hear with its ears? What is it like to smell with its nose, to taste with its tongue? What is it like to feel covered in its skin, to sense the world through its nerves?

What is it like to move with these muscles, sinews, bones? What is this animal's awareness of itself? How does it perceive the surrounding world? What are its desires, fears, joys, purpose for being? How does it feel about you?

When your experience is complete, become aware of the rhythm of your breath. And when you're ready, on an exhalation, separate completely from your animal and return as you came to the present time and place.

Journaling: You Within Your Totem Animal

What was it like to share your animal's body and breath? What was it like to explore the inner landscapes of its body and being? How was it to experience the world through its senses? Who are you to your animal ally and who is it to you? What is the meaning of your connection? What does it want to express through you? Can you allow its powers, attributes, and personality to move with you in your daily life?

Raven's Flight: Gina

Art: Sculpting Your Totem Animal

You have met and visited with your animal ally. You have shared body and breath with it. Now let the wisdom of its animal instincts inspire you to create. Experience for yourself how its powers, vulnerabilities, and personality show up in your sculpting, painting, and decorating.

Does your animal stand on legs, swim or slither on belly, glide on wings? What does your animal feel like? How can you express its movement, attributes, personality through your use of colors, brush strokes, viscosity of paint? Does it want to scratch, peck, burrow, or smear? What might form the heart of the animal? One student used an acorn as the heart of the deer. Another used a chunk of granite from the Rocky Mountains for the heart of a grizzly bear. You may want to write your animal's story on a special piece of paper and mold it into the center of its head, heart, or womb.

To sculpt your animal ally, apply the techniques used in maskmaking. You can mold your animal's form with newspaper and masking tape, then wrap it with single layers of plaster gauze wettened with warm water to embody your animal. You could even make your sculpture of your animal from a mask of your own face, which you may wear and move as your animal. (*See* "Sculpting the Mask" on page 115.)

You can add other materials to the sculpting process: wire, dirt, clay, sticks, cardboard, gel medium, modeling paste, fabric, natural fibers. What materials inspire you to create its skeleton, tissues, organs? What materials inspire you to create its feathers, fur, scales, skin? Then apply acrylic paints, beads, fibers, etc., for the painting and finishing.

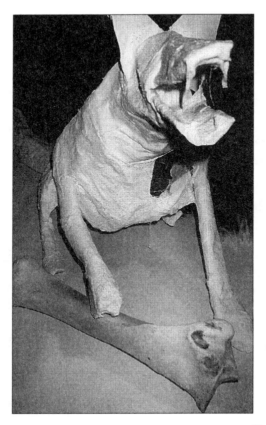 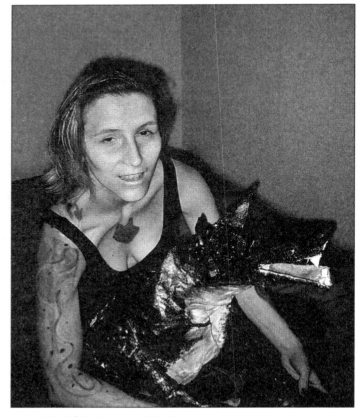

Becoming Wolf/Melissa and Wolf

The Nest or Den of Your Totem Animal

Guided Imagery: Your Totem Animal's Domain

Steps

1   Journey to the lower world with a gift and find the domain of your totem animal.

2   Observe the surroundings and signs until you meet the animal.

3   It leads you to its home.

4   Give your gift; share a meal.

5   Observe the animal up very close.

6   Return as you came.

Process

You are going on a journey to visit the habitat of your animal ally in the lower world and share its meal. What kind of gift from the upper world would you like to bring?

Sit or lie in meditation and allow the soft rhythm of your breath to bring you to the inner terrain. You feel safe and comfortable, for the way is familiar. You find yourself in a haven in nature, and as you explore, you discover an opening in the earth and descend a tunnel to the lower world.

Enter into the domain of your totem animal. Observe your surroundings. What is the geography? What is the relationship among water, air, plants, and earth? What other creatures abide here? Notice how they interact with each other.

Look around until you find traces of your ally: tracks, scat, fur, a feather, a shed skin, a discarded bone, a smell, a sound.

Follow the traces until you see your animal in the distance. It's happy to see you and is beckoning you to follow, inviting you like an old friend to its home.

It leads you deeper into its territory. When you arrive at its home you are welcome to explore. In what kind of habitat does your animal reside? What is its home made of? What size is it? Is it woven with sticks and strips of color? Burrowed or sculpted? Does it sit on an edge of a high mountain peak or in a dense forest canopy?

Present your gift from the upper world to your power animal. How does it react?

Your ally invites you to share its meal. It offers you part of its feast: berries, nectar, shoots, roots, bugs, fish, fowl, small creatures, or large mammal flesh. What are this meal's colors, textures, smells, flavors? You may prepare it for your own palate as you wish.

When you are done, your ally invites you to come closer, close enough to see the nuances of its outer covering—the mottled colors of its fur, scales, feathers, even the skin beneath, the smell of it, the feel of it. Now that you have become this close, this familiar, notice how your relationship with your ally shifts and deepens.

Now thank your animal for its hospitality and part ways. Ascend back up the tunnel the same way you came.

Writing and Art: Your Totem Animal's Domain

What kind of gift did you bring for your animal?

Describe the domain, the environment, in which it resides. Describe the habitat of your animal in the real world and in your inner experience. What do you learn about its habits and characteristics? How was your experience of sharing the meal?

Draw or sketch the tracks of your animal. Sculpt, carve, or weave its home. How would you create a burrow for fox? An eagle's nest? An undersea cavern? A cave for bear? A tiger's lair?

You might begin by looking at pictures of wolves at den or reading about where the deer makes her bed. The Santa Barbara Natural History Museum has a wonderful collection of nests of many different birds: the hanging pouchlike nest of the bushtit made of plant fibers and moss; the tunnel burrowed in a dirt bank where the belted kingfisher lays her half dozen eggs; the delicate structure that the Costa's hummingbird has woven from flowers, leaves, plant down, bud scales, and strips of bark bound together with spiders' webs. How amazing the artists of the animal world!

Communing with Deer: Jais

Let the resourcefulness of animal architects and builders, settlers and nomads be an inspiration to you to create the nest or den of your totem animal.

Suggested materials: jute, hemp, twine, yarn, raffia, chicken coop wire, twigs, branches, tree stumps, leaves, pods, moss, grass, tinsel, rags, dog fur, feathers, dirt, sand, rocks, shells, kelp, driftwood sticks, etc.

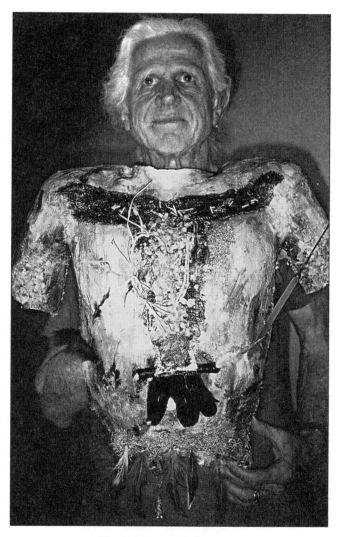

Eagle Totem: Othmar

Your Totem Animal's Story

Writing: Your Animal's Story

Journeying, art, dreamwork, and inner dialogue help you form a bond with your animal ally through intuitive activity. Research, observation, and interactive experience help you develop a practical understanding of your animal's characteristics, behavior, and ecology.

Consider the following questions:

- What do you know about your power animal?

- What do you believe about it?

- What is your sensory experience of it?

- What are its strengths?

- What are its vulnerabilities?

- What is the feeling tone of your relationship to your ally?

- What boundaries do you and your animal observe in relation to each other?

- What do you share with your animal ally?

- How does it touch you personally in a way that it perhaps would touch no other being?

Once you have gathered this wealth of intuitive and objective awareness, try bringing them together in your own personal myth of your totem animal through story, song, or poem.

Your story could start with an observation about the animal: its wild eyes, thick layers of fur, iridescent fins, the size and shape of its paws, its grace in flight.

Or you could begin with the theme of its symbolic qualities: the vision of the eagle, the sophistication of the wolf society, the trickster in the coyote.

Or you could describe the interaction of the animal and the personal in your own experience.

Or perhaps you become the animal, seeing the world through the animal's eyes.

Invite your muse to whisper in one ear, your ally in the other, and let their voices emerge onto paper.

Elise's Story: Arctic Wolf

When I became the wolf, I entered a world of black and white, white forever reaching for the black sea. There was no longer any question about where I was to go or what to do. All choice was clarity like life and death. I had wonder but was not confused. When I was the wolf, the world was white, black, and red like my mouth—teeth, gums, and tongue laughing for the taste of warm moist flesh. I loved the feel of my wide paws against the ice, thick pads of feet a neutral barrier between blood and ice. I loved how my narrow-set front legs and strong back haunches carried me in a lope across dunes of snow. I loved how I always knew where I was and was never lost. I loved the adventure of smells beyond my nose. I loved the sound of wind and the dance of the aurora.

I am wolf. I know survival. I know strength. I know loyalty, companionship, love, and play. I know how to use my senses to their limits. I know how to sing and how to sleep.

One day as I was running for the sake of running, I heard a strange noise from the sky and a bird bigger and more awkward than I could imagine swooped low and attacked me. Streaks of yellow came from its mouth, like little pieces of the warmth my human friends in borrowed fur sit with in the night. The bird sent a shadow on me, and I felt something tear my flank. I could run no more. I fell to the ice and the bird came down. I thought it would devour me, until it suddenly turned into a yellow ball of warmth bigger than I have ever seen and died. I thought I was having a very bad dream.

Then one of my human friends in his borrowed caribou skin came to me. He put me on his sled and carried me to his den. I felt humiliated to be pulled by dogs and touched by humans. It is not my way. But I knew they were helping me when I could not help myself.

When I became strong again, I left in the night. I hunted a caribou and brought part of it to the dark silence of their den door before leaving again for the freedom of the great white world.

Writing: Training the Scout

Animal habits have lessons to help us along our own life paths. Each animal has its own set of lessons for survival in the wild that can teach us on our journeys through the inner wilderness. Your totem animal has come to you for a reason, just as your dreams fill your sleep with their own reasons welling up from the unconscious.

As you follow Elise's journey with Coyote, you might want to jot down ideas for your own travels with your animal ally. What have you learned about your animal through reading, videos, observation in captivity or in the wild?

When and where do you find yourself? What is your ally's prey and what are its predators? Does it travel alone or in a group? What are its mating and parenting habits? What are its strengths in movement and its weaknesses? What are its strongest senses?

What signs does it discover as it travels—scent markings, movement from hundreds of yards away, the snap of a twig beyond the laughter of the river?

What signs does it leave—wads of emesis, distinctive tracks, mounds of dirt, aromas in the air or along the trail, scat with fur or seeds or fragments of bone?

How do these lessons help you on your own life's journey?

Elise's Story: Coyote Trail

It is near dusk on Mt. Shasta. I have just been to the native Wintu people's sacred spring past the road's end to bring back its pure clear water for ritual, in exchange for a small crystal sliver and a blessing. Many have been here before, leaving small natural gifts on the earth altar near the bubbling water. Now mine, along with the rest, is nestling into the slumber of winter.

Coyote's Tale: Rob

On the way down Everitt Highway, I stop above snowline and put back on my snowshoes. The near full moon has just ascended over the southeastern ridge, bringing the comfort of a blue glow to replace the receding pink over the fresh early winter snow. The quiet woods summon me for a few more moments among the mysteries of the mountain. The only sound is the gentle crunch beneath my snowshoes and the whistle of a mountain chickadee from the branches of a nearby white fir tree. Perhaps the great horned owl will come out soon with a low soul-stirring song to replace the chickadee's. But for now the longest shadows of day still hide the great winged predator.

My right foot is just about ready to crease the snow, but it stops in midair and returns to its last imprint. I squat to inspect a track. It is oval-shaped, with a heel and four toe prints, with the piercing dents of two inward slanting front toenails. Coyote's front foot has broken this sheath of snow before me. Close by is the rounder track of the back foot, its heel hardly registering in the soft snow. The prints emerge from the woods to my left and disappear into the woods to my right. I can tell by their regular placement and wide stride that Coyote is in a happy trot. To my right, in the distance beyond where the tracks disappear among the firs, blue snow arcs over a wide mouth of blackness—the secrets of a rocky ledge in the mountain's flank. Perhaps this is where Coyote dens.

Then I notice something that the shadows and my excitement have hidden from me—dark spots between the paw prints in this swath of white. I bring out my flashlight, for the moon is hidden now beyond the conifers. Sure enough: blood. Turning to the left I stalk alongside Coyote's tracks, rather than going to the right and disturbing the likely den site. As I track, the blotches of blood get bigger. My nostrils flare, longing for the powers of olfactory discrimination of my four-legged fellow traveler. My ears strain, wishing for the big pointed scoops that locate sounds and funnel them into Coyote's auditory canals, but I hear only the snow beneath my feet and my own rapid breathing.

A dark irregular mass lies at the base of a tree in the blue-white expanse before me. The kill is a deer. I do not know its story or why it succumbed to Coyote. Was it sick? Was it injured? Closer inspection with my flashlight reveals a doe whose back lower leg has been broken. A partly healed wound indicates that the fracture is older than today's encounter. The deer must have been weak and vulnerable, but from the frenzy of hoof and paw prints in the vicinity, she did not give in without a fight. Her rear end is ripped open and flesh removed, but the rest of her is left for another taking.

I take out some dried rosemary, harvested from our garden, and scatter it lightly around the remains of the doe without disturbing her. Rosemary is for memory and loyalty: remembrance of those who have passed this way before, loyalty to the spirits of earth and sky, a reminder to me as witness and participant in the mysteries of life that this moment is sacred.

A howl ascends into the sharp thin mountain night air from the darkness behind me. I feel a chill and a thrill at the same time. Is Coyote reminding me whose feast this is? Or summoning friends? Or just singing to the stars? There are millions and millions of them, layer beyond layer, more numerous than the crystals of snow that wrap the mountain.

Writing: The Trails of Your Soul Journey

As you accompany Elise on her journey into the past, pause in the story and begin your own journey—into the realm of those who have passed this way before, into the ordeals of nature, among the fellow creatures and spirits of the wilderness. Let the narrative trigger memories, from your personal past or from the collective past, that entice you to follow them into your own experience. When the intensity of your journey softens, return to the present. Let the journey unfold in chapters.

What lessons do you learn about yourself through the characters and events of your story?

Elise's Story: Following the Black Bear

Kaleo and I are just ending an eighteen-mile summer's hike in the Trinity Alps. The trail is flat and soft now and we trudge along in silence remembering the sounds of the waterfall and the coolness of the mountain lake at the top.

Suddenly, we hear a loud stirring in the pines to our right. A black bear cub quickly shimmies up a tree trunk and stares at us with big fearful yet curious brown eyes and twitching nose. We feel delight, appreciation, but also fear: Where is its mother?

We hear a deeper rustling on our left. We stand between her and her cub—not a good place to be. We show confidence with loud friendly talking and noisy stomping on down the trail to let her know our intention—to make distance between her and her baby and us.

She continues ambling parallel and a little ahead of us to our left. She seems to be guiding us away. Finally she crosses the path in front of us then runs back along the path to her cub. We imagine the little one still safe and still curious up in the branches of the tree.

When we feel that we have given them a safe margin of trail, we stop to rest against boulders and share our excitement. At last, we lapse into silence and doze in the late afternoon sun.

I remember:

Once there were Bear-women. Women of long ago. I recall one in particular. My oldest sister. I used to watch her, always from a distance.

Some say I was a Bear-child by nature, so reclusive, remote, like a bear, always finding a cave of distance for myself. But she took her bear wisdom into the world. I watched in awe from the shadows, tugging at my black braids.

Do you know the river?
Sometimes girls swim in indigo
so deep and dark it mocks the adamant sun.
They feel cool healing fingers along their arms
tickling their bare backs to laughter
as if girlish joys
were nymphs who sing forever.

Forgotten a moment:
rounding bellies
lengthening breasts
and eyes full as the beloved pools
with loss and hope
and so much living.

The oldest one
with the longest darkest hair
who is friend of She-Bear
and pounds secrets from the herbs
catches the wink of her own eye turning
turning with the looping of breath and bones
and knows the drops that fill the eyes
within the water of the dell
are amulets sent from her
who lives beneath the stone.

Sister had dreams every night. Sometimes she shared them with me—dreams of dark earth spaces and pungent smells, of black creatures with sharp claws, large jowls, and deep mysterious voices speaking a strange guttural language. Each time she awoke from one of these dreams, she described a new fragrance in her nostrils. Sometimes she would be able to find it among the plants in the meadow, or in the forest, or down by the river.

One morning when I woke up, she was already gone. It was still dark. I was puzzled, for I was always the first one awake. Just like her bear friends, she liked to sleep late, especially in winter.

I got up and followed her tracks in the light of the high waning half-moon down toward the river. I walked cautiously and silently, stopping when I heard a low groaning noise above the river babble. I stepped behind the wide bole of an oak tree and looked.

My mouth must've been as big as the opening to a bear's den. A big black bear, big to me anyway, with a wound in its side, was lying not far from the trail near a clump of yarrow. Sister was plucking leaves from the yarrow plants, mashing them in the palm of her hand, and sprinkling them on the bear's wound.

I had never seen anyone close to a bear before and had only heard about the men's bear encounters during the hunt. Women were not allowed near a bear until it had been cut open, skinned, and prepared, and its spirit freed. One whole night after a bear-kill a man would stay awake watching to make sure the bear's spirit did not return.

I took off running. I ran and ran and ran until my circles grew smaller and smaller and I found myself back home. I collapsed on my mat and fell asleep again just as dawn was coming. I did not wake up until the sun was high in the sky. Sister was sleeping next to me.

I do not know if my sister as healer to Bear was real or was a dream. I do not dare to ask.

The Adversary and Your Totem Animal

What in your being is no longer useful in its present form? What do you want to hunt, to trap, to transform into something more useful in your life? This could be a fresh emotional wound, a problematic relationship with another person, an old habit, an encumbrance of material possessions, a pattern of moods.

What are the shape, color, texture, smell, sound of this attribute? Where does it live in your body? How can your animal ally help you change this adversarial attribute into something of meaning and beauty for you?

Guided Imagery: Confronting the Adversary

Steps

1 Journey to the lower world, meet your totem animal, find your power circle.

2 An adversary emerges.

3 Your animal confronts the adversary.

4 It helps transform the adversary into something of use.

5 The animal instructs you how to complete this transformation.

6 Return as you came.

Process

Sit or lie in meditation and allow the soft rhythm of your breath to bring you to the inner terrain. You feel safe and comfortable, for the way is familiar. You find yourself in a haven in nature, and as you explore, you discover an opening in the earth and descend a tunnel to the lower world.

You enter into the domain of your totem animal, who awaits and greets you. You feel its great power, character, and wisdom. Together you find your circle of power. Enter it and look off into the distance.

Your animal senses that something is troubling you. What's going on? You share what in your life is causing hindrance, pain, or doubt. Perhaps it is a troublesome relationship, a fresh wound, an old trauma, a difficult character trait. What is this adversary?

If this adversary could take a shape, color, texture, or sound, what would it be like? If it transformed into an animal, what would it become? If it approached you, now, in the lower world, what form would it take and how would it act?

You are in your power circle, and your animal ally is nearby, ready to help. As your animal moves forward to confront the adversary, notice how they move. As they come face to face, what does your ally do? Does it engage the stare of the adversary and wait patiently? Does it need to shapeshift to become more effective in this challenge: Fawn becoming Stag with sharp antlers and flashing hooves; Cat becoming Tiger to pounce upon the back of the adversary, clamping its jaws down, breaking its neck; Wolf acquiring the ability to speak in words? Or does your animal in its wisdom realize that the adversary's core is fear and loneliness that can be transformed by acknowledgment and affection?

Witness the confrontation. How do the powers of your totem animal combine to bring the adversary under its dominion?

Once the adversary is overpowered, how does your animal transform it? Does your ally kill it, then breathe new life into it, turning what was harmful into something that serves you? Eat it and excrete the waste, transforming the flesh into the substance of its own off-spring? Bury it in the earth? Green things grow lushly around outhouses and graveyards. Or does your ally engage it in play and embrace and comfort it?

When your power animal has finished its work, it presents you with a task to complete this process of transformation. What must you do? Receive the instructions, knowing that you have the ability to perform this task. Can you make the commitment to yourself and to your animal to do so?

When it is time and you're ready, thank your animal for its help. You have learned much through this experience. Notice the shift in yourself. Then, part ways, as you return again from the lower world to everyday reality.

Writing and Art: Completion with the Adversary

What is the task of completion your totem animal presented to you? Is it a shrine to build, a ritual to perform, a noble deed to enact, or a pilgrimage to undertake? Does it mean setting boundaries; forgiving someone; purging your home to make space for thought, movement, and change; purging activities to make room for your sacred purpose? Is this task something you are willing to do, and if not, how can you modify it to meet your needs? What is the intention behind the task?

Begin by embodying the task in art. Sketch a blueprint of the shrine you are to build. Draw a map of the boundaries you are to establish. Make before-and-after collages of your home in need of purging. Write an elegy for your adversary. Paint or sculpt the transformation of your adversary.

Then try to fulfill the task in a way that you feel best honors this transformative process among you, your adversary, and your power animal.

How have you all changed in this saga?

Gifts and Your Totem Animal

Your relationship with your totem animal is one of reciprocity. You both have things to give to each other. To this point, what have been the gifts you have received from your totem animal? Perhaps you have received lessons in self-respect from the skunk. Or prayer has become a more meaningful part of your life from your association with bison. Or owl has shown you how to look in the mouth of death and not be afraid. Or spider has inspired you to develop your skill as a weaver of words. Or bear has deepened your powers of healing. Or otter has brought out of hiding the playful child in you. Or vulture has shared the freedom of tilting wings, the experience of a wider vision, the value of things that others have overlooked, rejected, or discarded.

What gifts do you bring to your animal ally?

Storyteller: Kira Sharing the Gifts of the Animal World

Guided Imagery: Gifts

Steps

1 Journey to the lower world and find the domain of your totem animal.

2 Return with it to its home.

3 The animal presents you with gifts.

4 You offer it gifts.

5 Lie down together.

6 Dream the same dream where the animal supports you during a life transition.

7 Awaken and ask your animal how you might be of help to it.

8 Make a pact to honor each other.

9 Return as you came.

Process

Sit or lie in meditation and feel the comfortable rhythm of your breath. Gently let your own animal breath fill the vessels of your lungs. Feel how this breath reaches into the farthest corners, as wind exploring the walls of a great cave. Then release your breath and listen to the silence within, and in that silence find yourself making that familiar descent down the tunnel to the lower world.

As you look around, your sharpened instincts sense the presence of your animal friend. It emerges from the wild shadows to greet you. It shows you a beautiful spring, where you both drink refreshing cool water. It invites you to return to its home.

As you enter, what do you feel instinctively? Has anything changed since your last visit? What is the light like? What smells does your nose detect? What sounds do your ears perceive?

Within this abode you find wonderful gifts that your animal has prepared for you. What are they? Receive them. You too have brought gifts for your animal friend. What did you bring? How are these gifts received? Take a few moments together to explore these offerings of friendship to one another.

You both become drowsy, lie next to each other to rest, and soon fall asleep. You're in the same dream! You find yourself in the scene of a significant life transition. What are you going through? And your animal is there with you, ready and eager to help you in any way it can. What happens? How are you changing? Feel your animal's support and loyalty to you and your life's journey. Allow yourself to sink deeper into this dream. Where do you go? What do you see? Together your wisdom, your strength, your compassion are exquisite.

Awakening from your dream, you find your animal curled trustingly next to you. Feel the comfort as well as power of your connection, your deep caring and commitment to one another. The animal stretches, awakening in your gaze. In this moment you are acutely aware of its balance of strength and vulnerability as a denizen of the shared shifting world.

Ask your animal how you can reciprocate its support for you. How can you contribute to its well-being? How does it respond?

You make a pact with each other, to honor each other and to protect each other's best interests.

Now take your leave, return back up the tunnel into the cave, and cross the threshold into everyday reality.

Art and Journaling: Gifts

What gifts does your totem animal offer you? Sculpt or paint them. You could possibly use pig gut, fish scales, rabbit fur, or bones to embody your animal's gift. Perhaps the gift is a talisman with symbols on it.

What gifts do you offer your animal? Look at the things now present in your life that honor your animal, perhaps things that invited it into your life in the first place. Realize that giving has a yin (inner) and a yang (outer) side: the inner gifts of awareness, appreciation, meditation, prayer, and creative process; the outer gifts of action in the world.

The processes offered so far in relationship to your power animal have included mostly yin activities, inner work. The yang part of your relationship might be sharing with your ally more deeply through action in the world. How might you do this? This is, of course, a question without a right or wrong answer.

Possible gifts of action to honor your animal:

· environmental activism

· recycling

· adopting through a monetary gift an animal at a wildlife haven

· supporting domestic animal rights organizations

· supporting wildlife organizations

· volunteer work that helps animals or preserves wilderness

· docent work at a wildlife refuge, nature museum or park

· leading nature outings

· joining park cleanup or trail maintenance events

· runs, walks, or bike-a-thons to preserve the wild

· sharing your awareness of the wisdom of the wild with others

However you choose to address this issue, realize that the connection may fall into place easily or your intention may take time to ripen. It may take research and exploration, as well as patience, on your part to find out the best path for you, the most appropriate place for you to put your energy. At a busy time in your life, your gift might need to be something as simple as a letter to a congressperson—for example, to preserve the habitat of the spotted owl or support the reintroduction of wolves into a national park; at another time your gift might be more vast, an afternoon out of your week to be a volunteer or perhaps even finding a career that connects you with the wild world in a mutually beneficial way.

Invite your animal to accompany you in your search: a research trip to the library, bookstore, or Internet or to the wildlife organization for an exploratory visit or informational meeting. Be honest with yourself and with your animal about what you are willing and able to give. If your intention is aligned with the blessing of your animal and the guidance of your heart, then your process is destined to be a meaningful one.

Lion's Gift: Dawn

Kaleo's Journal: Elise's World

Elise honors her connections to the animal world through membership in various environmental organizations and volunteer work with wildlife. She's worked with wounded animals near where we live in California, at the Lindsay Wildlife Museum in Walnut Creek, WildCare in San Rafael, and the Raptor Center in Davis, where she's met Thor, a ferruginous hawk, Kaeli, a merlin, and Aquila, a golden eagle. She's cleaned their cages, fed them, changed their dressings, and trimmed their talons.

At WildCare, they once received a fox. As a curious and playful pup, he must have gotten his front shoulder and neck stuck in one of those plastic hoops for a six-pack of cans. As he matured, the plastic started cutting into his growing muscles. When a farmer found him, he was very thin and had open wounds in his shoulder and neck. Everyone at WildCare was astonished to see that he was still alive because he was stuck in this plastic and had almost no mobility to hunt. Whenever he tried to run, the plastic cut deeper into his body. After surgery and months of rehabilitation, he was set free, back into the wild, a very fresh, robust, and sassy young fox. Now I always use scissors to cut the plastic hoops for six-packs.

Elise finds that the animals always give back to her. We live near a large nature park, where we often walk with our rambunctious Australian shepherd, Teekkona. I hear Elise conversing with rabbits, deer, coyotes, foxes, snakes, newts, great horned owls, red-tailed hawks, and many other birds. She dialogues with them also in meditation, through reading, journal writing, and art. They visit her at night in her dreams. She's created poems, stories, drawings, and sculptures of skunk, turtle, deer, bison, coyote, dragonfly, condor, and even a mask of bear. They're magical art pieces and reside on her altar, in our art studio, all over our house (ha, ha). Her drawing of a *koaʻe kea*, the white-tailed tropicbird that spirals in Halemaʻumaʻu crater, is tattooed on her shoulder. Her drawing of a bear's claw is tattooed on her ankle. The spirits of animals live in her heart.

Elise's Journal: Wild World

It's a windy day as Lynne, my raptor friend at WildCare, and I enter the empty sports field. Hinton, a seven-year-old Swainson's hawk, perches gingerly on my gloved left arm, waiting for it to stretch and rise, giving her room to spread her wings to their four-foot-plus span, to feel the closest she'll come to flying free.

Hinton was named for a woman who, during a raptor banding project, discovered her as a nestling with a stick in her right eye. Being blind in one eye might be a handicap an adult could adjust to, but an unfledged raptor could not learn to hunt with this limitation. So rehabilitation for this young Swainson's hawk meant a life in captivity, not the freedom to live free and wild, hunting, mating, nesting, breeding, migrating every year from the plains of North America to the pampas of Argentina.

I must always remember that Hinton is wild. The killing tools of hawks, their talons, are sharp and fast and strong. Even this 2.5-pound bird could inflict major damage, not out of any fault of spirit or temperament, but out of her own ancient instinct and quick reflex, combined with any lapse of focus or discernment on my part. These animals learn quickly and well what they need to know to survive. The very first time I tossed one-eyed Hinton a mouse, she missed it; the second time she did not.

Phoenix, a red-shouldered hawk risen from the ashes to get a second life as a WildCare resident, lost his primary flight feathers in a fire. His flight potential is a short sprint from perch to closely placed perch. The first time I took him out on the glove, I felt rather awkward. Never had I been scrutinized with such concentration in all my life, not just with his eyes, but with every nerve fiber of his avian being. He is a bit smaller than Hinton, weighing only 1.5 pounds, but smaller in the world of hawks also means quicker. What a fine model of presence and focus! My vigilance could never come close to matching his. He lets me know just how close on the glove to my body he wants to be by putting his head in one spot. It's my job to keep his body lined up beneath it.

Respect: Elise and Phoenix

Then there is Vladimir, the trickster turkey vulture. The first time I entered his cage, he ran up my leg and bit me in the calf. We always wear long pants for a good reason. Vladimir seems to need to know who's boss, and until it's proved otherwise, it will be he. Our rapport is taking a long time to evolve. Maybe it's having his business end, his beak, so close to my face that obstructs my confidence.

Every time I work with Hinton, or any of the other unreleasable wild animals that find homes in rehabilitation centers and wildlife museums to live as emissaries from the wild world, I have a sense of deep appreciation tinged with awe. Were I on their perch, so to speak, would I choose to stay in good enough health and good enough disposition to fit the federally regulated criteria to be kept as an educational resident? Never to be with others of my own kind? Just for the thrill of a predictable diet of dead mice and the constant amusement of the antics of those weird beings called humans? And as one of those humans, I also admire the dedication of the volunteers who give so many hours to help treat, care for, rehabilitate, and release (roughly 50 percent of the time) the sick or injured animals brought in for care, often by other caring individuals who bother to take the time. As a wildlife rehabilitation volunteer, you don't get many warm fuzzies. The great horned owl puffs out on one side to look huge and mammalian, hisses and clacks and greets you with talons first, its fourteen cervical vertebrae allowing its eyes to follow you wherever in its perimeter you go. Raccoon claws are razors, gull bills are vices, heron beaks are daggers to the unwary. Vulture barf smells wretched, and duckling poop is slimy and copious. Wildlife rehabilitation is as much about doing laundry and dishes as being a healer and savior. But if you feel your patients aren't grateful, well it's nothing personal. For me, gratitude comes from within, an enhanced awareness of interconnectedness with all living things.

CONDOR
by Elise

You walk to the edge of doom
on splattered feet
and cock your head like an ancient one
listening for the word
Your wings may not save you
but when you soar
the sky holds you motionless
as an Immortal

IV
Ancestors

Portal to Ancestral Realms

In our practice, we use Qigong meditation forms as gateways to the realms of the ancestors. We have found Zhan Zhuang standing meditation, the circuit of energy in the Microcosmic/Macrocosmic Orbit, and Spiraling Lotus Qigong to be especially effective.

Because we don't want to emphasize Qigong techniques in this book, but reserve these for our upcoming book on Qigong and the creative process, we encourage you on your journeys to continue practicing your own meditative forms as entryways to the ancestral realms. One person who practices yoga does *savasana* (corpse pose); another who practices craniosacral therapy uses the occiput and medulla oblongata; a photographer uses her eyes as the door to the ancestral realms.

During Spiraling Lotus Qigong, the practitioner may feel a strong connection to ancestral spirits along the path of the microcosmic orbit. A portal to travel into the past may be located at one of the chakras, or energy centers. The subconscious is highly intelligent and knows just where to go and where to land. There awaits an ancestral guide, who shares wisdom about life's journey.

Through what portal will you enter? Your guide may be a *genetic* ancestor (blood related) or an *ethnic* ancestor (related through culture and heritage). It may be a *geographical* ancestor (sharing the same homeland), an *inspirational* ancestor (related through your passion for the arts or social action), or a *spiritual* one (related through your spiritual practice).

Preparation: Discovering the Ethereal Thread

In Qigong the ethereal thread is a fine channel of energy extending through the core of your body and connecting it to heaven and earth.

Prepare yourself for a journey. Dress to be warm and comfortable and go to a natural setting that is sheltered from wind and disturbance. Find a flat spot and stand naturally and comfortably, allowing your body to be in relaxed alignment.

As you make contact with the earth through your feet, acknowledge all who have passed this way before. Be aware of the forces that have gone to make this beautiful earth: geographical (fire that creates and destroys and water that nourishes and erodes); biological (the birth, growth, migration, death, and decay of plant and animal life that help to shape it); the work of our predecessors reshaping and conforming it and ultimately returning to it as flesh or ashes.

Breathe naturally and easily and let the exhalation close the lids of your eyes. Softly, gently, receive your breath, then let it release. Feel how your whole body breathes—bones, muscles, tissues, and skin opening and closing with each breath.

Preparing to Meet the Ancestors: Jamie

Feel your breath as it shimmers on the surface of your body. Feel how tenuous the barrier is between the universe without and the universe within. Inhaling, let your breath slip through this barrier and bring you deeper into your core.

Explore this inner core. What are its color, sound, texture? What is its mood?

Enter deeper within. Observe the vertical ethereal thread at the center of your core. See how it shimmers. What color is it? What size? Is it a thin thread like a spider's or thick like a rope? Reach out and touch this thread. What does it feel like?

Bring your attention above your head. Notice the thread descending from the heavens down to enter the crown of your head. You may feel a tingling, pulsing or throbbing there. Let your attention travel along the thread as it descends through the crown, through your head, neck, torso, out your perineum at the center of the base of your torso and down into the earth.

Now observe your breath and feel how its pulse is the same as the pulse in your ethereal thread. Gradually, let this pulse expand and send its vibrations into your bones, muscles, and tissues. Let it softly slip through the pores of your skin and reenter into this familiar world.

Guided Imagery: Ethereal Thread Time Travel to Ancestral Realms

Steps

1　Contact the ethereal thread at the core of your body.

2　As the thread disappears, you travel back through time and space.

3　Enter into the ancestral realm.

4　Explore the terrain and observe the inhabitants.

5　Meet the ancestor.

6　Receive and don your magic cloak.

7　Interact with the ancestor and receive its teachings.

8　Receive a word.

9　Return to the ethereal thread and retrace your journey back to the present time and place.

Process

Stand, sit, or lie in meditation. Feel the awareness and presence of your breath as it enters and releases. Can you feel it shimmering on the surface of your body? What does it feel like as it slips through the tenuous barrier between the universe without and the universe within?

Breathing naturally, let each breath take you deeper, like a wave, into the core of your body. As you enter the core within, notice its color and sound. You easily find the ethereal thread. See how it shimmers. It is the landmark of your inner terrain, the axis of your inner world. Know that it is always there to guide you.

Inhaling, allow your breath to travel up and down the ethereal thread. If you want to stay within, you can stop at the crown and the perineum. If you want to experience more, you can travel up and down the ethereal thread into heaven and earth.

You feel comfortable and safe in this place of mystery and awe. As you travel along this thread, feel its texture. Feel how appealing it is. Ask this thread to take you on a journey through time.

The thread responds to your request. Feel it quiver and disappear, causing the dimensions of time and space to fold in upon each other. You find yourself traveling into the past, shifting backward through the dimensions. You may actually see the passing of days, years, decades, centuries. Continue on your journey until you reach a time and place that invite you to enter.

Feathered Cloak: Jais

Your travel slows and you pass through the entryway to this distant time and place. Be still and notice how the ethereal thread begins to shimmer again. As you inhale, it illuminates the core of your body. As you exhale, your breath expands outward, through the layers of your body and the surface of your skin. Your awareness enters the world of the ancestors.

Where do you find yourself? In a jungle, desert, city, on a distant planet? You feel safe and comfortable, and it feels so right for you to be here. Explore this terrain. What signs of life do you see? Just follow what direction feels right for you.

The ancestors have summoned you across the barriers of time and space to share their wisdom. They have summoned you to expand your awareness of your origins of blood, culture, land, or spirit. Take a few moments to explore. Where are you? In a family, tribe, village? Among whom do you find yourself? At what time and place have you arrived?

One of the ancestors comes forward to welcome you in the customary way of greeting a friend. Look at this face. Do you recognize it? Do you see a resemblance? As you look into the eyes, recognize your deep connection with this person. Look at the apparel. Do you see anything familiar?

The ancestor has something for you. It is a magic cloak that will help you to understand the ancestors' language and customs, so that you may visit with them as one of them. Receive this cloak. What does it feel like in your hands? Of what is it made? What are its shape and colors? How many pockets does it have? What do you find in them that may help you during your visit to ancestral realms?

Put on the cloak and feel yourself transform. You are now one of them, one of the tribe of ancestors!

Listen carefully as your ancestor speaks. What language do you hear? Listen to yourself respond in this new tongue. What is your ancestor's name? What name do you receive to use during your visit?

You're invited to stay awhile and visit. What is the ancestor's role in this time and place? Leader, warrior, midwife, or shaman? How do you interact with each other?

The ancestor understands why you have come. What does she or he want to share with you, teach you? Spend some time together. How does your relationship evolve?

The ancestor gives you special tools, gifts, mementos to take back with you. Tuck them in the pockets of your cloak.

When it is time to leave, understand that the wisdom you have gained is a valuable gift. The ancestor gives you a word. What does it sound like? This word is the seed of ancestral wisdom that will grow within you through time.

Your ancestor guides you back to the shimmering ethereal thread. You take your magic cloak with its pockets of gifts with you to wear on future visits. The word echoes within you, a connection to another time and place. Then as you inhale, enter the thread and feel its shimmering in the core of your body. It connects you to heaven and earth. It allows you to journey back through the dimensions to the present time and place. On an exhalation, feel your breath move outward through the layers of your body and the surface of your skin. Your awareness returns to the world of the present moment.

Journaling and Art: The Ethereal Thread, the Ancestor, the Magic Cloak

- Using words, pastels, pencils, clay, or paint, describe your journey.

  What was your experience of the ethereal thread as a guide through time? Where did you go? In what time or dimension did you land? Who is the ancestor you encountered? How did his or her background compare to yours? What were the culture and practices of the ancestor? What wisdom did she or he share? What is the special word you were given? How can the lessons from the past guide you on your journey of the present and into the future?

- Make a mask of the ancestor. (*See* "Sculpting the Mask" on page 115.)

   Is she or he healer, hunter, artist, sage, warrior, midwife, scout? One of our students used his son's umbilical cord in making his ancestral mask; another shaved off the hair on his head and applied it as a beard on his ancestral mask. One student brought a small urn of her mother's ashes and created a mask/altar. Another student made an ancestral mask/shield mounted on a torch. He took it to a secluded beach at night, lit the torch, and danced with ancestral spirits in ceremony.

- Make the magic cloak you wore to understand the language and customs of the ancestors.

   Out of what do you make it? What are its colors? Is it heavy or light? Does it fit loosely or snugly? Does it have a hood? How many pockets does it have? What do the pockets hold? How is it decorated? How do you feel when you put it on? What is your name as you become one of the ancestors and wear their cloak of transformation?

- What was your special word that symbolizes the wisdom of the ancestors?

   How is the word affecting you, deepening your own wisdom and understanding? Write the word and put it in a pocket of your cloak.

Ancestral Gates

Guided Imagery: Four Gates and Beyond

What difficult decision are you facing at this time of your life? You may be in the process of changing a relationship, choosing a different career, or moving to another city.

Hold it before you as an intention. Light a candle and place it before you in a darkened room.

Steps

1   Enter the forest and walk on the soft path.

2   Encounter the four gates at the end of the path.

3   Invoke an ancestor and ask for guidance on your difficult decision.

4   The ancestor guides you to one of the gates.

5   Pass through this gate and journey beyond, reaping experience and insight.

6   Take something with you from this realm.

7   Return to the gate and receive a signal.

8   Pass back through the gate and return through the forest to the present.

Process

In a darkened room position yourself for your inner journey in a comfortably supported sitting meditation. Light a candle and place it before you. Hold before you a difficult decision that you are facing at this time of your life.

As you breathe naturally, notice the temperature, texture, and sound of the darkness around you. Notice how the darkness covers you, like a soft, comfortable, cozy blanket. As you breathe, allow the darkness to enter your body. Tangible darkness and soft breath bring a calmness to you. As your breath guides you into a tranquil inner environment, you find yourself in the deep green of a heavily canopied forest.

You are walking with a lit candle down a spongy path, thick with humus of sodden leaves and long decayed logs. The path is soft enough to walk in deerskin moccasins. The forest is so soft your vision feels relaxed and at rest and your soft focus spreads out into the green foliage. Each step you take on this path brings you deeper into this magical forest. Your inner eye looks to the edges of the forest. Beyond, at the end of the path, you see four gates, each facing a different direction—north, east, south, west.

Sit before the gates. By the light of your candle, observe what they are made of. What colors are they? Are they plain or ornate? Are they solid or can you see through them? Invite an ancestor, one who cares about your well-being, to be your guide. Who appears to be with you? What is his or her name? By the candlelight, notice the ancestor's apparel, demeanor, personality.

Ask your ancestor for guidance. You are seeking insight for this difficult decision that you are facing. The ancestor guides you to one of the gates and tells you to release all expectation. Which gate do you approach? Reach out and touch this gate. How does it feel to your skin? Listen, what do you hear on the other side? Enter the gate with an open heart. What kind of shift do you feel as you pass through?

On the other side, you notice that the light from your candle intensifies, and you perceive with increasing clarity your new environment. What do you see? What greets you on this other side? Your ancestor guides you on a journey. Where do you go? What do you experience? Just keep an open and receptive heart and allow the experience to evolve. You may see a scene from your distant past or from a past life. Are there any sounds or voices? Are there any symbols, colors, icons? There's no need to understand any of this right now. Just take it all in.

When it is time to return, thank your ancestor. You have permission to take something back with you. What would you like to retrieve from this illuminated world?

Your ancestor accompanies you back to the gate. Before you say good-bye, ask if there is anything you need to know about contacting him or her in the future. Watch carefully for a gesture or a signal.

As you exit this world through the gate, you realize that the other three gates hold different experiences, different consequences. For now you acknowledge them and turn to leave. They exist for a future visit, or for the realm of the unknown.

You find yourself on the path through the forest. As you move through the forest, the trees thin and the light gets brighter. Blow out your candle and return up the path the way you came.

Journaling: Four Gates and Beyond

What difficult decision are you facing at this time of your life for which you are seeking wisdom?

What was it like to walk through the dark forest only with the light of your candle? What was it like to feel the presence of your ancestor? What is his or her name, relationship to you, position in life, position in the spirit world? Through which gate did your ancestor guide you? Describe the clarity and the light in this new environment. What evolved on your journey with your ancestor beyond the gate? Were there symbols, scenes, voices? What elements were prominent during this journey? Metal (or air), water, wood, fire, earth?

What insights fill you? How do they illuminate the decision you are holding? How is your relationship to your decision changing as you encounter it from new perspectives and with new illumination?

Art: Four Gates and Beyond

Light a candle. Draw a map of your journey. Build a model of the four gates on this map. These can be made of anything and can be simple or elaborate. What colors or textures do you choose for walking into the magical forest with candlelight? For entering and passing through the gate? For the brilliant clarity on the other side? For the journey with your ancestor? For the special signal your ancestor gave you?

Create a mask of your ancestor. Do you illuminate the mask?

Draw or sculpt the item you retrieved from this world. What color, texture, or shape describes this? What elements are involved? One of our students brought in her grown daughter's baby teeth and used them in making this item.

Guided Imagery: Two Gates

This experience should help you to clarify if a decision you feel poised to make is indeed true to your heart and to bring perspective to any lingering doubts. This time, you are invited to experience choosing between a decision you are planning to make and an alternative. For example, if you are planning to end an intimate relationship, your alternative choice may be staying and working on it. If you are planning to embark on a certain career, your alternative may be another career that attracts you. If you are planning to move to another city, your alternative choice may be moving to a more rural community close to where you currently live.

This process may be helpful for you in affirming your anticipated choice or in revealing hidden factors not yet considered. It is an invitation to try on a choice while it is still a choice and see how it might feel if you go with your plan or with its alternative.

See which option, which gate, you choose to enter the first time: the probable choice or its alternative. Then when you have completed this process, engage it a second time, trying out the gate not taken the first time.

Steps

1   Hold the decision and enter the forest.

2   Encounter two gates, representing your probable choice and its alternative.

3   Invite the ancestor and verbalize your two choices.

4   Reach out and touch the two gates: which one with which hand?

5   Choose one of the gates and enter.

6   Experience this world of your choosing.

7   Ask your ancestor a question and receive an answer.

8   Receive a gift representing the quintessence of this choice.

9   Return back through the gate.

10   Reconsider the two gates and the choices they guard.

11   Return along the path to the present.

Process

Get comfortable in sitting or lying meditation. Hold the impending decision that you are facing at this time of your life before you. What is your anticipated choice and what is the alternative? Again, you find yourself walking with your candle along that familiar soft path. Your vision spreads softly out into the green foliage. Each step you take on this path brings you deeper into this magical forest. Your inner eye looks to the edges of the forest. At the end of the path there are two gates. You understand that these two gates symbolize the two choices regarding your imminent decision.

Invite an ancestor, one who cares about your well-being, to be your guide. Who appears to be with you? Greet each other with respect and love. What is his or her name? Notice the ancestor's apparel, demeanor, personality.

You both sit before the two gates. There is a deep connection between you and your ancestor, and you communicate effortlessly through words, images, or telepathy. What is that imminent decision you are facing at this time of your life? Tell your ancestor. Make it very clear. What are the two choices you are entertaining, the probable one and its alternative? Verbalize them for your own clarity and for the ancestor.

You understand that these gates lead you into different dimensions. Each shows you how your life might be if you make each choice. One gate shows the decision you plan to make; the other shows you the alternative.

By the light of your candle, you see the shape of the gates. You see what the gates are made of. There is a symbol on each of the gates. One hand reaches for one gate, the other hand reaches for the other. Which gate does your right hand touch and which the left? How does each gate feel against the palm of your hand? What is it made of? Fire or water? Wood or metal? Which gate guards your probable choice and which the alternative? Listen, what do you hear on the other side?

Now make your choice, selecting one of the gates, the probable or the alternative. Release all expectations and enter that gate with an open heart. What kind of shift do you feel as you pass through?

On the other side, you perceive with clarity your new environment. This experience is very real. Where are you?

Observe carefully. Who have you become? What is your new life like? Who is involved in this new life of yours? Who is missing? What kind of career do you have? How do you feel about yourself? Just keep an open and receptive heart and allow the experience to evolve. You may find yourself interacting in a scene. You may overhear a conversation about you. You may see symbols with special meaning for you. You do not need to understand any of this.

Take some time now to really experience this world of your choosing. How do you feel living in this alternative dimension? Was it what you imagined it to be?

Ask a question of your ancestor. Listen and receive the response.

It becomes time for you to leave this dimension of your choosing. Your ancestor hands you a gift that is the summation of your experience in the world of this choice. What is it? Look at it. It represents the quintessence of this world of your choosing.

Your ancestor accompanies you back to the gate. You look back at this potential life you have chosen to understand what you are leaving. As you pass through the gate, notice what emotions come up for you. Look at both gates, one guarding the choice you made, one guarding the choice you relinquished. How do you feel about your choice now? Return along the same path back to the present.

Journaling: Two Gates

What decision are you facing in this time of your life for which you are seeking wisdom? What is your probable choice and what is its alternative?

Which gate did you choose to experience the first time you engaged this process, the one guarding the probable choice or the one guarding its alternative? How did you feel about the gate of your choosing and what you discovered beyond? What emotions came up for you? Who did you become? Who was involved in your new life? What was your daily life like? How did you feel about it?

Then, if you have not already done so, go back and engage the process and select the second gate this time. What happened when you engaged this process again, selecting the other gate? How do the two options compare? Has this process affirmed your probable decision? Or brought up new questions?

Art: Two Gates

Draw a map. Build a model of the two gates on this map. Draw or paint your experience of each of your choices. What was each new world like?

Draw or sculpt the gift you retrieved from the dimension of each of the choices.

Make a mask of the person you might become. The left side represents one choice, the right side, the other. What colors, textures, and shapes describe your process with each of these choices? Are there gates transitioning between the left and right sides of the mask?

One student wrote his decision on the protruding tongue of his mask, the tongue representing the gateway between the two sides.

The Council of Ancestors

In our journeys the ancestors sometimes gather together as a council. We find each member of our council plays an important role in our lives.

Preparation: Ancestral Fire

Choose one of these options:

- Go to a place that sells incense. Smell the choices. Select one of the fragrances for burning. At home in a quiet sacred space, arrange the incense and strike a match, observing the flame as it lights the incense and the smoke as it releases the fragrance. What memories emerge?

- Go to a candle vendor. Find a candle with shape, color, and fragrance that attract you. At home in your sacred space, light the candle, observing the flame as it flares on the wick, then settles to a gentle dance.

- At night build a fire in a fireplace or campsite.

Guided Imagery: The Council of Ancestors

Steps

1 Let the warmth and flicker of flames guide you to the ancestral circle.

2 Meet the ancestral leader.

3 Join the circle.

4 Meet each of the ancestors in the circle one by one.

5 Offer your gift.

6 Receive the elixir from the chalice and its blessing.

7 Return to the present.

Process

Sit before the incense, candle, or campfire and observe the flame. Let it be the object of your visual meditation. Breathing naturally, notice the smoke and sounds of the fire. Notice the fragrance of the incense. Allow your senses to be alive and receptive.

Place your palm over your heart and feel the fire of your heart as it continuously pumps fresh bright red blood through your entire body, transporting nutrients to every cell. Feel every cell bathing in nourishment, every cell breathing.

Then carefully extend your palm, toward (not into) the trail of smoke or burning tongues. Feel the energy of fire. Notice its warmth, texture, intensity. Notice its delicate balance between being a little too hot and painful or warming and soothing for you. Allow your hand to find that delicate balance. In this balance is the portal, a magical entryway to another fire in another time and place. Yes, you have been summoned to share a fire with a council of your ancestors.

You see their figures silhouetted by the flickering flames. These are your ancestral guardians. Observe your environment. What is it like? Are there sounds of music or laughter, aromas of food? What other beings or animals are present?

The ancestors welcome you into their presence. Who is the leader? She or he summons you to approach. How does this person look at you? The leader invites you to join the council, to make the acquaintance of each member.

Take your place among them and look into their faces. Meet them one by one. How do their voices sound to you? Spend a moment with each one. What is the role of each individual? Observe each one's appearance: the shape and form of the body, the color of skin, the type of apparel. How do the ancestors greet you? Whom do you choose to sit next to?

When you have met the entire council, reach into your pocket or pouch. You have a gift for them. What is it?

Before the leader, there is a sacred vessel with drink. What does it look like? What shape is it? Are there symbols, pictographs, colors? What is it made of? The leader offers you a drink of an elixir that will nourish you in a way you need right now. Smell the liquid. What is the aroma of compassion, courage, wealth, strength, or clarity? As the liquid enters through your lips, how does your body feel? For a moment, savor the nectar in your mouth. What does it taste like as it swirls around your tongue?

Feel how your body hungers for this precious fluid. It glides down your throat and into your core. It warms your heart, enters your bloodstream, and carries the blessing of the nectar throughout your entire body. Feel the blessing, this gift, from your ancestral lineage.

You feel the protective comfort and support of your ancestral council. You know when the time is right to take your leave. Inhaling, savor the aroma released by the fire. Exhaling, release your breath back into the present.

Writing: Ancestral Circle

In your journal describe your experience in as much detail as possible. What was the feeling of being carried by fire/smoke on your journey? How did the Qi of the fire feel? How did you connect with it? What was the portal into the past like?

How are these ancestors related to you genetically, symbolically, or spiritually? Who was the ancestral leader and what qualities did she or he possess? What was each council member like? How did each respond to you? What characteristics, strengths, vulnerabilities, and purpose did each one seem to have? What lessons did your encounters teach you?

Who did you choose to sit next to? What was the setting? Was there music? Were there aromas? Were animals or other beings present?

What was your gift to the ancestors? What was your experience of the nectar? What did the vessel look like? What were the color and aroma of the drink? What effect did the elixir have on your perception? What blessing did you receive?

Write a story or poem in which one of the members of the council enters your being. How is it to feel the presence of this person in your body, mind, and soul?

Art: Ancestral Tree

Sculpt, paint, and embellish a genealogical mask. Paint or sculpt a genealogical tree and write or hang symbols representing each ancestor of the council from the branches of the tree.

Blessings of the Ancestors: Brigit

Ancestral Lands

The land of the ancestors shaped who they were, how they survived, what they feared and revered, how they prayed and played, how they fought wars and what they did when they won or lost, how they lived, and what happened to their bodies when they died. If we as future ancestors have sometimes felt removed from the land of the modern world, the ancestors preceding us felt no such deprivation. Everything in their lives was interwoven with the shape of the great earth mother and the whims of nature.

A journey to the ancestral domain can offer much insight into the lessons the ancestors have to share. It is a pilgrimage into their territory.

The following journey into ancestral lands is an expedition that occurs over a period of time (in alternative reality). It is divided into five stages:

I   Preparing for the Expedition into Ancestral Lands

II   Day One of the Expedition into Ancestral Lands

III   Expedition into Deeper Territory

IV   The Battle

V   The Resolution

You may want to embark on this process as if it were truly an expedition, moving through it one stage at a time, over a series of days or weeks.

Guided Imagery: Preparing for the Expedition into Ancestral Lands

Steps

1   Make a fire at your campsite or at the hearth in your home.

2   Let the glow of the embers take you back to the ancestral council's fire circle, where you find yourself asleep.

3   An ancestor awakens you for a journey.

4   Who else is going?

5   Receive clothing, a pack, a weapon for the journey.

6   Observe the map of the ancestral lands.

7   Receive writing tools.

8   Take note of the journey preparations and the experience of your fellow travelers.

9   Pack your bag and change your clothes for the journey.

Process

You may want to prepare for this journey by making a fire, either in your fireplace at home or in a campfire circle in the wild. When the flames from the fire have turned the fuel to embers, let their glow guide you into meditation. It feels so pleasant to have the warmth embrace you as you enter deeply into your core.

As you smell the cinders, you find yourself sleeping in the near dawn after meeting the ancestral council. You feel the mystery of darkness enshroud you. Your body basks in the comfort and safety of sleep.

Someone is gently shaking you awake. One of the ancestors has come, summoning you for a journey through the ancestral lands. Who is it?

What are they wearing? What are they bringing? You receive special clothing to wear on this journey and a pack. What do they look like? You receive a weapon. What is it? How does it feel to hold it in your hands?

The soft gray of the early morning light welcomes you. Listen to the songs of the dawn. Notice the movement in the camp. Other members are also preparing for the journey. Which others of the council are joining this expedition into the wilderness?

The ancestral guide unrolls a map of the terrain in which you will be traveling. Look at the map. What kind of terrain lies before you? Are there mountains, a desert, bodies of water? You have no clue as to where you're headed, but you feel safe with your ancestors.

You are appointed scribe of the expedition, recording all that is seen and done. You are given writing and drawing tools and pages of parchment.

As scribe of the geographical expedition, you are a scout, observing and noting the surroundings, the trail, the changes in ecosystems, the signs of weather, the traces of those who have passed this way before. You will also trace your progress on the map.

As scribe of the communal expedition, you record the interactions of the group.

As scribe of the spiritual expedition, you record the signs from the heavens, the appeals to the heavens, the blessings and curses from the heavens, the way the Spirit pervades or eludes the spirit of the group of travelers.

And so, your ancestral guide helps you to pack your bag. What do you take with you on this expedition into ancestral lands? How do you pack your writing and drawing tools and the parchment? How do you carry your weapon?

Now change into your travel clothes and prepare to leave.

Art and Writing: Preparing for the Expedition into Ancestral Lands

Who and what greet you in the morning? Describe the movement and excitement in the air as the tribe prepares for the expedition. Which ancestor helps you to pack? Describe your clothing, your pack, and your weapon. Create artifacts out of fabric, leather, feathers, bones, stone, or iron. You may want to make a weapon or a medicine pouch filled with herbs. What items do you take with you on this journey? Describe your writing and drawing tools and your pages of parchment. As scribe of the journey, you may want to create your own logbook using natural materials or handmade paper. In it you will record your notes as scribe and include your observations of the landscape and of the group.

Guided Imagery: Day One of the Expedition into Ancestral Lands

Steps

1   Travel among the mountains to the bridge.

2   Cross the bridge over the chasm.

3   Travel through the terrain on the other side.

4   Descend the stone steps deep into the inner terrain.

5   Make camp, dine, sleep.

6   Awaken at night and go to the pond.

7   Meet the small creature and respond to its questions.

8   Return to camp, where someone watches you.

9   Record your experiences in your log, then rest.

Process

You find yourself with a small group of ancestors leaving to go on the expedition. Which ones are with you and what are their roles?

You find yourself among high mountain peaks with deep ravines, so close to the skies that you can almost reach up into the heavens. You come to the edge of a huge cliff with a long, old rope bridge with wooden slats stretching across a chasm. Approach it carefully, because even from the distance, you can see that part of it is in disrepair. Who built it and when? Look around for telltale signs. It is necessary to cross this bridge to continue your journey. What does it feel like to let go of the support of the land? Feel the wooden slats under your feet, the thick rope in your hands.

Look below. What do you see? How deep is this chasm you are crossing? What emotions come up for you? Is the wind blowing, or is the air very still? Look above. What do you see? Is there a sign above to accompany you on this journey? Proceed. What sounds does the bridge make?

Each step you take on this bridge brings you closer to the other side. As you come to the places of disrepair, what do you do to move on? When you arrive at the other side, step off the bridge. Feel your feet on solid ground. What is the landscape like? You and the group descend stone steps deeper into the terrain. All you hear, after a while, is the rhythm of your footsteps on this stone stairway. Your group walks on and on, descending deeper and deeper. How do the terrain and climate change?

When it is time to rest for the night, your group finds a beautiful setting. What is this place? Do any other living beings share it? What is the night light like? You are all tired from the day's journey. How does the fatigue manifest among this group? The group prepares camp for the night, then dinner, dines together, then prepares for sleep.

During the night, you awaken and go to the pond nearby. As you drink from the pond, a small creature emerges from the depths. What is it?

It introduces itself: "I've lived here for thousands of years and have seen a number of voyagers passing through. I ask them questions and receive many answers. I ask: 'Who are you and what are you doing here?'"

You are a little startled and reveal your name. The small creature just looks deeply into your eyes and asks again, "Who are you? Why are you here?"

You search for an answer to give. What do you say? And the small creature looks deeply into your eyes and asks again, "Who are you? Why are you here?"

"Ancestral Guidance" by Kaleo (mixed media drawing, 30″h x 22″w)

What is your answer to this small creature of the pond? How does it respond to your answer before disappearing back into the water?

When you go back to the circle of sleeping ancestors, you notice one of them is watching you. As scribe, you take out your parchment and writing tools and record the events of the day and night. Then you return to sleep.

Art and Writing: Day One of the Expedition into Ancestral Lands

What was it like to be in mountainous terrain and to cross the bridge? What came up for you as you stepped onto the bridge, crossed over the areas of disrepair, and stepped again onto solid ground? How was your balance? Did you see anything below or above? What does bridge as metaphor mean for you in this time of your life?

What was it like to enter the new terrain, persevere on the trail, and finally rest? Describe the mood of the group and any interactions. Describe the pond and the small creature. Did it have a name? What were your answers to its questions and its response to you? Which ancestor was awake and watching you when you returned to the campsite?

How do you feel after this first day's journey?

Guided Imagery: Expedition into Deeper Territory

Steps

1 Clear the path through the underbrush.

2 Encounter a bee stuck in a spider's web.

3 Scout the new trail.

4 Enter the clearing with the structure.

5 Choose a gate that leads under the ground or into the heavens, and enter.

6 Walk through the corridor.

7 Choose a door and enter the room with the altar.

8 Explore the altar and bowls of five elements.

9 Choose one element and apply alchemy to transform it.

10 Record the events, then rest.

Process

You and your group of ancestors are breaking camp. It is early morning and the sun has not yet risen. In the distance, you may hear the sounds of animals returning from the night hunt. Everyone is packing to go, refreshed and in good spirits.

The path you are traveling soon turns into thick underbrush. What is the vegetation? Is it bamboo forest, unruly madrone, or prickly briars? Your machetes hack an opening through this undergrowth. It is exhausting work under the hot sun. Insects pester you. Sometimes you come across poisonous snakes or scorpions with their wrathful stingers. Large spiders weave the brush, their webs studded with dying insects.

In one web, you watch a bee struggling to set itself free. Every time it frees one of its legs, another leg gets caught in the sticky web. At first, the bee, energized by fear, struggles desperately to get loose. Gradually, it starts to tire and becomes more and more enmeshed in the sticky thin lines. Eventually, the exhausted bee hangs there limply and the vigilant spider approaches it. What do you do?

Hush! The leader of your group signals for silence. There is total stillness among the group as you come across a small barely visible trail in this underbrush. You are summoned forward to explore ahead. Move along this trail; look for signs. Who or what has made this trail? What traces do you perceive? You are sweating with anticipation heightened by the company of insects, scorpions, and spiders.

Eventually, you emerge in a beautiful clearing with a large structure in the center. Notice the architecture. Is it Polynesian or African? European, Asian, or American? Inuit or Anasazi? Approach this structure. What elements is it made of? What colors and symbols decorate it?

Notice that part of this structure travels deep underground, while the other part reaches into the heavens. There are two gates. One leads into the earth, the other into the sky. Which do you choose?

Pass through the gate of your choice, and as you move through a long corridor, notice the change in temperature. Suspense fills you. Many doors line this corridor. Some of these you pass by; others you wonder about. Which one do you choose to enter? Why do you make this choice?

You find yourself in a large room. Its spaciousness permeates you with inner stillness. What is the shape of this room? Is it circular, rectangular, or triangular? Are there windows and are they open or closed? What adorns the walls? What covers the floor? Feel free to touch, to explore.

You feel drawn to an altar at the far end of the room and approach it. What is it made of? Somehow you understand that it was prepared just for you. Take a few moments now. Do you recognize the items on this altar?

Notice the five little bowls, each containing one element: metal, water, wood, fire, or earth. You feel summoned by one of the elements to transform its negative emotion: the grief of metal, the fear of water, the anger of wood, the alienation of fire, the worry of earth.

Choose one and create a ritual of transformation. If it is metal you choose, fire may forge its grief into something of beauty. If it is water, a basin of earth may create a safe vessel for fear. If it is wood, you may carve anger into a new form with metal. If it is fire, water may quench the sting of alienation. If it is earth, you may plant a tree to grow roots and loosen the grip of worry.

How does your ritual transform your relationship to the element and its negative emotion? What shifts do you feel inside your being?

As scribe you sit and write the events of the day. You draw the building and its room, the altar and your ritual. And now you find a comfortable spot in this room and lay your head down to sleep.

Writing and Art: Expedition into Deeper Territory

On a large sheet of paper, write or draw the emotion you chose to transform. Then through painting or drawing apply the alchemical process you chose for the ritual. Use white, gray, or silver to represent metal, blue or black for water, green for wood, red for fire, yellow, ochre, or brown for earth. You may even use elements to transform the drawing: massaging with earth, melting with fire, cutting with a knife, baptizing with water, or drawing with sticks.

Guided Imagery: The Battle

Steps

1   A beautiful being awakens you and takes you to paradise.

2   You meet friends, experience the luxuries.

3   Bathe with friends in a pond.

4   The small creature emerges.

5   A storm comes and the beautiful being turns into a huge monster.

6   The huge monster attacks the small creature.

7   You attack the monster, and the creature escapes back into the pond.

8   A weapon appears in your hand and radiates light.

9   The monster retreats, then transforms and dissolves in darkness along with your friends.

10   The small creature emerges and brings you the monster's shed skin.

11   Receive the creature's response to your questions.

12   Find the tree, sit down, record the events, then sleep.

Process

The night is wonderful. The air feels temperate on your skin. The room is a haven and you feel safe and comfortable. You fall asleep and your body enjoys a delicious rest. As you weave in and out of dreams, you hear soft music and feel a gentle touch on your face.

As your eyes open, you are startled to find the most beautiful creature before you. Who is it? Is it woman, man, a winged horse, a sleek dolphin, a furry wolf? Is it a guru, goddess, warrior, or what?

This beautiful being offers to guide you on a journey. You gather your belongings and leave this abode. Do you walk hand in hand, ride on its back, or fly through the sky? This journey takes you into enticing territory. Where are you? Your senses are so alive in this realm. Everywhere you look are wealth and beauty. Everything you may desire is here. Many of the residents recognize you and greet you warmly. You seem to have a multitude of friends and admirers. What a paradise this is! Luxurious! Intoxicating. Look, listen, smell, and feel the pleasures of this abode.

Take a few moments now to enjoy this place.

Later, you, the beautiful being, and your friends are bathing in the pond. The ambience is pleasant, and everyone is cheerful. Music soothes you. An abundance of food and drink satiates you. As you bathe, something stirs in the water and you have a sense of *déjà vu*. From the depths the small creature, which you met before at the other pond, appears. How has such a small creature traveled so far? It startles you. The creature stares deeply into your eyes and asks, "Who are you? Why are you here?"

You hear laughter from the others in the pond. The beautiful being is enticing you to come and play with your friends. Puzzled, you look back at the small creature. Again, it stares deeply into your eyes. Again, it inquires, "Who are you and why are you here?" Something within you stirs. Your friends in the pond become quiet and serious.

Suddenly the weather changes. The sky darkens and rain begins to fall. Thunder rages. Lightning splits the sky. A sense of danger saturates the air. You are shocked! Before your very eyes, the beautiful being transforms into a huge monster! What form does it take? It pounces on the small creature!

The monster is powerful, but the small creature is agile. They struggle. Suddenly, the monster gets a hold on the small creature and squeezes tightly. The small creature turns purple, is choking and gasping. It looks like it's about to burst. The monster laughs and tightens its grip, enjoying this moment. The small creature looks at you with its large eyes that are glazing over. It gasps, "Who...? Why...?"

Your friends in the pond laugh and mock the small creature.

Suddenly, you leap onto the huge monster, causing it to loosen its grip. The small creature, half dazed, slips back into the comfort of the watery depths.

A fierce battle ensues! Your friends are startled and back away. The monster snarls furiously and uses all its powers to overcome you. The battle continues and no one is winning. Then you hear an inner voice: "Who am I? Why am I here?" And you understand.

Your thighs clamp down on the monster's thick neck. One hand grapples with its sharp talons. Suddenly, the weapon from your ancestor appears in your other hand. The ancestors! Where are they? How could you forget them? The weapon begins to pulse, to hum, to glow. A brilliant light emerges from it. You jump free of the monster, and you both back warily away from one another. Its eyes are red with fury; its body twitches with rage.

The light! You focus the light. It pierces the monster's eyes. It illuminates the dark corners of its mind. The monster writhes in pain! It retreats! The light becomes stronger. The monster roars, shuts its eyes, and sheds its skin, showing its true form. What is it? You watch it dissolve in the depths of the darkness.

Your friends are fearful. As you shine the light toward them, you see its reflection in their eyes. They groan and wail, and they too dissolve into the darkness.

You look into the light. Its beam enters your eyes and spreads into your core. You receive its beauty, clarity, and illumination. You understand, and you peer into the depths of the pond.

The small creature swims joyously toward the light. It breaks the surface of the pond and your eyes meet. It retrieves the monster's shed skin and brings it to you. Reach for the skin. How does it feel in your hands? What color is it? What does it smell like?

Thank the small creature and ask, "Who are you? Why are you here?" What is its response?

Exhausted, you sit down under a magnificent tree. Being a conscientious scribe, you record the dramatic events faithfully.

When you finish, you stretch out beneath the tree. The moon covers you in a blanket of pale blue light. You feel deep comfort of body and soul. Crickets hum you to sleep.

Art and Writing: The Battle

You are the scribe. Record what happened as you experienced it.

Then using your chosen media, let the forces of light and dark do battle through art. You may sculpt the ancestor's weapon, depict the fury of the battle, draw what you saw behind the eyes of the monster, create an installation piece with the skin of the monster as a collage of scaly paint, shapes, and textures.

Guided Imagery: The Resolution

Steps

1   The sun awakens you under the tree.

2   Find the shed skin and five pouches.

3   The small creature brings the ancestors.

4   Share ritual and receive a new name and role.

5   The creature gives you a talisman.

6   Share your story.

Process

Rest is upon you. Deep, embracing sleep. Feel your breath nurturing and rejuvenating your body. Feel the transformation of healing deep within your cells.

Warmth begins to spread along your skin: the embrace of the emerging sun. Your eyes open to the magnificent tree above you. Observe its colors and textures of trunk, branches, leaves. As you lie under it, feel the energy from its body, the protection of its canopy of leaves and branches, the deep grasp of its roots. What kind of tree is it?

As you sit up and lean against the tree, notice your weapon before you. Also notice your pack with your writing and drawing tools. Sketch your impressions of the area.

You also notice the large shed skin near you. Touch it. How do the light and warmth of the sun affect it? What would you like to do with this skin? Make it into a garment to wear? Turn it into a sheath for your weapon? Shape it into a cover for your parchments? Turn it into shoes?

As you sit, you notice five pouches hanging from the tree, each containing one of the five elements. What are the pouches made of? Are there symbols on them? You understand that metal is divine inspiration. Water is endurance. Wood is motivation. Fire is connectedness. Earth is centeredness.

The wind blows and the branches of the tree sway. You hear a whispering telling you that the elements are yours. These pouches were made just for you.

Collect the pouches and thank the tree.

You hear voices in the distance. There's your friend, the small creature, happily bounding along! Following it are the ancestors. They're so relieved to find you well and immediately notice your transformation. They can feel your inner light, its glow emanating from you. They understand.

It is time for ritual. You are its center. Around you the ancestors arrange the five pouches, your weapon, the shed skin, your pack, and your scribe's tools and parchment. What is their ritual to honor you? They give you a new name. What is it? They also give you another role besides that of scribe. What role are you given?

The small creature comes forward, blesses a talisman, and gives it to you. Examine it. Of what is it made? Touch it. Is it rough or smooth, heavy or light, large or small? What symbols or glyphs does it reveal? Thank the small creature. If you are ready, you may make a vow on this talisman.

Now it is time for food and drink to replenish and nourish the body. Now it is time to relate your story to the ancestors.

Art and Writing: The Resolution

Write a paragraph as the tree. What do you as tree have to share?

Write a paragraph as the shed skin. What have you as shed skin left behind? What do you want to become?

Write a paragraph as the small creature. Who are you and why have you come?

Write a paragraph as the talisman. Describe your features in detail: size, shape, composition, symbols, textures, colors. What is your purpose? What do you bring? What do you ask of the one who wears you?

Then, as yourself, sit in meditation. Feel the response to this journey in your body. In your mind. In your spirit. Then allow your inner response to emerge on paper as the energies and forms of art.

Alchemy with the Ancestor: Wood and Fire Ritual

In the last journey into Ancestral Lands, you experienced the influences of alchemy and the interrelationships of the elements of metal, water, wood, fire, and earth. In this Wood and Fire Ritual, we invite you into the specific relationship between wood and fire.

Stuckness in the wood element brings anger in all its myriad forms, including rage, resentment, frustration, even some forms of depression. Health in the wood element means motivation and growth: growth so that wood may perform its alchemical function of birthing and nurturing fire.

Disharmony in the fire element can bring alienation and withdrawal, from others and from one's sacred life's path and purpose. Health in the fire element enhances the quality of connectedness: within oneself to one's highest good and among oneself and all other beings of the living universe, past, present, and future.

Kaleo's Journal: By the Fire

9/13/98

Elise and I are camping in Big Sur. It's early morning and the ancestor guides us. Twirling and swinging our wooden staffs, we build relationship between flesh and bone and wood. Certain wood (pine) has a sinuous feel of strength and resilience as it snuggles in the crook of the elbow, spins around bone, glides over flesh. The staff is an extension of the body as we parry and strike under the vastness and light of the stars. The air whistles. What fun!

9/14/98

Tonight at our campfire we're enjoying the soft juicy flesh of chicken and the sultriness of Merlot. Cooking over fire is as old as mankind. We thank the ancestors, the first ones who discovered fire and used it for cooking, illumination, ritual. *Ē Pele ē. Mahalo nui loa*—we thank also Pele, the goddess of fire.

As the flesh and skin of the fowl sizzle and blacken over the fire, I feel angst filling my body. The ancestors, peering from the darkness at the rim of our campsite, understand. They see the blackened scars of *pāhoehoe* lava over my heart.

As I inhale deeply, the angst fills my lungs and heart. I have worked with this and understand the lessons. Exhaling, my emotions flow through my body, into pen, and onto paper. I fold the paper three times, and stick it in my shirt pocket. The fire encourages the dance of Qi, Qi from my core— flowing from the undulations of inner organs through my flesh. My skin loosens. It begins to melt. It sloughs off to dance in the fire. It surrenders to the flames. My prayer for forgiveness ascends into the heavens. Thank you, ancestor, for your guidance. In the morning I gather the ashes for creative process. Pele is inspired.

9/15/98

It is late evening. Within the circle of campfire stones, I arrange a circle of sticks. *Pī kai*, anointing with salt water from the Pacific, a prayer, a strike of the match, and fire begins snapping and crackling.

My eyes close. Obstacles float by—obstacles that block my spirit. They tread before my mind's eye. When the procession feels complete, I draw symbols of the obstacles on pieces of driftwood. This wood has drifted with the Tao. It smells of salt. It has been shaped by many different ocean currents. It has traveled and visited distant lands.

Circle of Fire

According to Chinese five element theory, my strongest element is fire. Ancestors have instructed me to use fire in this process. As wood feeds fire and becomes earth, negative emotions transform so that I can continue my journey toward wholeness.

Picking up one of the pieces of driftwood, I say a blessing, aware of the dance of yin and yang, for the obstacle has been an important teacher to me. The blessing allows it to transform into an attribute that better serves my spiritual intention. I offer the sticks to fire, to my lineage of ancestors. I ask for guidance. The fire advises: forgiveness, loving kindness. I let the flames within me explode into my journal.

Writing and Ritual: Calcination and Purification

Write in your journal. How is your emotional relationship to wood (anger vs. growth)? In relationship to these qualities of the element wood, are there ways that you feel stuck? How is your emotional relationship to fire (withdrawal vs. connectedness)? Are there ways you want to bring more love and intimacy into your life? In relationship to whom? How warm is your relationship to yourself?

Plan a time when you can do your own wood and fire ritual. Set your intention for this ritual. Invite the guidance of the ancestors. Create your own ceremony with safety and responsibility. Gather your own pieces of wood, build your fire, shed your "old skins," and enact your wood and fire ceremony, using the same contents as above or modified to fit your own desires and needs for this sacred process.

What kind of wood do you gather? What symbols do you draw on the sticks? What do you want to let go of? What is the next phase for healing?

Art: Out of the Fire

Summon the guidance of the ancestors. Using ashes, charred wood, burnt sticks, singed hair, fur, or skin from an animal, and other art media, create a drawing or sculpture that helps you to purge old stuck or worn-out emotional skins of your psyche. Out of the cleansing fire may emerge an enhanced sense of connectedness.

Birthing (Hawaiian petroglyph)

Joining the Ancestors

Who are your immediate ancestors, those who have preceded you, taught you, directly or indirectly, before passing on to the spirit world? They may be ancestors of blood or spiritual kinship. As you follow Kaleo and Elise on their inner journeys of remembrance, allow them to inspire your own exploration of the intimate bonds of immediate ancestral relationships.

Kaleo's Journal: In the Hospital Room with Art, Elise's Father

1/23/00

The room echoes with his gasping—fifty-eight respirations per minute. The air is thick, humid. The muscles on his face and neck strain with effort. His mouth is open, the cavern of his throat heaves, its tunnel is dry and windy. Gases and humid air gush from his lungs. The room smells of dying.

Suddenly I am standing in the dry heat on the edge of a red cliff in the wild, ancient desert of southern Utah. From out of the blue expansive sky, raven appears.

Quickly, I swab the arid cavern of Art's throat with water.

A spot in the desert floor begins to heave.

My palm is drawn to his respiratory diaphragm. Immediately it's sucked in and pushed out with tremendous force. My palm moves over his sternum and listens to the roar of his heartbeat, the swelling and the emptying of his lungs. Zhong Fu, the opening into his Lung meridian, beckons and my palm begins to spiral into its vortex. Gently, I cradle his lung and heart. Art looks up at me, relaxes a bit, and smiles.

Large bruises from the IVs cover his forearms. Tubes for oxygen and nourishment snake into his nostrils.

Suddenly Art and I are once again hiking together in the forest. Under my feet, I feel the softness and tenderness of Gaia, the Mother. My body fills with the cool dampness of the giant redwoods. The smells transport us to our kitchen table and we're enjoying dark red wine and smoked Gouda, baguettes, chocolate, and fruit. I'm listening to his stories of his life and family and his thoughts of aging and dying. I listen to his prayers to Edith, his deceased wife.

At his bedside in this hospital, we continue our conversation. His eyes twinkle as I speak: "Art, how courageous you are. Remember our hike up Yosemite Falls? You were 84 then. And what fun we had during the holidays! At 88, half blind and with respiratory problems, you still flew on your own 3,000 miles to spend the holidays with us in California. Such fun we had eating at your favorite Thai restaurant and walking the dog at the Berkeley Marina. Remember our conversations about the meaning of life?"

Elise leans over, kisses him, and whispers in his ear, "Dad, the doctors say the stroke left your whole left side paralyzed. They say you may not make it through the night. We will honor your wishes. You've touched many people deeply and given much love in your life. We love you. When you're ready, it's okay, just let go."

Ē ka Dan Zhong, ē ka Shen Zhu, ma ke aupuni o ke aloha mau loa, e kahe mālie ka la'a kea e hiki 'ana ke ola. My heart chakra chant fills the room. By 2:00 a.m. Art's respiration rate is dropping and his systems are shutting down. At 3:30 in the morning he looks peaceful. His extremities are cold. Elise is on his right whispering in his ear. I'm on his left. Family members encircle him.

Suddenly white tiger appears, brushes against me, and sits at my side. His strong breathing comforts me.

Around 4:00 in the morning, Art releases his spirit into the universe.

Art, Elise's father, in Maui

1/26/00 Kaleo's Eulogy for Art in Church

"The other night, Art's family slept at his bedside in the hospital room. Throughout the day and night his breathing was loud, raspy, desperate. In time, his breathing became more peaceful. He felt our loving hands on him. As he felt Elise's lips kiss his forehead, Art let go.

"Last night. Elise and I are sleeping in Art's bed at his home. His presence, his smells are in the bedroom. The room has a breath of its own, a dampness, sound, fragrance—sweet like the earth. Art appears during the night. At first I'm afraid, but then, I remember his loving kindness. Just three weeks ago, he was in California visiting us. We sat talking story at our kitchen table. He looked carefully into my eyes and said: 'Always look for the goodness in people, even if they don't see it in themselves.' I thank him for his wisdom.

"Art used to love watching me do Qigong. For me, Qigong is prayer that integrates body and spirit. I know he wants me to share this Qigong meditation with all of you today. In this meditation, an ancestor will appear. It may be from the distant past or it may be from the present. It may be living or dead.

"Gently, just allow the lids of your eyes to close. And notice your breath entering, filling your nostrils, and gliding down into the cavern of your throat. Softly. As your breath releases, allow your body to let go. Surrender. Feel your breath descending down into your chest, into your belly, your pelvis, this chalice of your body. Feel your breath as it expands and fills your inner body, pressing gently into the walls of bone and flesh—pressing, softly, then releasing.

"Listen to the sounds of your inner body. Observe. Someone, an ancestor who loves you, is approaching. Which ancestor appears? Look into its eyes. Allow yourself to be filled with its love. What is the message it brings for you? Receive it. When you're ready, exhale and let your breath, your blood, and this message flow into every cell of your body.

"Inhaling, receive the blessings of the Divine. Exhaling, release the love into this room. Listen. You can hear the breath, the spirit, in this chamber. Listen. You can hear the beat of your heart. Of Art's heart. Listen as you offer your breath into the Universe."

2/14/00

Three weeks later. The grieving continues, mixed with gratitude for what he taught us.

The muscles in my body have been very tense, ropy. The grief resides between the fascial layers. My organs crave attention: Kidney (endurance and wisdom), Liver (loving kindness), and Spleen (nurturing and grounding).

Yesterday I received a massage from Barbara.

As I lie prone, she does shiatsu with her fists on my back. When I lie supine, her fists walk up the Spleen meridian on my inner leg. I start to release.

At Chong Men, in the bilateral caverns of my pelvic bowl, she presses her fists down and in with her full body weight. My belly distends and contracts powerfully.

Suddenly I find myself surrounded by gigantic rocks. A powerful tribal being dressed in furs holds a large wooden club. He is the guardian of the entrance. How can I get past him to enter into this lava tube? My body transforms quickly into a black spider and I scurry into the mouth of the tube. With my spider belly close to the ground, I feel the temperatures, vibrations, and hum of the earth. I feel the warmth of the earth's belly rising to meet the cool air in the cave. I'm quite proud of myself! My eight legs are quick, sensitive, aware. I go anywhere I desire. I crawl on the cave walls, hide in cracks, spin a web, and even dangle from the ceiling!

Quickly, I move through the lava tube deep into the earth. It opens up into a cavernous room and I'm drawn to the warmth of a fire. Shadows play on the walls. I hear wood popping, sparks crackling, and little breezes playing. An ancient woman with long gray hair squats before a black kettle. Bright colors of woven fabric, leather, and fur cover her. She stares into the contents of the pot while stirring. I smell fire, blood of fresh meat, ancient dust, herbs, and fruit. Rattles, drums, drying herbs, insects, and skins hang on the walls. Open gourds catch dripping water from long roots from the ceiling of the cave.

I move in closer. The ancient one is in trance. Her body is one with time, one with earth, one with the universe. The walls of the cave begin to heave. They weep with all the sorrows of birth, struggle, and death since ancient times. I realize that I'm in the den of the first mother!

My spider body weaves a beautiful intricate pouch designed to carry herbs. I give it to the ancient one, along with a large spool of webbing for further weaving. We sit together, spider and the first mother. We sit quietly and look into the fire. Our eyes turn brown, blue, green, then red. Fire brings joy, community, intimacy. Fire flows through the vessels and warms the body. Fire is passion. Fire is the blood urging a newborn into this world. Fire is the old blood passing with the cycles of moon. First mother gives me a vessel made of earth—of Art's body. In it is fire holding the gold friendship ring that Art gave me a few years ago. She cautions me: Do not be afraid to get in touch with the fire within. If the fire dies, there will be coldness. With fire there are passion, love, and strength, but there are also much sadness and loss. Understand it, use it wisely, revel in the presence of your fire.

Barbara releases her fists from my lower abdomen. The walls of my pelvis open and close, releasing ancient tears that bathe and cleanse the vessel.

Writing: Intimate Ancestor

Who has gone before you into the spirit world and left you with the most profound lessons, the most intimate connections, the most powerful memories? How did your relationship in life compare to your connection across the threshold of death? How do you feel this person's presence still in your life? And how do you honor that presence when you can no longer communicate in the flesh?

Write a eulogy for an immediate ancestor, parent, close relative, or friend who has passed on. Write a eulogy for yourself.

Art: Invoking Your Ancestor

Assemble tools for artistic process. What materials do you use? Herbs, earth, ashes, fire, water, wood, metal?

Sit in meditation.

Then bring awareness of the deceased's spirit into your studio to guide you in your process. Invite the spirit to express his or her message for you in this moment through art. Then inhale the presence of that spirit into the cauldron of creativity deep within your being and begin.

Ancestral Totems and Archetypes

Elise's Journal

2/8/00

Kaleo said, "Let's go to the ocean," so here we are at Drake's Beach. No one else is here right now on this blustery winter afternoon, just us and the raven.

Eat bread, chicken, sip peach tea. Light candles and joss paper to Mom and Dad.

Dad, just two weeks dead. The gathering at his funeral, an awesome array of relatives, of generations. Dad, the Patriarch.

This ocean makes me feel so small. Thanks to Mom and Dad for all the gifts of my life—every second of it, bringing me here—to the edge of the sea—a sea I could slide into like any old seal and never return.

That raven. Still there. Who else besides a raven would dare to hunker so close? Eye on the grub, eh? You're a rascal.

What trick do you have tucked under your wing today, raven?

"I bring a message from Art. He says his journey is going well. He says thanks for the send-off. He sends his love."

Raven croaks twice, so guttural, so emphatic, then spreads his obsidian wings and takes to the sky.

Writing: Totem Animal, Archetype, and Ancestral Spirit

What do you know about the relationship of animals to the person close to you who has died? Did this person have a totem animal in life? A favorite wild animal? A pet? Did you experience an interaction with an animal in close connection with the person's death? Have you had dreams of animals in relation to this person's spirit?

Often those who have touched us deeply have great stature in our lives. Perhaps the profound wisdom comes from a child who lived many spirit years before dying early. Perhaps it comes from an elder whose eyes, ears, and flesh explored enough wealth of life's lessons to fill years of stories. What archetype do you associate with that person's spirit?

Sometimes it is difficult to write about someone so close to us, especially one newly deceased. But perhaps that spirit can be honored by writing a story or poem whose persona embodies an archetype closest to that person, such as patriarch, matriarch, or wise child.

In story or poem, bring together the archetype you connect with your ancestor, the totem animal of your ancestor, and the archetype of yourself as witness.

VIGIL
by Elise

Wingbones fold against your ribs
sides heave, each breath a question
I seek behind your eyelids:
How is it

To grind slate to numberless points to fit the shaft
apply yarrow to decades of wounds
share tales with your brother
of maps of scars
and years of hearts still quivering in their sacs

Feel the weight of time
curving your spine like an old bow

Watch birth rip your love's womb
squeezing life into the world
and opening death's door

Feel the image of the waning moon
the crackle of dry leaves in the forest
the touch of your children
slipping away

All that you have loved and feared embracing
even as soul and flesh begin to separate
leaving you
sometimes the wise man, sometimes the fool
to watch it all molt like last season's plumage

Can you feel the warm wind
of the wings of the great bird
reaching along the path that parts the night?

Art: Ancestral Altar

You have traveled many journeys with the ancestors, shared trails, stories, gifts, questions, wisdom. Now construct an altar to honor the ancestors and your relationships with them. What will be the primary material: stone, wood, cloth, metal, clay? What will be its shape, its colors, its textures? What elements are present? What direction will it face? How will you embellish it? What sacred objects will it hold? What blessings and songs will waft over it? What ancestors are represented?

As you prepare to create your altar, what ritual do you perform to invoke ancestral spirits and their guidance? As you begin to create your altar, notice your inner experience. As you create, what emotions come up and how do they shift? Take your time with each step of creation. Realize that your altar may grow and contract with the shifts of time and the commands of experience.

Shared Journeys

Relationships with guides from the spirit world are often reciprocal. They may learn from you as you learn from them. Perhaps an ancestor has unfinished business where you could be of assistance. Perhaps a lesson the ancestor was working on during his or her lifetime was not complete, and you can help make steps toward fulfillment.

Honoring Ancestors: Lisa

Guided Imagery: Request of the Ancestor

Steps

1   Journey to a fire circle, where you are alone.

2   Invite the ancestors to join you.

3   Leave the fire circle while the ancestors confer.

4   Return to the fire circle.

5   An ancestor presents a request.

6   Respond to the request.

7   The ancestors leave except for the one.

8   You discuss the request and your response.

9   Return to the present.

Process

Sit or lie in supported meditation position. Close your eyes and watch your breath as it travels deeper into your body. Allow your heart to receive the blessings of your breath.

It is night. You find yourself sitting alone in front of a campfire. Where are you? What does this inner terrain feel like? All the ancestors you have encountered on your journeys are waiting beyond the light of the fire circle. Invite them to join you. Watch them enter the circle and take their places one by one. Who comes to join you in this circle?

They have gathered to make a special request of you. Now step back out of the fire circle. Wait. Surrender all expectation as the ancestors confer.

Finally the ancestors invite you to rejoin the circle. One of them rises. Who is it? What is their special request of you?

What is your response? Is assistance in this matter something you feel you can offer?

If so, how? If not, why?

The ancestor sits back down beside you while the rest rise and take their leave. You are left alone together beside the flickering fire to share thoughts and feelings about this request and what is to be done. Can you make a vow to your ancestral lineage?

When you feel finished, take your leave. Enter into the flow of your breath and allow it to return you to your present awareness.

Journaling: How Do You Respond?

Which ancestor made a request of you and what was it? How did you respond? Do you feel this is an appropriate and meaningful request for you to honor? How will your responding to this request enhance your own growth? What kind of effort is required of you? How does this request affect your relationship with the ancestor?

Life with Your Spirit Mentors

Now that you have met and come close to your ancestral, spirit, and animal guides, keep them always with you. Watch them in your dreams. Keep images of them by your bedside or around your neck. Keeping your spirit mentors with you means spending time with them in your daily life. Journal about and with your guides. Let them guide you in meditation or lead you on a journey. Introduce your ancestral, spirit, and animal guides to each other. How do they interact? How do their qualities influence you, inspire you, free you? Invite your guides, through your voice, to tell their stories. Allow their stories to evolve, like the events of a legend, the insights of a biography, the mythos of a dream.

Tribal Lineage: Raven

V

Sculpting the Mask

Maskmaking is about journeying beneath the masks we wear and touching the soul. It is about recognizing the Spirit in each of us as we connect with one other.

It is about community. Through maskmaking we have met people of all backgrounds, in many contexts. Whether working with inmates in the jail psychiatric unit, the homeless, celebrities, upper middle class, urban youth in San Francisco's Mission district or Chinatown, teachers, or psychotherapists, we are continually challenged on both creative and personal levels. We are continually reminded that we are all related, all of the same family.

Introduction: Maskmaking as an Ancient and Holistic Process

Our process of maskmaking involves the body, mind, and spirit. We begin with Qigong movement or acupressure facial massage to connect with the intelligence of the body and facilitate the flow of creative energy. Guided imagery and meditation experiences deepen your inner journey and evoke images and archetypes from the inner world. Writing and drawing manifest and further explore these images. As you sculpt, paint, and decorate your mask, you involve the senses and intellects of your body, your mind, and your spirit and come to deeper understanding of yourself. You also discover how your creative process mirrors your process of interacting with the world. The discoveries you make through creativity overflow into every aspect of your life, whether you are cooking, gardening, meditating, communicating with others, working, or playing.

In ancient disciplines of moving meditation, such as Qigong, the energy descending from the heavens and ascending from the earth fills the inner body to integrate the body, mind, and spirit. You enter an altered inner state, where space deepens and time slows down. Movement originates in the organs and flows out to the surface. Awareness of this flow of energy carries over into creative expression, as this practice inspires you to draw, sculpt, and shape the inner and the outer landscapes of your being.

Acupressure is an ancient healing art deriving from Traditional Chinese Medicine that facilitates health, harmony, and inner awareness of the recipient (maskgiver) and empowerment through sensitivity of the practitioner (maskmaker).

Guided imagery takes you deep into subconscious realms, where figures from your inner domain can bring forth themes, images, and ideas for creative expression.

The art of maskmaking deepens the holistic process of greater self-understanding and growth. It invites you to explore your inner experience with all your senses, to caress colors, palpate textures, drag lines onto your mask mold. The process moves energy from deep within. A single line or shape of color could be hesitant, bold, protective, aggressive, solitary. It gives clues into your inner feelings, the ones that are much deeper than those around or right beneath the skin.

Janette and Blair
and their children, Bennett, Genna, and Perry

Ancestors have also used masks in ritual, healing, and transformation. The manifestations through maskmaking of inner dimensions of experience—taking such forms as warrior, goddess, healer, demon, wounded child, matriarch, totem animal, and countless more—express and ground the transformative process in the world.

Each time you face your mask, you face that part of your being who asked for expression, reminding you to recognize it, work with it, dialogue with it. This may mean bringing, for instance, your inner healer out into the world. Or it may mean transforming a challenging part of your being by applying alchemy to your mask—burning it, ripping it apart, baptizing it, adding layers to it, a process catalyzing a shift that helps you in the world.

In the maskmaking process, you will be working with a partner, each making the other's mask. First, one of you will be the maskmaker, sensitively applying the techniques of massage, acupressure, and sculpting the mask on your partner, the maskgiver, who cultivates receptivity and meditative awareness. Then you will change places and the maskmaker becomes the recipient, and the maskgiver becomes the maskmaker.

The studio you work in is a sanctuary. A supportive ambience helps to shape what takes place—within you as individuals, among you as participants—what evolves between your hands as you form your self-images, what develops among you as you share creativity, self-exploration, and life stories. Some of our students have done mask workshops with their life partners, children, parents, and grandparents. Masks of relationships often evolve: of mother and child, father and son, generations in a family, intimacies with friends. Art becomes a sacred and sensory process in self-understanding and understanding others.

Preparation: Qigong and the Inner Sanctum

Both participants may want to do the following meditation and imagery before engaging in the dialogue of making each other's mask.

Meditation: The Inner Sanctum

Sit in Qigong meditation and close your eyes. Breathe gently and softly, enjoying the rhythm of your breath.

On an inhalation breath enters, ascending the nasal passage and spreading into the chamber of your skull. Your breath presses gently into the walls of your cranial vault, then slowly recedes.

The next inhalation lifts your skull gently off the atlas at the top of your spine, and your occiput floats backward and upward. Within your skull your brain floats in the sea of your breath. Your brain stem aligns in the large opening at the base of your skull and gently tugs the spinal cord. Exhale and relaxation spreads from your brain and spinal cord throughout the network of nerves in your body. On the waves of your breath, brain, spinal cord, and entire nervous system dissolve.

On the next inhalation, your breath enters your eye sockets: gentle breath expanding, filling both eyeballs and sockets, and softly massaging ocular muscles; healing breath cleansing stress and tension; sweet breath refreshing the eyes and their muscles; soft breath releasing fatigue from your eyes.

On the next inhalation, your breath enters gently into the ear canals and explores the tunnels. What colors, temperatures, and textures does it find? What sounds funnel in from without, and what sounds echo from deep within?

On the exhalation, breath glides down into the cavern of the mouth. It explores this cavern, finding ridges on the ceiling, noticing differences in temperatures and textures between the ceiling and the floor of your mouth. Breath moves into the muscles of your jaw, relaxing and releasing it at the hinges. Breath travels over your tongue nestled in its pocket and senses the intelligence and the heaviness of your tongue as it lies at rest. Breath tastes the saliva, the sweet, smooth elixir with nutrients for your body.

On the inhalation your breath ascends and flows along the inner walls of the back of your cranium, the vessel that cradles your brain. It notices the density of the walls and glides over the ridges and valleys of this terrain. The gentle wave of your breath fills the space between your brain and cranium, breath cleansing, protecting, and nurturing your brain.

Listen to the vibrations and sounds. Feel the wave rising, cresting, receding to rise again. Feel the opening and closing of the plates and sutures of your skull. Feel the breathing of your cerebrospinal fluid.

Travel into your inner core to the deep center of your body. Feel the rhythms of your body echoing in the stillness.

Exploration: Qigong Massage of the Facial Terrain

In the beginning of a maskmaking class, Kaleo teaches some Qigong massage, including meridian awareness with their acupressure point applications, for the face, head, neck, and shoulders. By working the head and face, the whole body is affected. Massage and acupressure relax, nurture, and heal. They prepare you energetically, physically, and emotionally for the process.

Rub your hands together and notice how your palms transmit energy. Observe the sensation of energy in the hearts of your palms. How do you experience it: as heat, tingling, waves, color, sound? Feel how energy flows out of your fingers and palms to cleanse and nurture your facial terrain.

With the energy that exudes from your hands, explore the energetic field around your face and skull. You may feel textures and temperatures, see shapes and colors, hear sounds. Using your fingers and palms, touch, massage, and move this membrane of energy surrounding your head. You can brush it, stretch it, caress it, and spiral into it. Feel how this energetic massage affects your inner face. Feel how it affects your whole body.

Now with the sensitivity of your fingers, enter through the energetic layers and explore your physical face. Observe the terrain of the facial sculpture. Notice the difference when you use fingertips, finger pads, or palms. Massage your face. What does touch reveal about your face? How does it feel to press into the cavities, ridges, and ravines of the facial sculpture? What feelings and emotions do you notice? Where do you feel stress, peace, vulnerability, strength, sadness, joy? What does touch reveal to you about yourself? Notice how this self-massage touches your soul.

Exploration: Behind Your Facial Terrain

Rub your hands together. Experience the energy and warmth in your palms. With your fingers, explore the terrain of your face using gentle touch and sensitivity. Then let go, and with the inner touch of your breath, explore the interior terrain of your face and skull. Inhaling, allow your breath to travel into the inner landscape of your head. What do you discover there? What images, sensations, sounds, smells, or tastes arise? What is around your face, inside it, behind it, above it? What sort of inner expression does it have? What kinds of feelings can you read there? Does an ancestor or animal ally reside somewhere in this inner landscape of your skull?

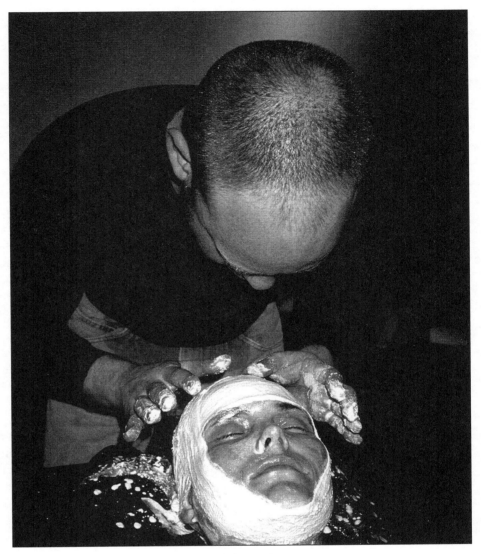

Facial terrain

Exploration: Behind Your Partner's Face

Now sit and quietly observe your partner's face. Look at his or her energy. Use your palms to feel the energetic membrane around your partner's head. What do you feel: shapes, textures, temperatures? Do you see colors or hear sounds? Look deeper through the layers of the energy. Enter beneath the skin. Can you see the sculpture of the face behind the surface of skin? Can you see ancestors underlying the facial terrain? Do you glimpse your partner's emotional history? As you observe the face, where do you discover areas of resonance, of human understanding and connectedness? When you feel a sense of resonance, close your eyes and notice where this sensation travels in your body. With this sense of connectedness, you are ready to begin making your partner's mask.

Practice: Acu-Massage for Maskmaking

The main thing to remember in making the mask impression of your partner's face is that you are engaging Qigong awareness. This awareness and its effects on both maskmaker and maskgiver are enhanced through Qigong massage and acupressure.

Maskmaking, like massage and Qigong, is an energetic, physical, and emotional process requiring trust and sensitivity. Gentle massage of the face relaxes and readies your partner for receiving the mask. Then, as you engage acupressure points, your partner sinks deeper into the process. Applying the plaster gauze is like layering skin on your partner's face.

The following acupressure points on the face, neck, and upper torso and on the hands and wrists are included to deepen the connection between maskmaker and maskgiver and to enhance the creative inner awareness and receptivity of the maskgiver. Descriptions of points are based on Traditional Chinese Medicine uses, sometimes combined with our experience, with a focus on their potential as applied to creative process. Included are points to relax tension, relieve anxiety, clear the mind, open the senses, remove creative blocks, stimulate intuition, and arouse the muse. Sometimes as maskmaker you may find you want to help the maskgiver become calmer and more grounded. Sometimes you may want to encourage the release of stuck emotions. You may want to massage and relax the shoulders. You may want to stimulate acu-points to facilitate the creative process of painting and embellishing the mask sculpture.

For example, the acu-point Tian Zhu (Bladder 10) is located on each side of the neck at the base of the occiput near the pons medulla and the brain stem. Pressing it guides your partner deeper into the subconscious. Feng Fu (Governing Vessel 16) is located at the top of the spine between the B10 points. It releases instinctive fear and stuck emotions. Tian Rong (Small Intestine 17), Ting Gong (Small Intestine 19), and Jia Che (Stomach 6) are great to release and relax the jaw, mouth, and throat to give voice to creative self-expression. Jing Ming (Bladder 1) releases the tension around the eyes and cultivates clarity. Dan Zhong (Conception Vessel 17) opens the heart. As you hold the Feng Chi (Gall Bladder 20) points beneath the occipital bone and feel their pulses come into balance, you and your partner meet in the sacredness and mystery of the inner world. All these things help to build trust and caring between you as you share the exploration of body, mind, and spirit through this creative process.

Once you have layered on the mask impression and the maskgiver sits quietly waiting for it to dry, we encourage you to release the tension in the neck and shoulders by pressing acu-points such as Nao Shu (Small Intestine 10), Feng Chi (Gall Bladder 20), and Shu Fu (Kidney 27). When the mask impression is dry, encourage your partner to inhale deeply and to feel the breath ascending from the abdomen up through the torso and neck into the face. The breath presses gently against the inner shell of the mask. On the exhalation the mask releases its embrace of the face. As the mask peels off, it feels not only like removing a physical shell, but releasing a psychological covering, as the maskgiver re-emerges in the world.

Whatever need you perceive as you apply the gauze or engage the acu-points, don't worry about performance; simply meet your partner with gentle intention and kindness. Allow the nurturing, healing power of touch to support you both in this creative collaboration of maskmaking.

For more information about and exact locations of the acupressure points, refer to Michael Reed Gach's book *Acupressure's Potent Points*.

NOTE: As maskmaker, select a few of the following points as you feel inspired for use on your partner to enhance the maskmaking process.

All points not located on the body's midline are bilateral. You may use a point on either or both sides.

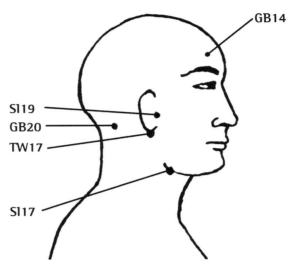

Acupressure Points: Profile

Acupressure Points: Profile

Gall Bladder	**GB14**	**Yang Bai: Yang White** Clears inner and outer vision. Stimulates memory. Relieves frontal headaches.
	GB20	**Feng Chi: Wind Pond** Improves visual and mental perception and clarity. Enhances memory and alleviates dizziness. Holding both GB20s until their pulses come into balance helps balance the right and left hemispheres of the brain and harmonize perceptions of one's inner and outer worlds.
Small Intestine	**SI17**	**Tian Rong: Heavenly Countenance** Resolves local swelling. Clears the throat to free the breath and voice.
	SI19	**Ting Gong: Listening Palace** "Third Ear for Inner Sound." Opens the ears and enhances perception of voices without, within, above, and below.
Triple Warmer	**TW17**	**Yi Feng: Wind Screen** Relieves stiff neck, temporal headache. Opens the gates of perception to higher consciousness.

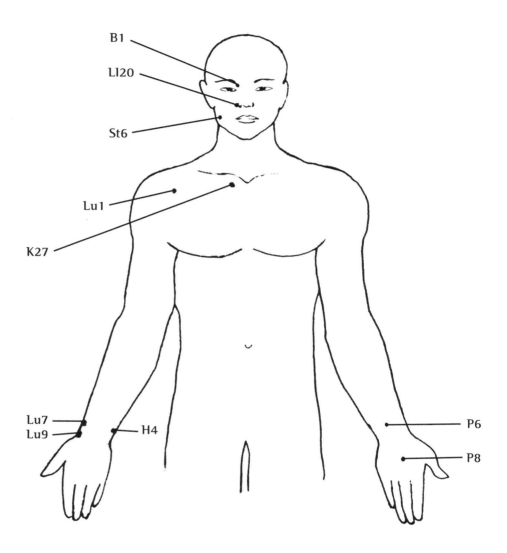

Acupressure Points: Anterior View 1

Acupressure Points: Anterior View 1

Bladder	**B1**	**Jing Ming: Eye Brightness** For any eye problems, sleep disturbances, tension, and headaches. Promotes clarity.
Heart	**H4**	**Ling Dao: Spirit Path** For speaking the heart's truth. Helps inspire the spirit of the heart, the Shen, in creative expression.
Kidney	**K27**	**Shu Fu: Elegant Mansion** Revitalizes and brings courage. Makes sure that the energy in the meridians flows in the proper directions.
Large Intestine	**Ll20**	**Ying Xiang: Welcome Fragrance** "Inner Smell." Cultivates the inner smile. Arouses the sense of smell.
Lung	**Lu1**	**Zhong Fu: Central Storehouse** Relieves stuck emotions (especially grief) and restores tranquility.
	Lu7	**Lie Que: Broken Sequence** Releases repressed emotions.
	Lu9	**Tai Yuan: Great Abyss** Enhances communication between blood and Qi, representing the yin and yang of vital substances, whose freedom of circulation is essential to the free flow of creativity.
Pericardium	**P6**	**Nei Guan: Inner Gate** Held with TW5 Wai Guan (Outer Gate) helps communication between the inner world and external reality during guided imagery and trance-work.
	P8	**Lao Gong: Labor Palace** "Inner Touch." Stokes the fire in the heart when depleted. Calms the mind and centers the emotions. Combine with SI10 Nao Shu (Upper Arm Point) to address writer's cramp, writer's block, and other blocks to creative process.
Stomach	**St6**	**Jia Che: Jaw Chariot** Relaxes the masseter muscle and relieves jaw tension.

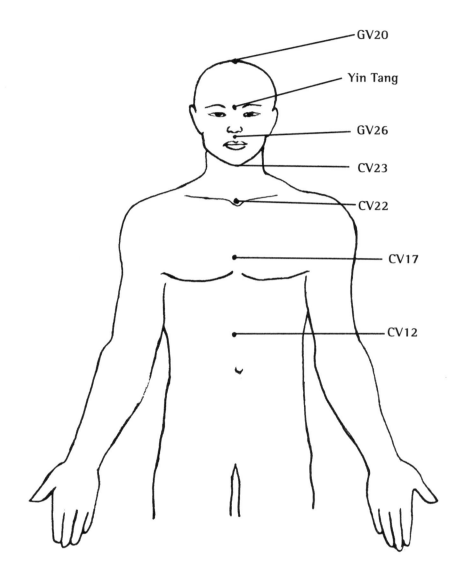

GV20

Yin Tang

GV26

CV23

CV22

CV17

CV12

Acupressure Points: Anterior View II

Acupressure Points: Anterior View II (Conception Vessel and Governing Vessel)

Conception Vessel	CV12	**Zhong Wan: Supreme Granary** Aside from tonifying the stomach and spleen, this point can also be used for grounding and centering one's sense of self and for tapping the inner sense of strength and power that comes from one's core.
	CV17	**Dan Zhong: Chest Center** Sea of Qi for the middle dan tian. Moves stagnant Qi in the chest, freeing the breath, as well as stuck emotions related to the heart and lungs (sadness, grief, anxiety, hopelessness).
	CV22	**Tian Tu: Celestial Chimney** "Inner Voice." Clears stuckness from the throat (5th chakra), freeing the voice/creativity, opening the throat to receive divine inspiration, and bridging the heart (4th chakra) and the mind (6th chakra).
	CV23	**Lian Quan: Corner Spring** "Inner Taste." In the soft pocket under the chin. Affects the tongue and speech. Helps heart to deliver its messages through the voice.
Governing Vessel	GV20	**Bai Hui: One Hundred Meeting Place** Meeting place of the yang channels. Clears the mind, lifts the spirit, and opens the crown chakra to receive heavenly Qi.
	Yin Tang	**Yin Tang: Third Eye** "Inner Eye." Promotes inner vision and clarification of intention.
	GV26	**Ren Zhong: Center of Being** Between the nose, which draws in the Qi of heaven with the air, and the mouth, which takes in the Qi of the earth through food. It is used to restore consciousness, whether it is the brain or the spirit that is in need of resuscitation. This point represents the human being as intermediary between heaven and earth and encourages standing tall and erect.

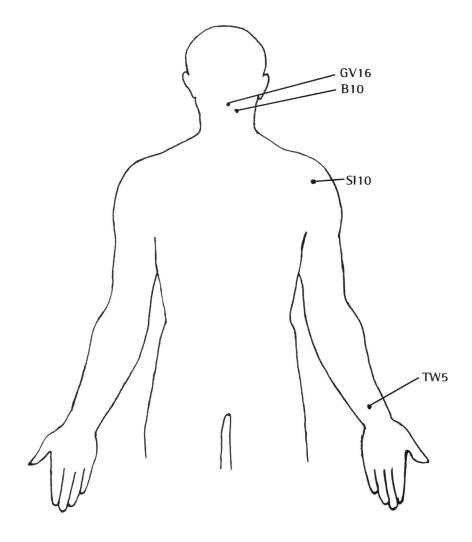

GV16
B10

SI10

TW5

Acupressure Points: Posterior View

Acupressure Points: Posterior View

Bladder	B10	**Tian Zhu: Heavenly Pillar** Clears headaches. Enhances vision, memory, concentration, and mental clarity.
Governing Vessel	GV16	**Feng Fu: Wind Palace** This point can be used both to attract beneficial wind in the form of Qi from the heavens and to dispel perverse wind that brings disharmony. It revitalizes the body and spirit and clears and invigorates the mind. Portal to the subconscious, to the land of dreams.
Small Intestine	SI10	**Nao Shu: Upper Arm Point** Relieves pain and stiffness in arm. Combine with P8 Lao Gong (Labor Palace) to stimulate creativity and free creative blocks.
Triple Warmer	TW5	**Wai Guan: Outer Gate** Held with P6 Nei Guan (Inner Gate) helps communication between inner world and external reality during guided imagery and trancework.

Practice: Sculpting the Mask

Kaleo's Journal: The Process of Maskmaking

I call on my ancestors for guidance. Our process begins. I, the maker of your mask, honor you, the giver of the mask, as we enter into our inner dialogue.

Ancestors watch over us as I apply plaster gauze to your face. Touching, listening, responding to your energy, I massage the wet warm skin of gauze onto the flesh and bone of your facial sculpture. I feel your inner face as well as the outer one.

What do you need? Do you feel safe? How can this gentle facial massage encourage you to enter and sink into trust? What images, sensations, emotions are emerging from your subconscious? All my senses are alert and receive clues from your body/mind about what this experience is like for you.

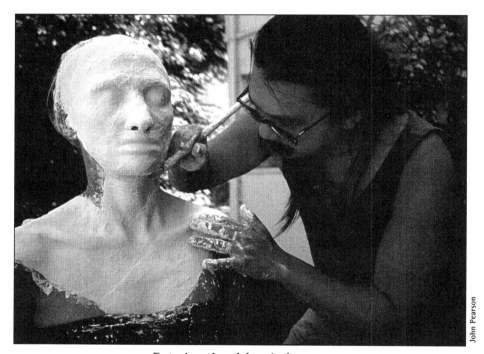

Entering the alchemical process

You, as maskgiver, question: Can I still my body, still my mind? Can I surrender to the nurturing fingers, to the warm wet plaster on my face? Am I vulnerable? Am I afraid? Will I like the impression of my face? Will the mask reveal an ancestor? What images will emerge from the silence and the darkness?

As you drop deeper in meditation, I feel your ancestors stirring within you.

As the mask on your face comes to completion, it is time for you to emerge. To release the mask, you engage your breath. Inhaling, you draw your breath into your abdomen. Exhaling, you settle into the comfort of the pelvic bowl. Then, inhaling, you draw your breath into your sacrum and up your spinal column. Your breath migrates into your throat and mouth, softening your tongue and chin. It now enters the space between your skull and skin. As you exhale, your breath expands gently and presses into the inner lining of your mask, shedding this new skin.

As your mask peels off, it reveals the wonders of the universe, your ancestors' legacy, the door of your heart.

NOTE: Maskmaking entails working with lotion, petroleum jelly, and plaster gauze. Avoid using materials to which you may be allergic. This is a dialogue between maskmaker and maskgiver. As maskgiver, inform your partner of any concerns you may have. If you have any respiratory problems, such as asthma, you may want to have your mask sculpted with your and its mouth open. If you are afraid of dark places, you may want to have your mask sculpted with eye-holes, so that you can keep your eyes open. Prearrange a signal, so that, if you feel uncomfortable at any time during the maskmaking process, you can signal your partner to remove the mask. Be aware that it takes only a couple of seconds to remove the mask from your face.

Maskmaking Supplies

- Oil based lotion to protect the maskgiver's face and under the chin
- Petroleum jelly to apply to the eyelashes, any facial or stray scalp hairs
- Clear plastic wrap to cover the ears and all scalp hair
- Plastic garbage bag to wear to protect the maskgiver's clothes
- Plaster of Paris gauze roll (four inches wide by five yards long)
- Warm water, about dishwater temperature, in a bowl
- Scissors
- Masking tape
- Brushes (a small one and a medium size one)

Reminders

- Maskgivers should remove any earrings, necklaces, and contact lenses.
- Always measure the gauze strips.
- Always double the gauze strip unless otherwise noted.
- Fold the gauze first, then immerse in warm water.
- Activate the plaster gauze by stroking it between your fingers.
- When applying the gauze strips, overlap them on the face. Then, smooth and massage the gauze gently with your fingers and palms or a brush.
- All instructions refer to a four inch wide fold of gauze unless otherwise noted.

Sculpting the Mask

1   Introduce your touch by massaging your partner's face gently. Remind your partner to keep the eyes closed during the entire process. Apply oil-based lotion to protect the face and under the chin. Apply petroleum jelly on the facial hair, making sure the eyelashes and eyelids are sealed. Protect the hair on the head with plastic wrap. Protect the clothes with a plastic bag.

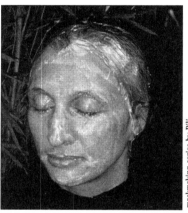

maskmaking series by Pili

2   Forehead strip: Measure from the front of your partner's right ear to the front of the left ear at the level of the eyebrows. Double the strip of gauze and cut it.

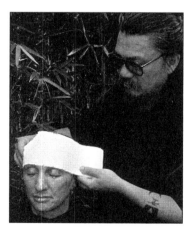

3   After immersing the plaster gauze strip in warm water, activate the plaster with your fingers; then apply the strip to the forehead. Massage gently into the forehead and temples, allowing your fingers, palms, and senses to be aware of the many nuances of the facial sculpture.

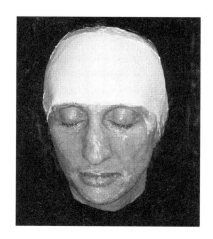

4   Head wrap: Measure around the head, under the chin, and alongside but not covering the ears, to overlap at the crown of the head, which is protected by plastic wrap. Cut the strip.

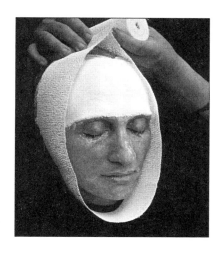

5   Fold this gauze strip in half, lengthwise this time, to double it.

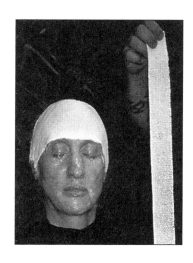

6 After immersing the gauze in water and activating it, wrap it under the chin and around the head, to overlap at the crown. Gently massage the gauze with your fingers and palms.

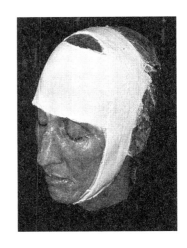

7 Half-moon shape: If there is an opening between the gauze strips on top of the skull just above the forehead, close it with a piece of gauze. Measure from temple to temple. Double the gauze; cut it; then fold it in half again. Holding the folded side in your left hand (fold facing left), cut an arch starting at the bottom right-hand corner (open-ended side) to the top left-hand corner (closed-ended side) of the gauze. Then, open it into a half-moon shape, which you will place rounded side downward.

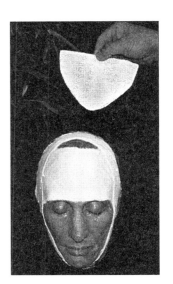

8 Immerse it in water and massage gently onto the crown of the head.

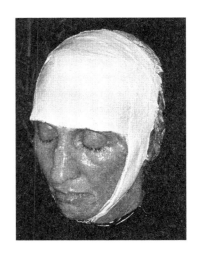

9 Nose strip: Cut a 1/4 inch wide single strip to place from the top edge of the upper lip, up under and along the base of the nasal septum, up the center of the nose, to meet the forehead piece. Immerse in water and apply.

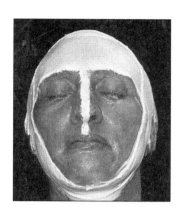

10 Nose triangle: Measure from the outer right eye to the outer left eye, double the gauze strip, and cut it. Fold this piece in half. Along the open-ended side, cut from the bottom to the top in a snaking line as illustrated. This piece opens into a bell shape that fits over the nose.

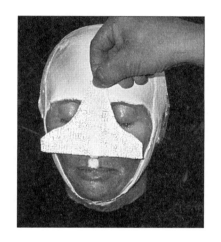

11 Immerse it in water and massage it onto the nose, beginning on the bottom at the ala (wings of the nose), leaving the nostrils open, and working up to the forehead.

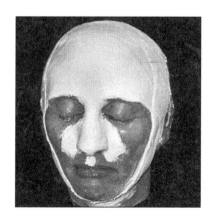

12 Mouth oval: Measure from the outer right cheek to the outer left cheek; double the gauze; cut it; then fold it in half. Round the corners on the open-ended side. Cut a small rectangle into the top closed-ended side to make a notch for the nose.

13 Open the piece into an oval shape, immerse in water, and place the oval with the notch under the nose.

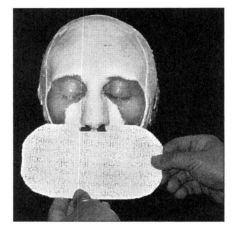

14 With sensitivity, massage and guide the gauze down over and around the mouth and between the lips for a distinct impression.

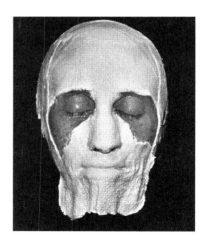

15 Very carefully, cut from the bottom center of the gauze up to the lower lip. Layer and massage one side down and around the chin.

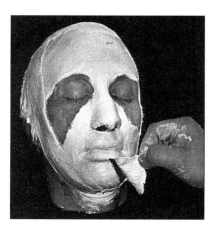

16 Then layer the other side to overlap it.

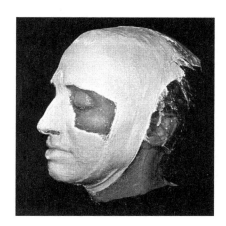

17 Diagonal eye strip: Measure from the top right corner of the head to the bottom left chin; double the gauze and cut. Immerse it in water; then lay the gauze from the top right corner of the head, diagonally down over the forehead, over the left eye, and down beneath the left chin.

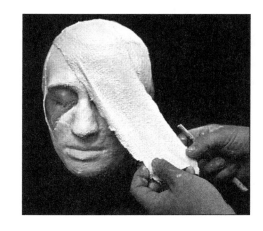

18 Massage the gauze across and down, over the left eye to the bottom left corner of the chin. Be very gentle and careful (you can use a brush) as you massage the gauze into the eye pockets to create a realistic impression.

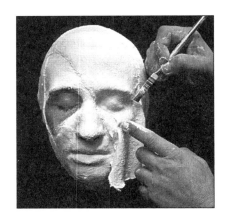

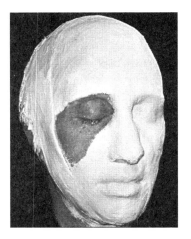

19 Now repeat on the other side, from the top left corner of the head, diagonally down over the forehead, over the right eye (be very gentle and careful over the eye), to the bottom right corner of the chin.

20 Birthing: When the mask is mostly dry (normally twenty minutes), loosen the plastic wrap at the back of the head. Encourage the maskgiver to inhale deeply and bring the breath into each dan tian, first the pelvis, then the heart, then the mind's eye. The breath, like petals opening, expands, and the mask blossoms forth.

21 Nostrils: Cut two single-layered circles; spiral each into a cone shape; immerse one in water and insert it into one naris; then repeat for the other naris.

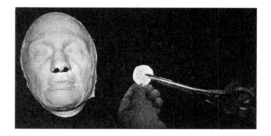

NOTE: Now the maskmaker and the maskgiver change places.

Emergence 1: Jane

Emergence 2

Reflection: Your Experience of Sculpting the Mask

Kaleo's Journal: Birthing

As your mask peeled off your face, you felt its gentle tug on your skin and heard the sound of its release. What did you feel and hear? As you emerge from your inner world, how did you respond to the light?

It's time now to commune with your mask. As you hold this fresh sculpture of your face before you, notice how surprisingly light and cool it feels. See your facial sculpture, its geography of ridges, caverns, muscles, and bones. Notice the subtleties, colors, textures of flesh and hair, of eyes and lips. Notice the changing facial expressions. Turn it over; look into your inner mask. What thoughts, emotions arise as you observe your original face?

Interacting with this mask is like holding and sculpting dried layers of your skin itself. You realize the mask captures the moment of your being at this time of your life. You realize that it reveals glimpses of your ancestors and of your descendants. The removal of the mask may inspire the shedding of inhibitions, the shedding of old skin, an experience of birthing.

Exploration: Your Mask Sculpture

Your mask sculpture is the outer expression of your inner core. It is an aspect of truth offered from your soul. Look at your naked white mask. Is it an ancestor, spirit guide, totem animal, member of your inner tribe? Look at the anatomy of your facial sculpture. Do you see colors, an aura, blueprints from your DNA? Using your healing palms, feel the energy exuding from the mask. What is its temperature? What is its vibration?

For the following exploration, you can wear your mask. Or you can look at it.

Close your eyes. Inhale and feel the presence of your mask. Allow the presence to enter into your body. What does it feel like as it slips into your skin, into your fascia and muscles? What does it feel like to have it wrap around your inner core? As it enters your inner terrain, where does it go: into the vessel of your cranium, your rib cage, or your pelvis? Where does it feel at home? Inhale and feel the nostrils of your mask open and close. As your mask breathes, the walls of your cranium, rib cage, or pelvis also breathe. They become moist with the humidity of the breath. Observe as the flesh of the walls, the blood vessels, and nerves pulse. What sounds are there: music, sounds from nature, laughter, conversation? Inhale: What are the smells and tastes? What emotion does your mask discover in the core of your cranium, rib cage, or pelvis?

Exhale and the wind of your breath creates a vacuum. You find your mask squeezing through fascial walls and reemerging back outside your cranium, rib cage, or pelvis.

Allow the breath to open your eyes. Your mask is before you, staring. Its nostrils flare. Its mouth opens. What does it say? Listen to its song, its chant, its story, your story.

Writing: Your Facial Sculpture

Record in your journal: What was your experience as maskmaker, sculpting the mask of your partner's face? What did you learn about sensitivity and the use of touch?

Then, after you changed places, and you became maskgiver and had the mask made of your face, what were your feelings? What did you experience under the layers? After the birthing of your mask, what was your initial reaction to it? Did your facial sculpture surprise you, enchant you, disappoint you, delight you? Notice the yin and yang of your reactions—the balance of pleasure and pain, like and dislike, excitement and fear. How can you bring the opposites into harmony, into dialogue, into dance? How can you work creatively with the natural asymmetries and whimsical eccentricities of this facial sculpture?

Then go back to the inner world behind your mask, and observe your surroundings. What do you see? What happens? The story begins here. Write your own personal myth.

Your Mask Awaits Transformation

The process of sculpting the plaster gauze mask with your partner is complete. Thank one another for this sharing of energies, touch, and heart. Now it's time to allow the mask molds to completely dry. We usually leave them basking in the hot sun, lay them overnight next to a fireplace or heater, or bake them in an oven or microwave.

The mask molds have been birthed into their raw white forms. They await transformation into one of the many faces of your soul.

Raven Medicine: Jane

VI

Faces of Your Soul

We offer many guided imagery explorations in this book. You can use any of these to inspire creating a mask. The chapter on totem animals offers guided imageries that inspire totem animal masks. The chapter on ancestors offers guided imageries that complement the process of making ancestor masks.

Guided imagery, ritual, and invocation summon the guides from the spirit world to join you in creative process. Their breath, your breath, moves in harmony. You sway to the sensuality of *nā mele o Hawai'i* (the music of Hawai'i); or dance to the rhythms of Africa; or smell the ochres, reds, and siennas of the Southwest; or walk softly in the cool, wet silence of the Pacific Northwest; or bow before the mysteries of Asia; or pause in awe of the mystics of Europe.

You breathe life. You are the creator as your mask transforms into sculpture, painting, totem; raw materials into meaningful whole; self into Self.

We are complex beings of many layers and have many masks waiting to emerge from our inner depths. The following explorations invite you to make mask molds based on the guidelines in the previous chapter, "Sculpting the Mask," and transform them into embodiments of a multitude of archetypes, the beings of your inner tribe, the faces of your soul.

Kaleo's Journal: The Splintering

Amanda, you become quiet and withdraw into yourself, then reveal to me that your life in the corporate world is very demanding. For years, you've had to suppress your creative, spontaneous inner child. She lives caged and locked in a metal box hidden deep within your body. This child has been stirring lately and craves the physicality, wildness, and discovery of the creative process.

In the beginning, your breath is shy, fearful, uneasy. Your body is stiff and uncomfortable and doesn't know what to do with itself as the class moves in Qigong. Over the semester, however, your body and breathing soften, deepen, surrendering to the fluid movement of Qi. You find comfort within your body.

The surrendering of your mind to the creative process, however, is more stubborn. I watch as you sit staring at the raw white mask mold of your face held between your hands. Your mind is blank, your fear palpable. The mask, too, stares petulantly back at you.

In ritual, you invite your muse to accompany you in the creative process. At home one morning, as you peer into a large mirror, your muse stirs. You recognize her, remove the mirror from the wall, and let it fall. The cracking of glass is startling! A metallic blue flashes through you, and you smear this blue on the outer skin of your mask. Anger and frustration surge through you as you jab with your paint brush. Then you gather the long, jagged shards of glass and stab them into your mask. Holding the mask in your hands, you stare in disbelief that you surrendered so easily to the explosive surge of creative energy.

Again, your muse beckons, this time trailing the scent of roses and tickling you with their velvet petals. You caress the passionate reds, daring pinks, and exuberant yellows and plant them in your inner mask. Your cleansing tears moisten the petals.

Your Mask of Self-Reflection

This encounter is meant to be a catalyst for self-exploration. Its relationship to the creative process of maskmaking may be close or may be remote. Your creative experience and the direction you take with self-expression are your own. As you look into the pond in your psyche, honor your own inner processes.

Guided Imagery: Beyond Your Reflection

Steps

1   Walk through a forest to a clearing with a pond.

2   Go to the edge of the pond.

3   Note the flat stone on your right with three objects. Explore each one.

4   Observe your reflection in the depths of the pond.

5   The face ascends and changes into your mask.

6   Your mask breaks through the surface.

7   Receive its message.

8   The face descends.

9   Note the objects on the stone. Are they the same or different?

10   Take one with you and leave an offering.

11   Return back through the forest to the present.

Process

Position yourself comfortably for your inner journey. Put on some calming, undulating music that mirrors the mood of calm water. Inhaling, invite the waves of music into your body, and let them drop you deeply into relaxation.

You find yourself traveling through a pleasant forest. It feels so safe here. Inhale the fragrance of forest, and marvel at the colors and textures of this friendly natural world. The trees begin to clear and you come upon a pond.

Shaman's Invocation: Diana

This pond feels so familiar. It beckons you to its edge. A very light breeze skitters over the surface of the water.

Notice the large flat stone on your right. What kind of stone is it? On this stone are three objects, placed there just for you. What are they?

Listen. Something's stirring in the pond. The surface stills and becomes clear. You scan across the water, then peer easily into the depths. On the bottom of the pond, you find your reflection looking up at you. How does it appear?

Listen. Notice your breath as it enters and descends into the core of your body. Notice how it settles in the floor of your pelvis. As you breathe softly, feel the stirring in the bottom of the pond, and watch your reflection as it lifts off the floor and begins to ascend toward you. Notice how your reflection transforms into a mask as it advances through the different layers of light under the water. How does it look as it nears the light of the surface?

Listen. As your mask breaks through the surface of the water, what sound does it make? What colors, symbols, or metaphors appear on your mask? What do you see when you look into its eyes?

Its gaze probes your depths. What does it find?

The Request: Natalie

Its mouth begins to move, opening and closing. At first there's silence; then sounds pour forth. Listen. Do you recognize the voice? What does it say? What gift of awareness does it offer you?

When you are ready, thank your mask for coming and sharing with you. You inhale deeply, and your exhalation sends your mask back into the pond. What sound does it make as it submerges? How does it transform as it descends into the watery depths? What is the sound of its descent?

A breeze riffles the surface of the pond, and you turn to your right. That stone—what objects are still there? Have they changed? Pick them up one at a time. Feel each one, its weight, temperature, texture. Observe its shape, its materials, its use. Then choose one to take with you, and leave an offering in its place.

Now you move away from the pond and return through the forest. How has the feeling in your body shifted as you walk back along the path? The trees begin to recede. On the next inhalation, you find the sounds of the water music flowing through your body. When you're ready, on an exhalation, let the sounds bring you back to the present.

Journaling: The Reflection

Using the present tense, journal about your experience at the pond. Describe the pond. What is it like? Describe the stone and the objects. What are they and how are they placed? Describe your reflection and how it looks up at you from the depths of the pond. As your reflection ascends, how does it transform into your mask? Describe any symbols, colors, textures, shapes that you see. What awareness does it offer you? Do you recognize its voice? How does it appear as it descends back into the depths of the pond? What are the objects on the stone like now? Which object do you take with you? What offering do you leave in its place? Observe your body. How do you feel now?

What ideas for your mask are inspired by the forms from nature, objects on the stone, images from the pond, the changes you feel inside?

Art: The Reflection

Begin by painting or drawing the pond and your reflection. Move beyond the visualization, allowing colors, textures, and images to present themselves in this moment as you re-enter the world of the pond. As the night sky takes you into the deep inner world from above, allow the pond to do so from below.

Art: Object on the Stone

What object on the stone did you take with you? What was it made of? What were its textures, colors, symbols, energies? Let it manifest its power through creativity. Where do the power of this symbolic object and the power of creativity take you? Do you find yourself sculpting the object out of stone, clay, or wood? Does it inspire movement or dance?

Art: Embodying Your Mask of Self-Reflection

Now you are ready to begin the process of embellishing your mask mold. Sculpt with more gauze, carve with tools, layer with paint, massage with your hands. Choose from a feast of art supplies. The muse is aroused by the horn of abundance: wire, bamboo, furs, wigs, fabric, natural materials, shells, herbs, spices, clay, beads, toys, collage materials, and a variety of tools, paints, and brushes.

Begin by invoking your reflection in the pond. Affirm your connection and set your intention. Your mask has a life of its own. Ask it what it wants. Give it permission to manifest, to evolve, to express. Then jump in! Sculpt, paint, embellish, and decorate! Let your mind surrender to the rhythms of your body, your intuition, the guides from the spirit world that inspire you in this moment.

Continuing the Journey: Encounters with Your Mask

You may engage these further explorations with any masks you create, from the mask of self-reflection, to the oldest ancestor, to the youngest child of your inner tribe.

The Sound of Your Mask

Every mask has a form, a sense of visual wholeness and integrity. It has its own Qi. It has its own sound.

Kaleo's Journal: White Tiger Totem Animal

White tiger paces: breath vibrating from the source, the dan tian, deep within his core, deep within my core. I am the fragrance of the forest. I am the sound of rain dropping softly on leaves. I am muscles coiling and releasing, body moving through the mist. Earth gives way to large paws sinking into moist grass. Breath, guttural, rasping, resonates through the dark.

Stand or sit in meditation with your mask. Listen to the sound of your gentle breath, each breath spiraling in, filling your body, then releasing, each breath softening your muscles into deeper relaxation. You find yourself letting go, sinking into the earth, and grounding. See your mask before you. Look beneath its skin into the core. As you place the mask on your face, you find yourself slipping deeper into the core.

Listen. Listen to the sounds within. How far in do you enter to hear the sounds? To feel their stirrings in your body? Listen. What are the sounds like? What are they saying? Go deeper. You may hear sounds of birthing, sounds of dying, sounds of grieving, sounds of joy. Continue on your way, until you enter into a place of comfort and safety.

Listen. Within this core, a sound embraces you, cradles you, bathes you. What is its pulse? Its color? Its texture? Enjoy. It is a sound that resonates throughout the universe. Inhale into its source. You are one with the source. You are one with the Divine.

When you are ready, notice your breath moving like waves in your body. Inhale and lift a wave of sound up into your throat; then exhale it out. Feel its vibrations around you. As the sound dissolves, you become aware of the air against your skin, its temperature, its texture. You feel the surface beneath you, supporting you. You feel the blessing of sky above you. Your body begins to awaken. You can still hear the echo of the sound within you as your eyes open to receive the light.

Now, have a large sheet of paper and writing tools before you (we like to use a 30″ x 40″ sheet and different color pens or pastels). Introduce yourself to the paper by feeling its textures. Listen. The paper has its own sound. Then write down your sound. Allow your sound to move your hand in the rhythms, beats, and tones of nonstop writing.

Then pause.... Go inward and listen to the echo within.

Finally, look at what you have written. What are the colors, size and textures of your words? What are their moods? Pick out key words. Allow them to expand into a story, poem, or song.

Rob Lee

Journey with White Tiger

Movement with Your Mask

Kaleo's Journal: White Tiger

White tiger moves in Qigong. He stalks through rainforests and beds of lava and accompanies me into mysterious realms. And yet I still have doubt, fear, loneliness.

I close my eyes, chant, then listen. He approaches. He shoves his massive head into my chest. We wrestle. He wins, of course, and stands over me, glowering, then lets me rise.

Still glaring at me, he rips a patch of flesh, blood, and fur from his body. "This is for you. You are never alone. This is my promise to you. What more do you need? I will be your guide, even in your final passage." With that he flicks his tail and disappears.

Place your mask in front of you, as the focus for meditation; then get into a comfortable sitting or standing position. Be mindful of your breath. Breathe naturally and fill your abdomen. Watch as your breath builds in the lower, middle, then upper lobes of your lungs. Observe as your internal body stirs, moves, and changes.

When you feel your Qi is gathered (your entire body will feel energetic and alive), focus your attention on your mask. Your eyes are portals that receive and transmit Qi. Receive the image of your mask into your mind, focus on this image, then transmit rays of Qi through your eyes back into your mask. Observe the aura of light around your mask. Observe its colors, textures, forms. Observe your mask as it transforms in the rays of Qi.

Notice how you are affected—what emotions, bodily sensations, intuitions arise in you? What memories, dreams, images come and go as you keep your focus on your mask?

An inspiration to move wells up in you. Your body has its own language. Allow it to speak through free flowing movement. Feel the tingling in your skin, your muscles coiling and releasing. Feel the strength and stability of your bones as they glide. Feel the suppleness of your joints in movement. Listen to the fluids as they cleanse, wash, and lubricate your body. Feel the expanse of your nervous system, its rhythm of signals, sensations, reflexes, and emotions. Listen to the pulse of your heart, to the flow of your blood as it courses through its network of tubes and valves. Marvel as you feel your internal organs all working together in harmony—one pulse, one reflex, one breath.

You may find yourself inspired to wear your mask as a layer of bone, muscle, or skin over your face. Feel how it encloses you, protects you. The sounds are different within. Allow your eyes to peer out of the darkness. Let the mask speak its truth. You and your mask are one, dancing an ancestral dance, moving in harmony with the flow of universal Qi.

The Dialogue

Sit before your mask in a comfortable setting. Ask your mask: Who are you? How old are you? Where do you come from? Invite it to share its history.

Then go deeper. Ask your mask: Who are you to me? What part of me do you embody? Why did you come to me now in my life? In what ways are you pleased and fulfilled? In what ways are you dissatisfied? What do you need?

Now listen. What questions does your mask ask you: Who are you? Where are you going? What issues are important to you right now, and how can I help you?

Exchange whatever questions and responses feel important to you to uncover each other's story and to understand the significance of your relationship to each other. What do you ask and what answers do you receive and how do you put them together?

Tiger's Breath Qigong

The Observer

If you have made two masks, or complementary mask and drawing, be an observer. As observer what role do you play?

In what setting do you find yourself and your creative works? Are you all on a mountain-top, in a place of worship, or at home having a nice meal together? Watch as your creations interact in this setting. Watch as they dialogue with each other. What do they do and say? Perhaps they act out the dualism of yin and yang: inner being and outer being; spiritual being and material being; masculine and feminine; light and shadow; birth and death. Perhaps they sit and talk, asking questions of one another, expressing opinions, sharing experiences and wisdom. Or perhaps they are inspired to go on a short journey together.

Record this dialogue and interaction on paper. As observer, what role did you play? What do you understand more deeply about yourself from listening to and observing your two creations as they interact?

The Storyteller

What significant adventure or fantasy rivets your attention? Does it involve meeting and spending time with a spiritual mentor? Flying into the future or traveling into the distant past? Questing for your own holy grail? Embarking on your life's mission?

Your mask is about to take you into that adventure. Wherever you may go, it knows the way and where to land. It may take you into the future, into the distant past, into the mind and body of another person, or into the fulfillment of your dream. Wherever you may go, understand that you are safe and protected. Your mask has the ability to help you adapt, to blend in, even to make you invisible if necessary. It may bestow you with powers, skills, and knowledge that help you as your journey unfolds. Sometimes the journey may be challenging and arduous, sometimes incomprehensible, sometimes revelatory. Always remember there is a reason for the events of this journey. It is your journey, your initiation, into deepening growth and wisdom.

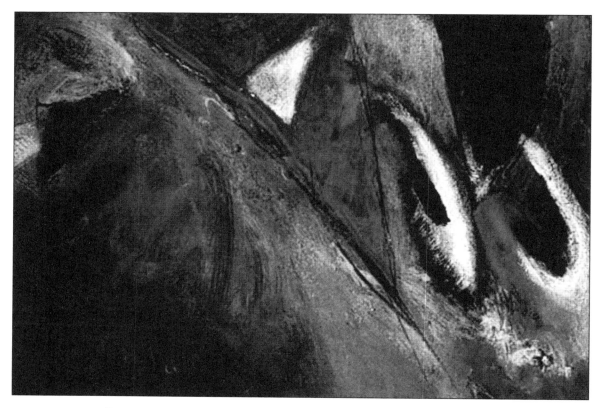

"Voice of Stone" by Kaleo (mixed media acrylic painting, 24"h x 32"w)

Now get comfortable, close your eyes, and enter into a meditative state with your mask. As you sink deeper into meditation, you become aware of your mask before you. Follow it to a portal. How large is this passageway? What sound vibrates from it? Your mask goes first and beckons you to follow through the portal. Go. Then follow your mask as it takes you on your journey.

Where do you go? What is the environment like? Are you and your mask alone or are others present? Who are they?

What circumstances and events unfold? Does supernatural intervention come to your aid? Do you meet your muse or a mentor? What task do you perform? What transformation happens? What destiny do you fulfill? What mortal lessons underscore the immortal events? Continue to explore, to discover, to live this journey.

Then, whenever you're ready, your mask leads you back through the portal. Feel the experience alive in your memory, alive in your body. Now record your journey with your mask through writing or art, keeping in mind the question: What did you learn through this adventure about yourself and the adventure of your life's journey?

Mask of Your Warrior-Healer

The Warrior-Healer archetype is embodied in Greek mythology by the Centaur, Chiron. Most Centaurs were savage beasts, half-man, half-horse, rowdy and violent. But Chiron was famed for his goodness and wisdom. He was a visionary, gifted in both healing and martial arts, so respected that even the gods sent him their children for tutelage. Among his pupils were the great warrior Achilles and the great physician Aesculapius. Chiron was an immortal, so he was able to mentor many heroes to maturity. But one day he was accidentally wounded in the foot by an arrow tipped in his own poison concoction. Being immortal, he did not die, but his leg festered and brought him great pain. The gods came to his mercy. He could exchange his life to release Prometheus, who had angered Zeus by bringing mortals the gift of fire and then paid for his crime in chains on a mountaintop where an eagle repeatedly ripped at his flesh and fed on his liver. Chiron's sacrifice would free them both from suffering. This he chose. To honor him Zeus sent him to the heavens to become Sagittarius, where he regained immortality among the stars, as well as his status of guide to the mortals who follow his path through the night.

In Chinese arts, healing and fighting are closely yoked. Certain acupuncture points can be used by the skilled physician to heal or by the skilled martial artist to incapacitate. Taiji's graceful movements can be practiced slowly and intentionally to bring balance and harmony to one's being. Yet each movement in a carefully choreographed Taiji form has a powerful and specific fighting application.

On the surface, the powerful warrior exhibits qualities of leadership, strength, endurance, courage; the successful healer exhibits qualities of sensitivity, compassion, discernment, wisdom. But beneath the surface, the qualities of the complementary archetype must be strong. A warrior without sensitivity, compassion, discernment, and wisdom would not be a great warrior but only a brute. A healer without leadership, strength, endurance, and courage would soon falter under the rigors of a healing practice.

As you encounter your own inner Warrior-Healer on this journey, notice how the balance between both aspects is embodied. Notice which attributes of each are strong in you and which you would like to cultivate.

Guided Imagery: Encountering Your Inner Warrior-Healer

Steps

1   Breathe with mindfulness into your bones.

2   Walk through the forest to the pond.

3   Go to the edge of the pond.

4   Note the flat stone.

5   Observe your reflection in the pond.

6   Note the reflection of your areas of imbalance.

7   The image shapeshifts into the Warrior-Healer.

8   The Warrior-Healer takes you on a journey of empowerment.

9   Return to the pond.

10 Look into the pond and observe your transformation reflected back from the depths.

11 Receive the Warrior-Healer's gift lying on the stone.

12 Return back through the forest to the present.

Process

Be comfortable in standing or sitting meditation. Align yourself properly and watch your breath. Be mindful of your bones and their structural integrity as they stack one on top of another. Notice how the bones were created to fit naturally into one another to provide structural stability. How intelligent is the creative spirit of the universe!

Now, simply watch your breath. Watch how it moves as it brings the current of Qi to spiral through your body and into your bones. Observe how your bones interact with your breathing. Notice how they vibrate, sway, and respond to the caress of your breath. Observe how your bones breathe, expanding and contracting, in rhythm with your breath, each breath naturally feeding and strengthening your bones, softly, gently. Feel your bones filling with your breath, filling with the power of universal Qi.

And when you're ready, journey through the forest to the clearing with the pond. Breathe and smell the fragrances. Feel the fresh Qi entering and feeding the tissues of your body, all the way into your bones.

Feel the familiarity of this setting that cradles the pond. Walk up to the edge of the pond, and stand next to the flat altarlike rock.

Look into the deep still water. Allow your gaze to travel down through the layers of liquid and observe. You see your reflection in the depths! Who are you? What are you wearing? What is your attitude? What surrounds you?

As you observe, you may notice areas in your reflection that seem out of balance with the rest, areas calling for attention. Observe. How do these imbalances manifest in your being, in your life? Acknowledge this picture of yourself, then let it go.

Pause now and be mindful of your breathing. Feel the strength of your body and bones. Notice how the image before you in the depths of the pond begins to transform. Behold the Warrior-Healer, your guide of personal empowerment. Feel the power. Who is this being? Look at this being's stature, clothing, demeanor. What does your intuition tell you about the characteristics of this powerful and personal guide?

Warrior-Healer: Gilles

Somehow you feel very familiar with this guide. You feel protected. This Warrior-Healer invites you on a journey. This is a journey to teach you what you need to do to move more fully toward your power. What do you need to release? How can you nurture harmony and wholeness where there are imbalance and deficiency? How can you cultivate inner strength and resolve?

Follow the Warrior-Healer. Do you descend down into the mysteries of the pond? Beneath the pond into the secrets buried beneath the surface of the earth? Over the earth into the adventures of wild terrain? Or up into the boundless wonders of the sky?

Where do you go? What do you experience?

Who do you become? What are you doing? What have you left behind? How are you dressed now? Do you have new tools, herbs, books, or instruments to aid you? Feel your strength, your resolve, your intention lodged deep within your bones. Feel your fulfillment. Feel your joy. Be mindful of your breath filling your bones, as your entire being embraces these qualities that belong to you.

When your journey is complete, the Warrior-Healer guides you back to the pond. You are standing beside it once again, looking into the depths. You recognize the Warrior-Healer within your reflection. How you have changed! You feel the harmony and strength from the depths mirroring the harmony and strength within your being.

The Warrior-Healer smiles then disappears beneath the depths. As you turn to depart, you notice the rock. The Warrior-Healer has left you a gift. Pick it up and take it with you as an aid for your journey toward greater self-empowerment. Then leave the pond and return through the forest to the present time and place.

Journaling: Your Journey with the Warrior–Healer

Describe yourself: How is your physical and energetic strength? What are your strengths of character? What are the strengths you share for the benefit of others? What areas are in need of attention, healing, and empowerment? What do you keep in your medicine bag that brings you more harm than good? What habits, attitudes, or personal relationships do you need to let go of? What concepts of yourself need to shift to carry you forward on the journey that is your destiny?

How did these aspects reveal themselves in your reflection in the pond?

How did your reflection transform to become the Warrior-Healer?

Describe this guide's attributes as you experienced them in your encounter. How did the qualities of warrior and the qualities of healer come together in this being? How do they come together in you?

Where did you go and what happened on your journey? How did you change? In appearance? In attitude? In tools and aids that support you? In people who surround you? What guidance did you receive? On the stone, what gift of empowerment did you receive from the Warrior-Healer?

What actions do you need to take to continue this process of empowerment in your life's journey?

Art: The Warrior–Healer Mask

Make a mask of your inner Warrior-Healer. What attributes of yourself does the mask portray? How do the warrior and the healer manifest? How do you embody them in colors, textures, images? You may want to paint and decorate the inside of the mask to show you as healer and the outside to show you as warrior. Or you may want to paint and decorate the outside to show who you have been and the inside to show who you are becoming. How does the mask embody your own life's journey toward greater wholeness and empowerment?

Maskmaking in Jail

Kaleo was employed by the California Arts Council, the National Endowment for the Arts, and the Haight Ashbury Free Clinic's Jail Psychiatric Services to teach in the San Francisco County Jails. He spent five years on a part-time basis teaching the holistic process of Qigong, guided imagery, art, and maskmaking to psychiatric maximum security inmates at the San Francisco facility and minimum security inmates at the San Bruno facility. The following are excerpts from his journal.

Kaleo's Journal: The San Francisco County Jail

2/95 The Process

I'm grateful to San Francisco Sheriff Mike Hennessey, the Haight Ashbury Free Clinic's Jail Psychiatric Services, Jo Robinson, Ruth Morgan, the Jail Medical staff, and all the deputized staff for being supportive of this process. To walk through those big iron doors, feel them slam shut behind me, into the support provided by these people makes this process possible.

The holistic process of Qigong, meditation, art, and maskmaking in jail has so much potential for transformation. But here the rules under which change may take place are somewhat different. The balance is more precarious. The stakes for self-expression, self-discovery, and self-transformation are higher, for such a process requires vulnerability and openness, not attributes that help one survive in jail.

I have a basic rule in jail: My class is a sanctuary, a haven. Close the door and it's a place of safety, integrity, and creative joy. The room fills with a vibration of peace and creativity. It permeates all. That's when the magical process works. The mundane transforms into a world of colors, shapes, and creativity. Art bridges the conscious and subconscious, the body, mind, and spirit. There is an openness, a space providing for self-awareness, affirmation, and healing to happen.

The joy and inner peace start in that classroom. They grow, spread, and affect everyone.

4/95 In Class

Silence—total presence—just the sounds of brush on paper.

"Listen everybody—to the sound of concentration. Watch the quality of the air around you, the quality of your breath inside of you. Feel the brush in your hand, the viscosity of the paint. Does the color bring you joy, melancholy, rage, calm? Do you stroke gently, carefully, thoughtfully, or do you jab, punch, strike, bleed with the brush? It's Qigong—the brush is an extension of you. What does it teach you?"

8/95 San Bruno Jail Inmate "Bo"

The energy in the jail classroom can be electric. Teaching is Qigong—centered, rooted, flowing. At times I am open and receptive, at times closed and guarded, at times neutralizing and warding off, at times assertive. Watching and waiting, walking like a cat, dodging and moving in, setting emotional and physical boundaries. And always, always watching my back.

"I'll kill that motha fucka if I find him! He took off, left my mother, when I was two years old!"

I look at him and ask, "But 'Bo,' when did you last see *your* own children?"

"Bo"

DIFFERENT QUESTIONS

"Another shot of blackness, man!"
You grin, stabbing your paint brush into the black liquid.
"This is me, African warrior, Kunte Kinte."

Your laugh reveals a gaping hole empty but for a few rotting teeth.
Your skull is completely shaven.
Bullet shaped. Smooth. Clean. No scars there—yet.
The scars on your body and face protrude when you laugh.
Fluorescent lights make them shiny, eerie,
against the warm black of your skin.

"No, man, Kaleo, brother, that's not from a knife.
That's from a bullet! Can't you tell?"

Interesting how the scar starts at your wrist at the point of entry
then moves like a long centipede up your arm to the point of exit—
snaking through tattooed religious icons covering your arms.
I ponder: Legends of life, John Henry, steel-driving man,
are made from men of your physical size and presence.
"Hey, Bo, I know you're really just a sweetheart!"

Your chest swells. You have honor.
You take care of your block, your turf.
Nobody from the outside comes in to play.
You watch out for the old folks, too.
And you take care of your women.
They are even free, like you, to move on or around.

"No one fucks with them. Fuck with them and you fuck with me."
Your children are in good hands. Raised by their mother somewhere in L.A.
"Bo, what do you tell your children?"
"You mean so they don't end up like me? In and out of jail?
Shit, man, what else? Learn to fight, be warriors among gangsters.
Survival, that's what it's about."
You're quiet now. Then chuckling to yourself,
"Kaleo, home-boy, you sure ask a lot of different questions."

10/95 The Cycle

For some, jail is debilitating, for others, a system they've learned to play to
survive, offering more safety and comfort than living on the streets. At
least in jail you get your meds and specs and your teeth fixed. In jail you
don't worry about being killed for a blanket while sleeping on cardboard
in an alley. In jail there are a shower, toilet, dry bed, three squares. Jail
gives a break from the patterns of abuse, addiction, violence. The question
is: Where do you go when you get out of jail, with no money and few job
skills? How can this cycle be broken? You need help and a support system,
so you return to where it's familiar, to family and friends. Back to what
you've known all your life. Often the cycle continues.

FRIENDS

"Not to worry about me, Kaleo. They know me. They all know Bo.
On the block I got friends. I'll do good, man. I know how to play the game."

"So you're going back to what you know. But it's a tough game.
Be careful. It's called Nowhere To Go."

You never look at me when we talk like this.

12/95 Final Words

Sixty inmates live in F-Tank. I'm visiting "Bo," soon to be released from jail. Deputies in the glass tower watch every move. Their eyes penetrate the back of my head. It feels weird and intrusive but it also gives me a sense of security. I'm glad they're there. Orange shadows, inmates, are alert and watch with all their senses. Like wary cats. To escape, some burrow into their bunks, looking like big fetuses covered with army blankets. A broad yellow line on the cement floor separates "Bo" and me.

"Warrior": Mask of "Bo" by Kaleo (16″h x 14″w x 7″d)

FINAL WORDS

In F-Tank
in a moment of silence, the kind that lurks in jail,
we had final words.

"Do good, Bo. Remember,
Legends of John Henry, steel-driving man,
were made from men of your size and presence.
Look to Gandhi, to Martin Luther King when it gets tough.
One man, one ideal. Be good to yourself and good to others."

You took me by surprise. Your arms ripped the silence,
tore rank air, crushed the distance between us.

Your embrace came from your heart, from deep within your bones.

4/96 Dying in Jail

Martin. My immediate impression of you is that of intelligence, creativity, and sensitivity. Then I notice your vulnerability, fear, and desperation.

Your background reads: white, gay, educated, middle class.

I wonder why you're here. On the "outs" your background could mean a world of privileges. Why are you dying of AIDS in jail? Here, the color of your skin, your background, sexual orientation, your disease could mark you—if you don't know how to play well.

You don't know how to play well. Your large nervous eyes give you away. It's the animal in you—anxiety, fear, desperation—cornered, hunched, poised, ready to leap. Caution, I feel. But your eyes are intense, needy, and vulnerable, not hostile. They draw me in. I feel their protective shield give, and I wonder at its thinness.

I listen. Your mouth nervously opens and closes: "You never know who's in the bunk next to you. You may know what they're in for now but you don't know what they've done in the past. No history. I never sleep well. Always watching, sleeping with one eye open all the time. It takes extra vigilance, for my immune system has abandoned me. Sixteen years ago it began. At 13 I had my first male lover. My parents never forgave me. They screamed, 'Perversion! Abomination!'"

I listen. You tried rebellion, drugs, suicide attempts. So alone. So much to carry. So much to hide. I listen as you rage at your parents, society. As you rage at yourself.

And then you're quiet. You look down at your hands and realize the cardboard art project you've been working on has evolved into an arch, a portal, a structure with no face.

We decide to make a mask of your eyes. As you close them, your body gently relaxes. I apply the wet plaster gauze to your eyes, and as you sink deeper, I wonder what God has in store for you. Will you die in jail, painfully, alone? If your parents knew and you were free, would they welcome you home?

You are asleep as the plaster gauze dries on your face.

As I gently remove the mask, I can feel your burden lifting.

Later, you paint the front of the cardboard arch white. "Eternity and freedom," you say. Then with a rubber band you hang the white mask of your eyes from the arch. The mask swings back and forth between present and future. You look at me and say, "If it ends up on the other side when it stops swinging, it means I'll soon pass on to the other world."

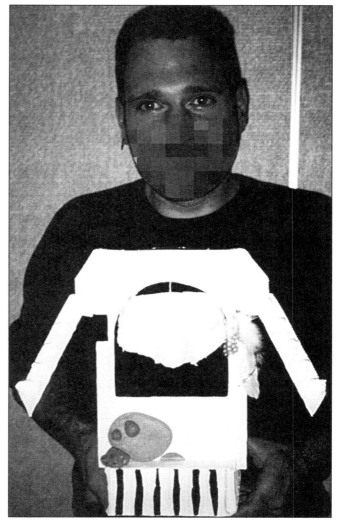

Martin

3/97 Guided Imagery: The Guardian

I'm teaching in the Jail Psychiatric Unit. Thirteen inmates and I sit together in meditation. As we sink deeper into our core, we find freedom. Freedom from the heavy metal doors with the fish tank windows: their skin of paint, scratched, bruised, and worn down from clutching hands, hands of despair, hostility, apathy.

As I lead the group in guided imagery, my breath is dry wind entering the humid cavern of my throat, then descending into the tunnel. I uncover subterranean textures, the smell of moist earth, acids, dripping liquids, the smell of underground roots. Deeper into the tunnel, my breath descends and explores the changing colors and textures until it enters the golden light at the end. A cool breeze sends large auburn leaves spiraling. Thousands of tiny bells shiver and ring, and I find myself on a mesa overlooking a sienna desert. The air is dry and cool. It feels so comfortable and safe. With my wooden staff I draw a large circle around me in the sand. The circle immediately turns red and suddenly my body is splashed in white pigment. A tattooed being wearing orange robes and prayer beads approaches. He has a message for me and speaks.

As I focus on his words, a shift occurs. I find myself stirring, awakening, opening my eyes. I'm back in the Psych Unit, emerging from my own inner journey.

'Turo is looking at me. He wears County Jail orange. He looks very old for being only 55. Heroin and homelessness have aged him. His face is tense, and his fingers grip the sides of his chair. "What happened, man? Where did I go? Shit. Heavy, man." He shakes his head, looks at me, and then explains how he descended into the tunnel, crawling, sliding forward on hands and knees. Crawling into that blackness. Deeper until the smell started to come back to him. The smell of fear, sweat, death, and he is back, back in Vietnam: "I'm 'Turo, the tunnel rat. The mad fucking tunnel rat from fucking El Paso! Mad Dog! Pissed off! Scared shitless!"

Cool, humid blackness is thick in the tunnel. He continues his descent, crawling deeper into the tunnel with his weapon. He swears, "Same old shit! Rats, snakes. Kill 'Cong! Wait! Something's different! The smells, the sounds. They're not the same. What's changed? What's that pink light ahead in the tunnel?" He stops. Paralyzed. Can't move forward. "*Chinga.* What the fuck!" A dark figure emerges from within the pink. It approaches him. An echo resonates through the tunnel: "'Turo, forgive. Go in peace and love." 'Turo jams quickly back out of that tunnel into the light of the sun.

And into the present, into the psychiatric ward in the County Jail. He looks at me intensely; then his face softens in sadness. "*Escucha.* Listen. You know, I lost my best friend in 'Nam. We were surrounded in a heavy firefight. We were back to back and shooting. All of a sudden this warm mush splashed my face. I turned. It was his brains. Heroin is my savior, man. Kills pain. You think that was him in the tunnel? The angel was him?"

That day 'Turo got oil pastels and drew the figure in pink light. Afterward he taped the drawing on his cell wall. Later 'Turo and I talked, and as he told me stories he had been hiding inside for so long, he released ghosts he had been carrying for thirty years.

Death and Transformation

Kaleo's Journal: Death and Dying

1/29/04 Mom's Passage

Elise and I just returned from a long stay on Oʻahu, Hawaiʻi. We were with my mother, Nancy, during her dying process. Mom had Alzheimer's and was unable to verbally communicate for the past five years.

Kaleo's mother sings and plays ʻukulele as father dances *hula*

In the past six months, her condition worsened. She was at home, totally bedridden, with chronic pneumonia. She communicated with us through her body. Her face was pained. Her body was extremely tense, angry, and frustrated. Her hands clamped shut and would not let go of their tight grip. Her doctor recommended Hospice. When Kuʻulei, a Registered Nurse from Hospice, came and talked to her, telling her that we were going to stop giving her the medications and syringe feedings that her body no longer wanted or needed, Mom finally relaxed. She looked up at us and smiled. We understood what she wanted.

During the week, our family gathered around her, talked to her, massaged her tenderly, or just sat and held her hands. Her hands—I remember them holding mine when I was a child. I remember them boiling Chinese herbs, rolling sushi, mixing *poi*, wrapping *laulau*, and frying *man doo* (Korean dumplings). I remember them strumming her *ʻukulele* as she gleefully sang her beloved Hawaiian music. Her hands— they have early memories of working the soil on the sugar plantation where she grew up in Pāhala, Kaʻū, near Kīlauea volcano.

Sometimes my sister, Robin, and her husband, Keith, read to her from her Bible. Often, we piped Hawaiian music into her room and strung flower leis all around her bedside so she could smell the fragrances of her beloved Hawaiʻi.

One evening my sister's friends, Kaʻopua and Kanani, brought their *ʻukulele* and played and sang to her. Our family sang along as I strummed on Mom's sixty-year-old *ʻukulele*. Because of her Alzheimer's condition, her eyes often looked empty. This time, she smiled and her eyes shone with tears.

The next morning at 5:00 a.m., her breathing shifted. Our family gathered at her side, our hands touching her. I gently encouraged her to breathe in the fragrance of her favorite blossom, the *ʻawapuhi* (ginger). We reassured her that Dad would be okay and be taken care of. We told her, "Not to worry, you've done a marvelous job taking care of and raising us. We will stick together as family. Not to worry about us. Take care of yourself, now. Just move into the light when you're ready. Christ awaits you. The ancestors will welcome you."

We encouraged her, breathed with her, held her, reassured her. She must have felt Elise's palms cradling her head. Mom simply sighed and released her final breath as Elise lovingly drew her hands up and out past her crown chakra. Her transition was so peaceful, calm, like the *makani nahenahe,* wind leaving, oh, so gently.

During her services, a beautiful *ānuenue* (rainbow) embraced the Makai chapel at Mililani.

I am deeply touched by my father, sister, and brothers and their families. Our personalities, politics, beliefs are all so different. This experience stripped all the layers away. What we discovered is a deep bond of loyalty, integrity, and love. My mother's dying meant a birthing for our family.

Mahalo Ke Akua mau loa (in gratitude to the Divine).

Your Mask of Death and Transformation

Death and life are yin and yang. Their dance is everywhere—in the air we breathe, in the seasons, in the faces of friends and strangers, in dreams and symbols, in meditation, creativity, in movement, and in standing still.

Acknowledging the intimate partnership between life and death brings us face to face with our limitations and our accomplishments, our disappointments and our joys. From death we may learn to fear, yet from acceptance of death, we can learn to take risks, to succeed and fail, to embrace and let go. In doing so parts may die—parts outgrown, transformed, transcended.

Then can come rebirth.

The following guided imagery, journaling, and art explorations invite you to explore your life in relationship to your own future dying process and beyond. They invite you to imagine that death is close at hand, even though it may in actuality be decades away. Work through them in your own time and your own way. Allow your contemplation of dying to become a spiritual exploration that deepens your own experience of your unfolding life as you live it moment to moment to dying moment.

Guided Imagery: Life Review

Lie in a comfortable meditation position. Your breath becomes slower and deeper. It becomes very peaceful, and you find yourself lying in a comfortable position in your bed. The room is dim and cool. The candle's flickering light creates a rhythm of shadows. There's incense in the air. You feel relaxed yet brimming with anticipation. Your spirit guide hovers over you, watching, caring, protecting, and whispers a message: You are dying and have only one month to live. How do you respond?

Your guide whispers to you, telling you to be mindful of your breath, to enjoy its rhythm. It tells you to feel each breath gently relaxing your body, each breath a soft comfortable blanket embracing you. You feel your body becoming heavier and sinking deeper into your bed. You surrender and find yourself traveling backward through your life, as if the pages of a calendar are turning back in time. You can still hear the encouraging voice of your guide telling you simply to observe.

What has your life been like? As you travel through time, notice the important times, people, places, and choices that have shaped your destiny.

Observe. Is there anything unfinished in your relationships? In your life's sacred purpose? In your spiritual practice?

What of yourself are you leaving behind? You have one month left of living. How should you fill it?

When you are ready, come back to the present time.

Art and Journaling: Life Review

Write in your journal. Make a collage of the life you are leaving, telling your story, through words, collage, color, symbols, shapes.

What has your life been like? What events, people, places, decisions stand out as important?

What plans have you made for your worldly possessions? Which ones mean the most to you? If you were to write your will, who would be your beneficiaries and why?

What business do you need to complete in your last month of life? What people and activities will you let go of to make room for the process of completion? What do you have left to do to complete your legacy?

What of yourself are you leaving behind: body, mind, and spirit? What plans have you made for your body and its parts when you die? What of your psyche will remain: artwork, letters, journals, books? What of your spirit: soul connections with others and with the earth?

Guided Imagery: Your Dying

Lie in a comfortable meditation position. Your breath becomes slower and deeper. It becomes very peaceful. As you sink into relaxation, be aware: Have you had any premonitions about your own death—age, cause of death, karma surrounding death?

Your slow, deep breathing invites you into the time of your dying. Are you ready to experience this? If so, feel the presence of your spirit guide, hovering over you, guiding and protecting you, as you begin to let go. Your breath is changing. How? You feel your breath suspended between the urge to live and the urge to release this life. You feel how your body lets go, becomes heavier, and sinks deeper toward the unknown.

Where are you? What is the cause of your dying? Are you struggling or are you peaceful? Observe your surroundings. Are you at home, in a hospital bed, or where? Listen. What sounds do you hear? Speeding traffic or sirens approaching? Voices yelling or loved ones crying? Birdsong or chamber music? Roaring fire or rushing water? Inhale. What do you smell in this place of your dying? Feel. Who is at your side?

Observe your dying body—its color, texture, shape. What is your breathing like? What is your awareness like? Feel your senses beginning to wane, sound being the last to go.

Journaling and Art: Your Dying

Write in your journal. Make a collage of yourself dying. What words, images, colors, textures do you choose to embody the scene, to set the mood, and to convey the power of the moment?

What is your experience of the circumstances surrounding your dying? Are you in the middle of rushing traffic, in crashing waves, or at home in your bed? How do you feel facing this moment? What emotions do you experience? Are you surprised? Perhaps you experience grief or pride. Perhaps rage or fear. Perhaps disbelief or gratitude.

What is the ambience around you? What are the light, the smells, the sounds that surround you?

Are you alone? What people and guides come to you to be at your side in this hour of your dying? How do they help you in the process?

Guided Imagery: Your Final Rite of Passage

Lie in a comfortable meditation position. Your breath becomes slower and deeper. It becomes very peaceful. As you sink into relaxation, be aware: The moment of your final rite of passage is at hand.

Observe your body. Has it served you well for all these years? What are your body's memories? Being an infant, rocked in loving arms? Being a child at play with a fuzzy puppy? Being a youth in your first love's embrace? Wrestling and killing an enemy in war? Holding a child of your own?

Observe your body as it becomes still. What are its color, texture, shape? Is your breathing fluid or shallow, soft or gasping? Listen to the beating of your heart. Feel it changing. Notice your body's shifting temperature, texture, rhythms. Experience how your consciousness changes moving from life into death.

Is there anyone at your side? Loved ones? Ancestor? Spirit guide? Totem animal? Listen. Do you hear the pulse of the Universal Spirit? Do you see a portal, a door, or an entrance to a tunnel? Do you sense anyone on the other side?

The time has come for you to let go. You release your final exhalation. Do you cry out as a warrior, gasp in awe, sigh in surrender? Does your spirit leave your body easily, struggle, or leap forward? What sound of departure does it make? Where does it go?

Journaling and Art: Your Final Rite of Passage

Write in your journal. Collage the moment of your passing over the threshold between life and death. Dreams of death may offer hints, yet death remains a mystery. How do you embody the unknown?

How is your awareness of death evolving as you experience the future of your own dying? How clear are your ideas and beliefs? How are they changing? What do you believe your final passage and the afterlife will be like?

Journaling and Art: Death Mask

Describe your Death Mask in your journal, not only how it appears, but what it means to you in this moment of your life. What is your intention? What hopes, fears, resistances, or expectations do you encounter?

Make a mask of your face that represents your final passage. Who do you choose as your partner to mold the mask over your face? What emotions emerge as you sit in darkness while the mold cools and hardens? What does it feel like as the dried mask mold is shed from your skin? What does it feel like to look at the shell of your Death Mask?

How does your Death Mask evolve as you paint and embellish it? Do you complete it all at once or take the process slowly over days or weeks? Does it appear as planned or is it a surprise?

Does your mask rest on your altar, become an urn for your ashes, hang on a wall, suspend from a tree? Do you use it in ritual? Will it be buried or cremated with you? Will it accompany you to the other side?

Observe your relationship to this mask over time. Like Death itself, your mask is your companion and teacher.

Then write your epitaph to accompany your Death Mask.

Guided Imagery: Your Funeral

Lie in a comfortable meditation position. Your breath becomes slower and deeper. It becomes very peaceful. As you sink into relaxation, be aware: You are observing your funeral.

Your spirit guide hovers over you, watching, caring, protecting.

What's happening? Where is your body? In a casket, embalmed, dressed in your favorite outfit? On a funeral pyre? In an urn as ashes? What favorite items of yours are placed around your remains?

Are you situated in a place of worship, at the ocean, on a mountaintop, in your home? Who are among those gathering to honor your passing? Is it a large gathering or just a few loved ones? Imagine if you could move in and out among the crowd: How would it feel? See their faces, hear their voices, feel their emotions. Do they carry anger, grief, remorse, laughter? People are speaking about you and your life. Listen. What are they saying?

What ritual celebrates your life and honors your death? What is the mood? What do you smell? Are there candles burning? Is there food? Listen. What music do you hear? Who speaks your eulogy? What does it say?

Who carries your body to its grave? Or scatters your ashes into the wind? Or finds a special place for your urn?

The funeral ends and the crowd leaves. How do you feel as you observe?

Art and Journaling: Your Funeral

Write, draw, paint, or sculpt the scene of your funeral. What medium entices you? What textures or words does your death invoke? What colors and shapes? What forms emerge from wood, metal, or clay?

Our good friend, Franciscan Sister and Seneca elder Mary Jose Hobday, lives and works on a Native American Reservation in New Mexico. At 76 years old, she, taking a vow of poverty decades ago, has very few possessions. Often she refuses payment for her work in the world. For a long time, a carpenter friend insisted on giving her something in return. She finally consented and had him build her a coffin, a simple but functional box, complete with handles. Being the practical soul that she is, she had him make it with removable shelves. It presently sits on its end in her living room and serves as a temporary bookcase and conversation piece, until needed for its original purpose. Children and adults in her community in Gallup drop by her living room just to see this piece.

Creative Writing: Voice of Dying

Write a poem, chant, or story to accompany your mask of death. Is the storyteller yourself? Or do you create a persona to tell the story? What are the time, the place, the surroundings? What does your persona have to teach you about dying and death?

WHEN THE RAIN BEGINS
by Elise

I say not to worry.
One year there was no harvest.
One night Earth ripped apart
like the gut of a sick deer.
One moment I saw myself
in the eye of the Moon
and I was afraid:
Even she is being licked away
by the black mouth of Heaven
and next to her this life
is a small dry stick burning.

One year the Bear plunged among us mad
and tore many lives
before the arrow stopped his pain.
I cried for us and for the Bear.
One day Ocean came across the land to our doorways
took some of us to feed his creatures
sent the rest into the mountains
leaving new Gods among us.
One moment I looked down the chasm of the past
into the red river of my birth
and readied myself to leave
my children and their children.

I grow old.
Sun has clawed my face.
Earth has bent my spine.
My eyes are clouded moons.
My ears are closed to song and terror.

Lay me in a plain canoe
without ceremony
and when the Moon is hidden
and the rain begins
give me to the River
to the whims of stones and currents
and a violence
that is natural and becoming.

Mask of the Ancestor

Kaleo's Journal: Into the Distant Past

Soaring! I'm soaring through time, back 1,000, 1,500, 2,000 years! Click! My body, following seconds behind, finally catches up to my soul. I find myself in a huge cave in an ancient world. Outside, wolves are howling, defining space, distance, and time as the pack moves. Inside the cave I smell fresh mammal milk, saffron, tangerines, nuts, and dates. It's very dim. From the fire in the center, a circle of warmth exudes, spreads, and presses gently into the rock walls. Around this fire hover shadows of men and women—voices droning softly in chant. White tiger lolls comfortably before the fire.

Sparks fly. My ancestor emerges in crimson-red robes. I observe him very carefully, his stature, clothing, and facial expression, and I begin to understand where I come from. His chest is tattooed—five circles with Chinese characters representing Metal, Water, Wood, Fire, Earth. He approaches and hands me a Taiji sword—sharp, shiny, double-edged. As I hold the sword, its message is clear: Be Taiji—focus, awareness, balance of yin and yang.

With deep gratitude I thank my ancestor. He turns and reenters the heart of the fire. The pulse of the chanting increases. It gets louder and louder. It begins to throb. I leap onto tiger's back. We are swept away in a river of blood. The sounds of the pulse and the river are deafening. I am aware I exist 2,000, 1,500, 1,000 years ago. Click! I exist now.

Guided Imagery: The Ancestor's Legacy

Steps

1   Go to a favorite private place and lie comfortably.

2   Allow your breath to connect you with the pulse of blood in your pelvis.

3   Allow this pulse to take you into the past.

4   What ancestor do you meet?

5   What lessons and tasks have been passed down to you?

6   What does the ancestor want to express through your creativity?

7   What balance of yin and yang does the ancestor embody?

8   Return to present awareness.

Process

Go to one of your favorite places of safety and privacy. You may find yourself lying in the quiet of your favorite room, or under a canopy of trees tucked away in a rainforest, or perhaps under the moonlight in a large sand pit at a private beach. Allow yourself to lie comfortably. Feel your body relax as each breath takes you deeper within. Notice how your breath coaxes your body into a shape that naturally fits the contour of your environment. Do you find yourself prone, supine, or in a fetal position?

Ancestral Totem: David

When you are ready, allow the breathing to expand in your abdomen. Observe how, on each breath, your abdomen expands and releases. If you listen carefully, you will become aware of the abdominal aorta behind your navel. Feel your life pulsing, your blood flowing into the arteries in the basin of your pelvis. Allow your breath to ride with the flow of the blood in your pelvic bowl.

As you inhale, your breath gently presses into the glistening membranes lining the walls of the pelvis. As you exhale, the tissues of the pelvis sigh in surrender. The breath, synchronized with the rhythm of the pelvis, opens and closes, expands and contracts. The pulse in the pelvis becomes stronger and louder.

Stronger and louder! And you find yourself being drawn into this pulsing river. You hear a sound and you recognize it. It is the call of your ancestor beckoning you. You are being swept away, back to a distant era.

How far back do you travel to meet your ancestor? Where are you? Who has summoned you today? Whose blood pulses in your pelvis? Observe your ancestor's presence. What sort of garments is she or he wearing? Does she or he carry weapons, tools, ritual objects?

Ask your ancestor what lessons and truths your grandparents and parents received and passed along to you. Are you the one destined to break the cycle of heredity? Are you the one to carry forth the destiny? What tasks do you inherit from your ancestor, and how do they become clearer and more meaningful through this encounter?

Observe your ancestor and your interaction. What is the balance of yin and yang: in the personality and role of your ancestor, in the lessons revealed, in the tasks passed along to you?

When your encounter feels complete, thank your ancestor and return to your breath opening and closing the walls of your pelvis. Feel the pulsing of your own blood and let it return you to the vessel of your body in the present time.

Art: Ancestral Mask

Make a mask of the ancestor you encountered. Do you use a mold of your own face, to honor the connection between past and present? Or do you make a mask mold of your parent or grandparent? Do you use sacred or personal embellishments to honor your relationship to your ancestor, as David, who shaved his head and used his hair to create the beard of his ancestral totem?

Is your mask's dominant essence yang or yin: totem or vessel? Do you mount it on a staff, carry it like a torch, wield it for protection? Or do you mold it into a sacred container, shaped and decorated in honor of your ancestor, an incubator, a womb, where your sacred intention can develop?

Writing: Your Ancestor's Voice

Write the story of your ancestral totem or vessel. You may want to affix this to the staff of your totem or to the walls of your vessel.

Unmasking the Faces of Your Soul

Creativity may embody aspects of your personality expressive of emotional or intellectual process, spiritual path, or cultural and ancestral sources. Creative expression materializes out of dreams, fantasy, mythology. Drawings, paintings, and masks evoke inner figures, such as warrior, healer, shaman, peacemaker, rebel, lover, trickster. They summon the influences of spirit guides and ancestors. With them you may share life's passages: birth, marriage, journeys, death.

Write about the prominent aspects of yourself. Then make a number of masks of yourself representing these aspects. Who are you? How many aspects of yourself do you know? Rodney has made many masks over the years. Each mask reveals another aspect, another truth, another voice of who he is.

Inner Voices: Rodney

Rodney's Journal: Five Masks

The five masks that I made under the guidance of Kaleo and Elise came forth from inner voices of my unconscious realm. Letting the creative juices flow through your hands after yoga allows the expression to be of the mind, body, and breath. The masks are a visual diary looking into a colorful blossoming future all housed in the present moment.

VII

Body Totem

Introduction to Body Totem

Elise's Journal: Healing Journey

More than twenty years ago I shattered my left femur in a motorcycle accident when I collided head-on with a pickup truck. Three surgeries, five months in a hospital lying still in traction, and two casts later, my left leg worked but not quite the same. I was lucky to be alive, to have a leg. But my spirit hedged. I used to ride and train horses, would ride any wild thing, and loved most riding bareback, because I feared nothing. But now fear was too familiar. The healing journey goes on years later.

A few years ago I started to have a lot of pain in my left knee. X-rays showed nothing. The orthopedist was sympathetic but noncommittal—the underlying message: Just live with it. I quit jogging, adjusted my Qigong practice, did yoga with intention to strengthen my knee, did physical therapy exercises, fretted.

Kaleo and I decided to collaborate in ritual and creativity. He made casts of my left leg, upper and lower. He transformed the cast of my upper thigh into sculpture: using skewers, inserting metal rivets at the seams, suturing the halves together with cordage, lathering the skin with painful red, burnt orange, then healing green colors. Inside along the inner fascial sheath of the thigh, he layered earth, leaves, crimsons, and pthalos.

I began working on the lower part of my leg cast: a spirit canoe. From it, I hung prayer rags, soiled and tattered pieces of red, blue, and purple cloth, remnants representing blood vessels and rough laps of the journey. I skewered dried fish, suspended for smoking, life altered and preserved to bring life. I strung the ends of the cast (foot and knee) with spider web adhesions. The inside was a cave dotted with cairns, pointing the way out.

We find that creative process helps to facilitate and deepen the dialogue among body, emotions, and spirit. Through dialogue comes understanding. Through understanding comes healing. Through healing comes acceptance. The mirror the work of the muse holds before us fosters integration on a soul level.

A part of your body is calling to you for attention, for exploration, caring touch, healing energy, and creative expression. What part calls to you this season, this day, this moment? Is it your lower back, perhaps injured years ago in an accident? Is it your chest, the area of your heart, asking for opening, laughter, engagement with the world? Is it your shoulders, tired and slouched from working too long at the computer, or from sharing too many of the world's burdens, now wanting to spread their wings through nurturing creativity? Or is it your pelvis, the cocoon of the muse, who is ready to come out of incubation?

Chrysalis: Sinh

Making a body totem follows the same process as making a mask mold of the face. Once you have learned the maskmaking techniques, you can work with a partner again to make a mold of a body part eager to be sculpted. The exercises in meditation may show you a lot about where in your body you store tension, where there is need of nurturance, what is crying for release. Be sure that it is not a part that has suffered a recent acute injury or that may not tolerate well being worked on. The creative process should not be a stressful one, but a healing one.

Let your inner wisdom guide you as you choose a region of your body for sculpting. Also, because of the intimacy of working on your body, select a partner with whom you share mutual comfort, trust, and rapport. Use whatever degree of modesty and privacy feels right to you and your partner to make the process safe.

Awakening Dragon: Sinh

Discovering, Exploring, and Healing the Inner Terrain

Preparation for Discovering, Exploring, and Healing the Inner Terrain

Do the upcoming three explorations in discovering, exploring, and healing the inner terrain in sequence. They will prepare you for working with a partner in making your body totem.

For the guided imagery, practice simple lying meditation. If you are experiencing pain in this posture, come out of it and adjust your position until you are pain free. Your posture should be one you can hold comfortably. You should be able to nap in it. If you are experiencing lower back discomfort, you may want to place a rolled blanket under your knees. Place a rolled hand towel under your neck if the back of your neck is pinched. This is also important if you are experiencing tension headaches, for they could be aggravated by tight muscles at the base of your skull. If your breathing feels shallow and constricted, try elevating your head and chest with blankets and pillows.

For scanning, use the hearts of your palms (P8 Lao Gong). They are connected to your heart. Your hands have remarkable intelligence. Chefs, surgeons, artists, herbalists, massage therapists, all those who work with their hands, understand their wisdom and intuition. Healers often use their palms for scanning the client's body, in order to understand more deeply and to perceive and transmit Qi (energy). We believe each human being is blessed with the power of healing touch. One just needs to acknowledge, develop, and practice using it.

For the art, have ready paper and an abundance of drawing supplies.

Guided Imagery: Discovering the Inner Terrain

Steps

1 Observe your body's surface.
2 Travel on your inhalation down through your throat.
3 Exhale and enter the dan tian.
4 Explore the inner landscape of your body.
5 Note areas of stuckness, pain, imbalance.
6 Mark the site most in need.
7 Return to the dan tian.
8 Inhale your awareness up your throat and exhale back to the present.
9 Scan your body with your palms to receive its energetic messages.

Process

Get very comfortable in lying meditation. When you're ready, close your eyes and feel the heaviness of your eyelids pressing together. The soothing darkness brings a gentle relaxation, and your body sinks into the surface you lie on.

With your inner awareness, observe the surface of your body. As your inner eye travels along it, notice the textures, contours, colors. How does the surface of your body respond to being observed?

Your awareness settles before your face. Inhale and let the breath enter your nostrils. Follow it into the cavern at the top of your throat. As you exhale, your awareness travels down the tunnel of your throat, and you sink deeper into relaxation and safety.

Observe the walls of the tunnel, the echoing sounds, the texture and temperature. Is the climate hot, dry, humid, windy? On an exhalation let your breath fall into the core of your body, and down into your pelvic dan tian. Observe its surroundings.

Then explore the entire terrain of your inner body. What path do you take?

As you travel, observe the landforms. Perhaps you find hills of muscles, boulders of bones, forests of connective tissue, rivers of blood, or streams of energy. Do you discover caches of food, reservoirs of fluid, or caves of wind in the organs?

Traveling throughout your body, note any areas that seem to be inviting further attention: stuck areas, where the landscape is congested, wounded, out of balance. One site calls to you. It's asking for special attention. Leave a cairn to mark the site.

When you have traveled throughout your entire body, return to your dan tian. On the inhalation your awareness travels back up the tunnel of your throat into the cave behind your mouth. Exhale and return to outer awareness.

Now rub your palms together vigorously until they feel warm; then place them several inches above your body. Feel the aura of Qi exuding from your body. Feel its membrane, its skin. What temperatures, vibrations, or densities do you feel? Now move your palms over the site you marked. How does your aura's temperature, vibration, or density shift here?

Journaling and Art: Discovering the Inner Terrain

Now journal and draw your experience on a large piece of art paper. With words, lines, and colors, map the landscape of your body. Use charcoal pastels for dusty dry desert. Use oil pastels and oil bars for lush, humid caverns or tropical forests. Use charcoal for scorched earth or alpine summits. Use watercolors for mist or gentle rain. Use glitter or beads for the cairn.

Then look at the terrain you've created. Notice how the arrangement of words and the space around and within the words have their own energy. So does each line, curve, and dot. How do the colors, lines, and textures complement your words? How do you portray the aura of Qi exuding from your body with its colors, vibrations, densities? How do you draw the site in need of attention?

Guided Imagery: Exploring Deeper into the Inner Terrain

Steps

1   As above, enter your inner landscape.

2   Return to the place you marked.

3   Explore it in depth.

4   Retrace its history.

5   Listen to its story.

6   Return to the dan tian.

7   Exhale and return to outer awareness.

8   Scan the area and receive its messages.

Process

Lie in meditation. Close your eyes. Inhale and your awareness reenters your pharyngeal cavern and glides down your throat. Exhale and descend into your pelvic dan tian. From there journey back to the site in your body, the place of holding, congestion, pain, or imbalance.

Explore this site in depth. Notice the nuances of the immediate landscape. What is the climate? Are there sounds or movements?

What is the history of this site? Who and what have been here before? What struggles have occurred here? What caring has it known?

When you are done exploring this area, return to your pelvic dan tian. Inhale and ascend the tunnel of your throat. Exhale and return to outer awareness.

Again place your palms several inches above the area. Allow your breath to travel down your arms into your palms and feel how your palms begin to pulse. Notice how sensitive and alive they become. Observe how they listen for information. The site is communicating to you more deeply now. What messages well up? Feel. Listen. Receive.

Journaling and Art: Exploring Deeper into the Inner Terrain

Now, from your deeper exploration of the site in your body calling for attention, return to your drawing. Through words, colors, and shapes, bring the nuances of your discoveries to this drawing. You may add to it, cut it, rip it, or take away from it. You may use a new sheet of paper to layer over it, build on it, extend it, sculpt with it.

Then use your palms to scan the drawing. Feel its different textures, climates, sounds, vibrations. What do you learn through the hearts of your palms?

Guided Imagery: Healing the Inner Terrain

Steps

1   Enter the dan tian of your mind.

2   An image of healing appears.

3   Send it down through your body to the lower dan tian.

4   Then it travels out to the site in need of attention.

5   Experience the healing interaction.

6   Return awareness to the lower dan tian, inhale up your throat, exhale back to present.

7   Scan the area receiving healing and transmit cosmic Qi.

Process

Lie in meditation. Close your eyes. As you enter darkness, your breath becomes deep and relaxed, encouraging your body to surrender to rest. Allow your breath to travel to the area behind your third eye, the dan tian of the mind. Allow it to bring the word "healing" there. As your mind wraps around the word, an image of healing forms. It may be an abstract shape, a symbolic object, a color, a sensation, a sound. It may be the face of a guide. It may be the hands of Christ, the voice of Quan Yin, the breath of Pele. How does the power of healing shape itself in your mind at this moment?

Then send this healing image down from your third eye, down along the bridge of your tongue, down the tunnel of your throat, into the core of your body in your pelvic dan tian. From there it travels out to the site in need of attention. As the healing image enters that area, notice what it does there, how it interacts with the environment, how it performs its task of healing. Know that its power is your power, its intention is your intention, its blessings are your blessings.

When the healing feels complete for now, for healing is a process and may occur in stages, return to your pelvic dan tian. Inhale, and your breath ascends through your torso, up into your throat. Exhale and return to outer awareness.

Now place your palms several inches above the site. Notice how they care for this area. How does it feel now? How has its energy shifted? Is there anything else it wants? Your palms also transmit energy. It may take the form of vibration, temperature, sound, color, or light. Your palms are connected through the meridians of energy to your heart, which pulses with the rhythm of the Universe. The Universe is a huge field of energy. Allow yourself to transmit this healing energy from the Universe into the site. Feel how this gesture is like placing a soothing compress over the site, sealing in the caring cosmic Qi.

Journaling and Art: Healing the Inner Terrain

Now, with your drawing before you, close your eyes. Invite the healing image back into your mind and from there down into your body, down into your dan tian. From there, it travels out into your hands and onto your drawing. Through words and images, it performs its healing magic.

How do your hands apply healing to your drawing? Do they make a balm of herbs and art media? Do they surgically excise scar tissue from the flesh of your drawing? Do they use translucent patterned Japanese rice paper to layer veils of protective Qi?

When your artistic process feels complete, lie down and place your drawing over the site in your body that called for attention. Notice the messages it sends to your awareness now.

Your Body Totem

Process: Sculpting Your Body Totem

You have learned how to sculpt a plaster gauze face mold with a partner. Now you are ready to apply those techniques to a part of the body. Through discovering, exploring, and healing the inner terrain, you've become aware of what part of your body you want to have sculpted. Assume the best position for the sculpting to take place. Set yourself up with props and supports in a comfortable position for the sculpting session. Let the environment be set up for comfort, privacy, and stillness, so that you may use your casting session for meditation and intuitive work.

Show your partner the area you want sculpted. You can draw an outline on your body with body paint or charcoal or simply trust your partner's intuition.

Follow the same principles as for facial maskmaking, but have plenty of warmth available (blanket, space heater), as the plaster gauze takes plenty of heat out of the body as it dries. You may cover the part of your body for sculpting with plastic wrap or lather it with oil-based lotion and/or petroleum jelly, being sure to cover well any exposed body hair.

If you feel it is desirable and appropriate, ask your partner to use a few acupressure points, light massage, or healing energy work around the area to be sculpted, prior to making the cast (*see* "Practice: Acu-Massage for Maskmaking" on page 120). This helps to release stress, to promote relaxation, and also to prepare the body and the psyche for the sculpting of the body cast. For example, CV17 Dan Zhong calms the heart and relaxes your breath; CV22 Tian Tu supports the throat chakra; Lu1 Zhong Fu is a portal into the chest and also benefits the lungs, scapulae, and shoulders.

When you and your partner's intentions are aligned and you feel relaxed and ready, invite your partner to proceed with the plaster gauze casting. Just enjoy and receive this experience as a gentle massage. Enjoy the landscape of your body, how your skin vibrates, how your connective tissue moves like waves. Explore the ridges, valleys, and caves. Notice the images and sensations you experience while your body area is being sculpted.

After your partner has completed molding the body sculpture, she or he can tap on it to see if it's dry and hard enough for removal (it may take a half hour to one hour for the whole process, depending on how large a body piece you want sculpted and how warm and dry the atmosphere).

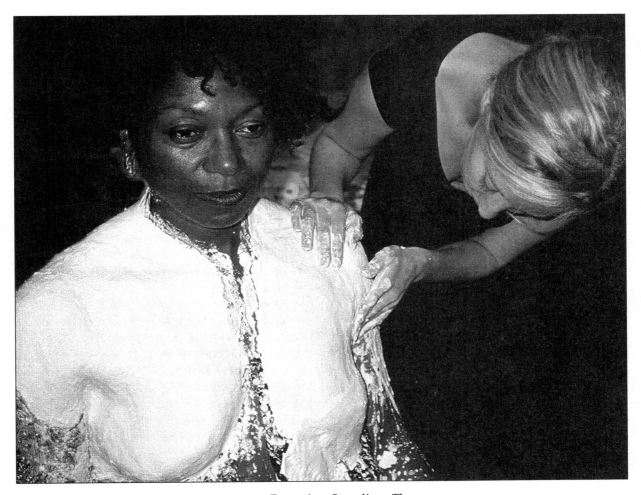

Emerging Guardian: Theresa

Once this mold is removed from your body, reinforce it with extra gauze and/or patching compound on the inside to strengthen it, especially around thin and narrow parts (joints, neck, groins), which may be especially vulnerable. Then, let it dry completely overnight (you can place it near a heater if you want). Sometimes, to give it company at night, we put a little night-light next to it.

You may want to live with your naked white totem for a while. You may want to touch it and feel where it is strong or vulnerable, guarded or transparent. You may want to sit and cradle it in your arms. You may want to use your palms to scan it energetically or to massage parts of it and see what additional information it offers you.

You could suspend it from your ceiling, sit it in a chair at your kitchen table, let it sleep next to you in bed, lay it by your altar. Place it where you can feel its presence and dialogue with it, where you can allow it to influence you, just as you will influence it when you begin painting and adorning.

Writing: Dialogue with the Cast of Your Totem

Sit with your journal before the cast of your body totem. Center yourself in meditation. Honor yourself and your totem with silence and focus.

Realize that your totem is a messenger from a part of your body, a part of your self. Then ask your totem the following questions and record its answers in your journal. These questions may prompt questions of your own. Allow your dialogue to evolve in its own way.

Ask your body totem:

· Who are you? What can I do to encourage you to share with me?

· What are your emotions?

· What needs healing? How have you experienced injury or stress? How have you experienced protection and strength?

· What would you like from me? How can I help you in your process toward healing and wholeness?

· Are there things I need to let go of or to create in my life to nurture our relationship?

· What creative process will support you in healing and growth? What art process would you like for me to apply to your freshly sculpted form? Would you like me to wash, cleanse, or fill you with colors, energies, sounds, textures, fragrances? Would you like me to write a letter or make a prayer bundle for you? Would you like an offering of forgiveness and loving kindness? Would you like me to wear you and empower you through the freedom of voice and dance?

· Would you like to go on a trip with me back to that place where the emotions first arose, to do ritual or healing? Would you like to go to the ocean, sit with me on the warm sand, and listen to the waves? Or would you like me to use the elements of metal, water, wood, fire, or earth in initiation, absolving, healing?

Art: Painting and Adorning the Cast of Your Body Totem

Your body totem cast is now dry. You can tell when it's ready to change from its naked white form, when it's ready for your creative dialogue of painting and decorating.

Gather your paints, tools, and whatever you might want to use as embellishments. Students use family photographs, love letters, personal mementos. One student incorporated his son's umbilical cord in the sculpture; another brought some of her beloved deceased dog's ashes and made a vessel for them from the body totem of her heart.

We recommend acrylic paints for their relatively low toxicity and their effectiveness when applied to the plaster gauze medium. You may want to add acrylic gel medium to the paints to create strata of colors revealing layers of depth and meaning. You may also use it in mixing additives, substances you have chosen for meaning and for texture (for example, dirt, ashes, herbs, glitter, joss paper, flower petals).

Before you begin this creative process, sit with your body totem cast in front of you. Set your intention for your relationship with your totem. How do you want to change together, to grow, to experience healing? You may notice images surfacing that symbolize this process.

When you are ready to begin painting, breathe gently and deeply into your pelvic dan tian and begin. Your body moving paint onto your body totem is your own intimate dance.

As you paint your body totem, ask it:

- What colors and textures do you invite to your skin? Would you like the red of fire, passion, birthing? Would you like the blue depths of the ocean? Would you like earth, sand, glitter, herbs?

- How would you like me to apply your skin of colors and textures? Massaging with my palms? Stroking with brush, bone, fur, twigs?

- How is our relationship changing through creativity?

Winged Guardian: Theresa

As you embellish your body totem, ask it:

- What do you want? Would you like me to cut or rip away layers? Would you like me to suture your parts together? Would you like me to open a portal and fill it with blessings?

- How do you want to be adorned? How would you like me to join the adornments to you? Should I use wire, yarn, raffia, glue, gut, hemp? Would you like me to weave, braid, cord, or tie special knots?

Writing: Your Personal Myth

Now your creative journey of sculpting, painting, and embellishing your body totem is coming to a close, at least for the time being, for your totem may always ask for creative transformation in the future. As you sit before it in meditation, ask it the following questions. Record its responses in your journal.

Ask your totem:

· Who are you? What's your name?

· What tribe are you from? What are your origins?

· What lessons do you have to share with me?

· What changes do I need to make in my life to facilitate our healing journey together?

· What voice or movement expresses your journey of transformation?

Unravel and create your personal myth. Through the gift of poetry or narrative, shape the lessons and insights of your dialogue. Give it voice through song or chant. Give it movement through dance.

Kaleo's Journal: Supporting the Healing Journey

What a beautiful experience! Elise and I just taught our four day long "Body Totem" class in the Arts and Consciousness Program at John F. Kennedy University.

Each day, through Qigong, guided imagery, and art, the students went deeper into a space of comfort, protection, and discovery. On the second day, after Elise's guided imagery, Kathy asked her partner to make a body cast of her throat, heart, belly, and thighs. She received the soothing massage of plaster gauze on her body.

The layer of gauze goes on like a protective membrane. Then it dries and contracts on the body into a hard shell. When it's peeled off, it takes with it old emotional debris ready to be discarded.

At home, during the following week, she laid her body totem next to her in bed at night and dialogued with it before falling asleep.

When our class gathered for the next meeting, she propped her body totem on an easel. They stared guardedly at each other. Quickly she invoked her power animal to accompany her on her journey. Snow leopard appeared, and she painted its hide of white with black spots on her totem's abdomen.

But then the struggle began. The beautiful pearlescent gold she layered on her totem somehow felt forced, constricted. It was not breathing.

I watched her. Kathy looked confused and frustrated. I asked her to lay her totem on the floor. As she stood hovering over it, it looked up at her quietly. It felt so vulnerable. Kathy began to weep, and the totem received her tears and prayer.

Then, we squatted down together right in front of her totem. She gasped! In the intimacy of this space, she could feel the Qi, the life force, radiating from the totem! She understood what it wanted and excitedly used hands and brushes to massage and spread paint. Her totem stirred. It began to pulse.

I left her immersed in her process and went to check on the other students. When I returned to Kathy, I asked her, "Why did you leave this area below the navel the raw white of the plaster? Why didn't you paint it?" Kathy whispered, "Sexual abuse." More of her tears rained onto her body totem.

Journey of Healing: Kathy

Then, a deep pthalo-crimson darkness began bleeding from her paintbrush and ran from the navel downward toward the pubis. She jabbed and stabbed with the brush. Gradually her strokes softened, and the crimson expanded into a cushion of soft ochre, forest green, and luminous gold. It was magical to see the triumph of her painting spreading into the smile on her face.

On the last day of class in our ritual of sharing, Kathy lay supine on the table. Lit candles encircled her. Her body totem fit snugly on her. Inhaling, she drew in blessings. Exhaling, she felt the totem sink deeper onto her body. Inhaling, she felt her skin press gently into the shimmering stars and indigo night sky she had painted on the inner lining of her totem. All of us in class surrounded her, and as she exhaled and surrendered, we lifted and removed the totem. Her hands folded together in *namaste*. We all shared in her prayer and awe.

Jeri's Protection: Yang and Open Wound; Yin

Jeri's Journal: The Art of Healing

My knees provided me with the ability to soar and dance. They were my wings, facilitating the movement from the inner toward the outer, expressing fluidity. Wounded in ungrounded movement, they now force me to remain grounded.

I am ready to soar again. The armor is needed to facilitate that soaring. It gives me strength and flexibility together in one structure. Being lined with fur, it comforts and holds my transition.

Your Secret Garden: Further Journeys into the Landscape of Your Body

As you contemplate your finished totem, allow it to serve as a companion for your explorations on the following three journeys into the realm of your secret garden. You may find parallels between the landscape of your body and the landscape of your secret garden. Some of the processes in the garden journeys are familiar from previous journeys; however, the terrain is new, and fresh wisdom may surface through exploration of this very personal inner sanctuary. Thanks to Pili for his guidance on journeys that first led us to explore the possibilities of the personal secret garden.

Guided Imagery: Your Secret Garden

Steps

1   Descend the path to the boundary and portal of your garden.

2   Offer the password and enter.

3   Explore the garden landscape.

4   Plan and build your shelter.

5   Invite a caretaker.

6   Return as you came.

7   Ask: Where is the garden within your body?

Process

Sit or lie in meditation. Allow your breath to deepen and lengthen, becoming soft and comforting. On the next inhalation, feel your breath gently entering your inner terrain. You find yourself walking along a comfortable path in nature. How does the path feel beneath your feet? Where are you? What kind of terrain invites you in further to explore? You wander to the top of a small hill and descend it. Each step invites your body to relax more fully as you descend deeper into your inner landscape.

At the bottom of the hill, you find yourself in front of your own secret garden. This garden has a boundary. What is it made of? Wooden fence, mud wall, thick trees, a ring of fire, a veil of mist? Search carefully and you will find the gateway, the entrance, into your garden. What is the password that you need to say in order to enter? Offer this password into the wind, and the portal to your inner garden opens.

You are now in the realm of your own secret garden. It feels so safe and lovely in this place. No one and no thing may enter without your invitation.

You find yourself walking on a path wending through your garden. What kinds of flowers, trees, shrubs, and herbs are growing? Their fragrances fill the air. Inhale them deeply; feel their textures on your skin. Listen. What sounds do you hear? Are they sounds from water, wind, other creatures?

As you move through the garden, how does the landscape change? Find a place that calls to you. You can feel its energy drawing you. Its attraction feels comfortable and welcoming. Observe this place carefully. What does it look like?

If you could imagine a shelter, any kind, just for you in this place, what would it be? A hogan? An art studio? A Taoist temple? A tree house? You have the ability to create whatever you wish your garden's shelter to be.

What do you need to build your shelter? Who do you invite to help you design the plans, assemble the materials, and erect the structure? Everything and everyone you need come together to help you. Then, once the structure is complete, how do you furnish this abode to make you feel comfortable and at home? Whenever you feel their work is done, you can dismiss your helpers.

You understand that there will be times that you are away from your garden. Invite an intimate friend, a caretaker, to tend your garden and shelter. This is a person or being from the spirit world whom you can truly trust with the well-being of your garden. Who comes? Is it one of your ancestors, inner guides, or healers? What is its name? What are its special skills or attributes?

You may have special instructions for your caretaker. You will have plenty of time during future visits to explore all the secrets of your garden. This is a place of deep inner awareness, which invites you to return.

Now get ready to leave your garden, trusting it to the capable and caring hands of the caretaker. Return to the portal, exit your garden, ascend the hill, and return along the path to outer awareness.

Before you arise from your place of meditation, ask yourself: Within your body, where is the secret garden located? Is the gate to your garden behind your sternum? Through the membrane of your diaphragm? Through the vortex of a spiraling chakra? Where have you built your shelter?

Then, when you're ready, emerge from your meditative state to everyday awareness.

Journaling and Art: Your Secret Garden

Write, draw, paint, or collage your garden onto paper or directly onto your body totem.

As you create, allow the participants, the parts, and the experiences of your garden to take shape through art.

How do you form the shelter? What is it made of? Who helps you build it?

How do you portray the caretaker? Who is it, this competent and trusted friend?

Guided Imagery: Tending the Needs of Your Garden

Steps

1 Scan your body where you found your secret garden.

2 Return to your garden and meet the caretaker.

3 Find an area in your garden in need of special attention and explore it.

4 With your caretaker, perform a ceremony of healing and apply healing remedies.

5 Receive the reminder of connectedness between the inner and outer worlds.

6 Return as you came.

7 Scan the place in your body that asked for healing: How has it shifted? What else does it want to continue the process of healing?

Process

Sit or lie in meditation. With your palms scan the part of your body where you found your secret garden and feel its energy. If, for example, you found your secret garden in the area of your solar plexus, place your palms over CV12 Zhong Wan. Feel the vibration of its energy. This rhythm guides you inward, downward, back to the gateway of your garden.

You find yourself standing before the portal, offering your password. The portal opens, and you enter. Notice the climate of your garden. Inhale the fragrances of plants and flowers, of earth and water, of shadows and light. Listen to the sounds of other creatures. Has anything shifted since your last visit?

The caretaker of your secret garden welcomes you. Together you wander through your garden and admire its beauty and wholesomeness. As you explore, you find a new area, one that you may have noticed but not ventured into before. As you enter into this uncharted territory, the environment shifts. This place has a different energy from the rest of your garden. Within it you discover an aspect that somehow is in need of attention. You find it easily, because its disharmony is obvious. Somehow the energy is out of balance. It may be very dark and murky. Wild and overgrown. Dry and parched and in need of water. Scorched by fire. Or flooded by water. How does imbalance manifest? What emotions surface in you as you observe this part that needs healing?

Ask your caretaker to assist you in restoring harmony to this spot. Together you perform a ceremony. How? Do you invoke the Great Spirit through prayer or incantations? Then what do you do? Use special tools? Till, purge, irrigate, rearrange?

When the work feels done for now, you clean and put your tools away. The caretaker gives you something to remind you of the connection between healing in this inner world and healing in the outer world. What do you receive?

Now get ready to leave your garden, trusting it to the caretaker. Return to the portal. As you exit your garden, feel how your garden has shifted. Ascend the hill and return along the path to outer awareness.

Stay in your state of meditation. Where in your body is the area that has been worked on? With the hearts of your palms, scan it. How does it feel after the ritual of healing? Ask it: What do you need to continue your healing? Is it something you can give to yourself: a massage of special salve; gentle touch of acupressure points; Qigong energy work; a daily prayer to the Great Spirit? Or is it something for which you need assistance: a therapeutic session of acupuncture, moxa, deep tissue massage?

Then, when you're ready, emerge from your meditative state to everyday awareness.

In Her Garden: Annalisa

FACES OF YOUR SOUL

Journaling and Art: Tending the Needs of Your Garden

On your body, locate the area that needs healing. With body paint, write, create symbols, or draw in this area its colors, shapes, and climate. Illustrate the feeling of disharmony in this area.

Then, write, draw, paint, or collage onto paper or directly onto your body totem the area of disharmony. Include the healing ceremony you and the caretaker performed. How do you use art to create it? Mix acrylic medium with herbs? Use layers of colors that mirror the healing changes? Cut away adhesions? Or add skin with acrylic medium and Japanese rice paper?

How can you continue this healing in outer life? What art processes do you apply to paper or to your body totem that embody the continuation of this energy of healing?

Guided Imagery: The Heart of Your Garden

Steps

1   Return to your secret garden.

2   Find the river and the small boat.

3   Ride the boat along the river of blood into your heart.

4   Enter the chamber of the heart.

5   Note the altar and objects of relationship.

6   Choose one object and receive its communication.

7   What change is it asking you to make?

8   Thank your heart and leave a gift.

9   Return to your garden and find the entrance.

10 Return to outer awareness.

11 Scan the area of your heart and receive its energetic messages.

Process

Sit or lie in meditation. It is time to return to your secret garden. Your breath guides you within and helps you descend into your core. You easily trace the way back to the gateway of your garden. Stand before the portal, offer your password, and see how it allows you to enter. Notice the climate of your garden. Inhale the fragrances. Listen to the sounds. Has anything shifted since your last visit?

Move through your garden on the path, inhaling and exhaling, each comfortable breath taking you deeper into your core. Notice how the environment changes as you go deeper. The changes themselves draw you deeper still, inviting you to explore. You come upon a smoothly flowing river. A small boat sits on its bank. The river invites you to enter. You climb in the boat, shove away from the bank, and paddle easily as the current draws you along. Notice that the color of the river is red. This is a river of blood wending its way into your heart.

The current draws you into a chamber of your heart. How magical it is to be here! What is the light within?

Notice the walls of the chamber. Reach out and touch them. Feel their texture, their temperature. Feel their vibration. Notice the beating and the pause between beats. Slip through the pause into the solitude of your heart.

And now, see a grotto within. Explore it. What is it made of? In the grotto stands an altar. It contains objects with special meaning for you. Each object represents a strong emotional relationship for you. Which one calls to you most urgently?

Pick it up. Examine it. Who or what wants to communicate with you? What does it say?

This object is an emissary of your heart. Do you understand its meaning? Go deeper still. Interrogate it. What does it mean? Ask it to show you, that you may better understand. It wants to reveal its truth to you, but it may have a different language. Does it speak to you through voice, written message, or intuition?

Somehow this communication is asking you to make a change. What is the change? Is it to empty out, to fill, to move forward? How? What are you being guided to do? Is it a change of habit? A change of awareness? A change of attitude toward yourself?

Ask this emissary for further guidance in making this change. Become it, transform yourself into this emissary, that you may understand its lessons firsthand. Or journey with it. Or observe it go through the metamorphosis it is inviting you to make, teaching you by its example.

Notice how your awareness has deepened through your journey. When you feel it is time, thank your heart for all that it has done for you, and leave a gift on the altar.

The beating of your heart is calling for your return. You enter the boat, and the current pushes you out of the heart and back to your secret garden. Walk through your garden to the entrance.

Now, allow your breath to carry you out and up, back to outer awareness.

Stay in your state of meditation. Now use the hearts of your palms over the center of your chest (CV17 Dan Zhong) to scan the area of your heart. You feel your heart's pulse within and receive its message. How does its energetic pulse feel as it radiates from your body into your palms?

Then, when you're ready, emerge from your meditative state to everyday awareness.

Journaling and Art: The Heart of Your Garden

Write, draw, paint, or collage onto paper or directly onto your body totem the river of blood to the heart and you traveling in it. As you explored the heart of your garden, what memories, images, emotions appeared? Did its sounds take you back to the pulsing of blood in your mother's womb? Did its fragrances transport you to your grandmother's kitchen in your childhood? What connections did you experience?

Make the altar in the grotto in the heart. Is it a wooded grove, a stone cave, a niche behind a waterfall?

Create the object of relationship on the altar. What do you use? Who or what does it represent? What does it communicate to you? How do you create the messages trying to come forward? How do you create the process of change? How is this creative process bringing you closer to understanding your truth and to living your truth?

When you are finished, step back and look. What shifts have occurred in your inner and outer being as a result of your garden journeys? How has your relationship to your body totem changed?

Now with your palms, scan your creation. Feel its aura. What colors, textures, shifts in temperature do you notice? Ask your creation: Is there anything more it would like? Anything that it wants added or taken away for greater integration on the path toward wholeness?

Into the Garden of the World

What teachings, journeys, transformative processes do you want to bring into the world? Where and in what context do you find yourself being drawn to share your most meaningful work?

Transforming Ego into Divine: Robert and Nancy of Eth-Noh-Tec

Robert and Nancy, the husband and wife team of Eth-Noh-Tec, based in San Francisco, travel throughout the United States sharing the wisdom, stories, art, and culture of their Asian heritage through performing arts.

Art: Yourself and the World

Make a mask or body totem of a part of yourself representing your relationship to the world.

What statement does your piece want to make? What audience does it want to address?

What part of your body do you choose? Your face? Hands? Heart? Spine?

With what movement, ritual, or healing energy work do you prepare your body, mind, and spirit for the process of creative expression?

What guided imagery do you choose to invoke images from the subconscious?

Do you involve journaling, collage, storytelling, or song to express the uniqueness of your muse?

What colors, textures, symbols, and embellishments do you use to shape your intention?

Then, when your process feels complete for now, ask your creation what it has to teach you about integration: of your creative process, your spiritual practice, and your relationship to the world.

Finally, realize that this creative art piece may be an evolving project. Like your life itself, it may be more of a process than a product, changing over time, along with your relationship to yourself, to your path, and to your world.

Nā mele o ka ʻāina aloha: Aunty Bea and Pili

Appendix A: Gallery

The following images and poems tell the story of some of the members of our inner tribe. We hope they all encourage you in your dialogue with your own inner sources through movement, meditation, and creativity.

To view more of Elise's poetry and Kaleo's masks and paintings in color, visit **kaleoching.com.**

Photographs by Lee Fatheree

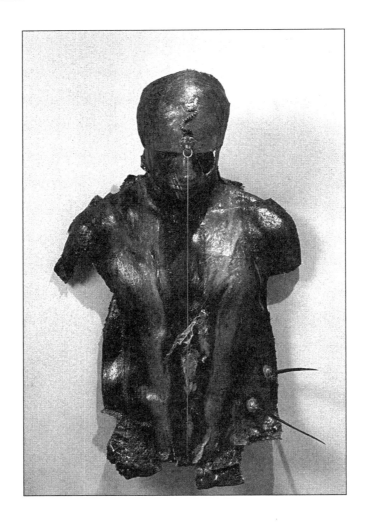

DAWN CLIMBER
Mixed media mask by Kaleo Ching
Poem by Elise Dirlam Ching

I leave the hunt among last night's embers
and reach like a child's awkward arrow for the morning.
I smell new life among night moistened leaves
and gray vapors juicing pine branches.
All that I have known now blends into this dawn
tracks, seasons, scars, longings
like seeds spitting life then falling back as hulls
barter for the midwife dirt.
I find that I am no center.
Only two legs and borrowed fur
with gift and luck of fire and spring fed water.
I am child of the blue sky that thickens into night.

I am lesser kin of moon sharing
moods, repetitive journeys, the need to hide and to be seen.
I sacrifice my rage against suffering
and bow to the spirits of the dawn.

EARTH PRAYER
Mixed media mask by Kaleo Ching
Poem by Elise Dirlam Ching

Such places
breath opening to a clear sky
wolf tracks in simple mud
sash of stars on black night
arrow of geese
notched against the string of blue
sweet flesh flung from the sea
a long moment
curled in fine white waves
on the edge of the world

May they last
a prayer and a pact
to feed the ancient elements
with kindness etched
into the membranes of our hearts

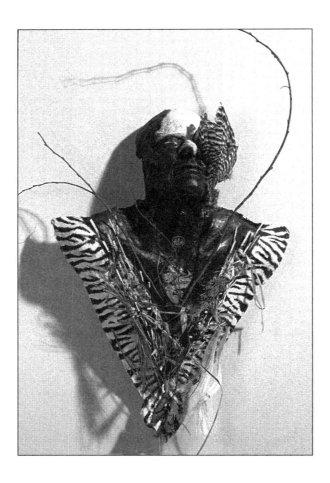

INITIATION
Mixed media mask by Kaleo Ching
Poem by Elise Dirlam Ching

You ride the back of night
into the low hum of moonless wonder
adorned in dreams for the dawn of your man-making.
You curl like a cub seeking a lost comfort
even bones pulsing with premonition.

Morning drinks the sky
licking away the silver studs of darkness.
Your eyes widened with night
narrow to the summons.
Unfed muscles beg for new power.
Wits gnash at fear crouching in crevices behind you.

Digging into a source
hidden from your humanness
but known to beasts guided by survival
you pull your name from doubt.
The Holy One is calling.

SURRENDER
Mixed media mask by Kaleo Ching
Poem by Elise Dirlam Ching

This long road:
neck arched as the heron's
to seek through moss on forest fingers
where silver throated owl makes song
and larvae of the spirit
work in silence to make a new world.
Oh, fertile darkness where misery sulks
a drunken shadow with no attachment
and moist earth trembles toward the light
that glows regardless of all suns.
All the while the heart full knowing
thumps its way to the pull of the polestar.

THE CRUCIBLE
Mixed media mask by Kaleo Ching
Poem by Elise Dirlam Ching

It has been your protection
fed you like a bowl
guided you like the full moon

But now, parts sundered like earth
her crevices and tunnels
groping for warm center

Open like fingers
broken fragments
a gift of softness

An open mouth whispering
up the shaft of your interior
ringing the walls of your throat

Exploding
in the clear cry
of a fearless voice

GHOST
Mixed media mask by Kaleo Ching
Poem by Elise Dirlam Ching

I awaken; he sits beside me
curling from my dreams onto the blanket.
I call him Ghost.
In arms of smoke he holds a thousand solitudes
and his eyes are misty openings
to the grimaces and ecstasies of a universe of souls.
He nibbles my ear savoring a moment the taste of flesh
along his formless tongue then whispers: Listen.
I am the wind who speaks through amber lips
the voice of autumn through the underwood.
You know what that means.
You hear the crackling.
The frost is on your lashes.
Your breath is my mirror.
Sing for your life!
Sing into the gaping sky.
Send your soul among the stars.
Hurry, while your eyes are bright
and your heart can still bend into the journey.

CHARON
Mixed media mask by Kaleo Ching
Poem by Elise Dirlam Ching

Oar churning swiftly
against black water
ferryman of souls
grief and fear
beating black wings
about your shoulders
face like marble
feet feeling the stern
bow pointing toward the light
oar dipping silently
into black water.

NOMAD
Mixed media mask by Kaleo Ching
Poem by Elise Dirlam Ching

Somewhere the flutter of a nova
sends a mourning for things
that blaze and die quickly
young heroes riding their vigor
like some bareback mustang
into the sputter of the sun

I have straddled a wild hope
then set my lips against the wind
felt cracking ice beneath my feet
lost sun and stars beneath the mountain
gave flesh to granite
and innocence to the path

At last, I arrive and I pray
at the rugged shrine of solitude

RAVEN
Mixed media mask by Kaleo Ching
Poem by Elise Dirlam Ching

We follow from the source to the river
to the mouth of the great water
the great water
whose sides heave to the sky's end
whose eyes blink on every wave like stars
whose body is deep as the night.
Who is friend or god in this mystery?

I know many:
hairless human
soul-eyed seal
otter child who never grows old
salmon with skin of silver suns
and caribou who move like ghosts
across the twilit tundra.

But Raven here prevails.
The Old Ones say
he first made a world of love and comfort
with no war nor death nor troubled heart
nor vermin nor leaking boat nor pestilence
then from boredom wrought mischief
our familiar and constant mate.

That same one wise as he is foolish
in kindness and treachery
accompanies the firm of heart.
He shows us prey to share the spoils
summons wind and storm
and sorts stars scattered on the night
like drops of mist on his obsidian wings.

Some call Raven a friend who is not true.
But what is truth among the wild?
Not promise nor loyalty nor certainty of reward
but a nudge
keeping our wits honed
as flint upon the arrow
to pierce sure the flesh for the sharing of souls.

Appendix B: Healing Herbs

The muse's garden is covered with herbs and spices. She is often inspired by their aromas, colors, textures, and healing abilities. Welcome their healing qualities into your drawings, paintings, masks, and sculptures.

Elise, Kaleo, and Teekkona in their herb garden

The following catalogue of herbs is intended to arouse your muse, not as instruction in herbal remedies. The functions of the herbs are intended for you to apply symbolically to your creative process. Descriptions of herbs are not comprehensive but highlight key actions.

Bathe or weave lavender into your canvas to comfort and calm and to treat its skin. Make a salve with comfrey, calendula, or *pa'akai* (Hawaiian sea salt) combined with acrylic gloss gel, and paint it onto the wounds of your art piece. Use aloe vera to heal the emotional as well as physical skin of your art. Put thyme or borage blossoms into your totem animal nest for courage in making changes in your life and leaving the nest. Use yarrow stems in your drawing of the ancestor for divination.

Western Herbs

Allspice
Relieves colic, flatulence, rheumatism.

Aloe Vera
Heals skin lesions, burns.

Anise
Relieves digestive problems, cramps, coughs by loosening phlegm. Since the Middle Ages nursing mothers have used it for lactation.

Astragalus
For diabetes, heart disease, hypertension. Enhances the immune system.

Black Cohosh
Traditional use for inducing menstruation, relieving menopausal symptoms, and facilitating labor and delivery.

Borage
From Celtic word for courage. Alleviates melancholy and soothes the heart. May tonify the adrenal glands.

Burdock
Excellent tonic for the lungs and the liver. Good blood purifier. For endurance and strength.

Calendula
Soothes and softens the skin. Antiseptic. Heals burns and wounds.

Chamomile
Soothes, reduces tension, helps insomnia, neuralgia, and skin problems. Relieves menstrual cramps. Calms the nerves and stomach.

Cinnamon
Antiseptic, astringent, stimulant. Relieves nausea, diarrhea. Clears the brain.

Clove
Antiseptic. Relieves toothache.

Comfrey
For irritated skin, eczema, burns, sores, aching joints. Helps mend broken bones.

Corn
"Giver of Life" for many Native Americans. Important in their art, religion, and ceremony.

Dandelion
Builds and strengthens the blood. Combats anemia. Very good for liver diseases.

Eucalyptus
Cleanses the lungs and lymph system.

Fenugreek
Good expectorant for coughs and colds. Relieves sore throat, skin irritations, diabetes (lowers blood sugar).

Flax
Laxative. Used as poultice for boils and inflammations. Helps pulmonary infections.

Garlic
Antibiotic. Helps prevent heart disease and cancer. Treats tuberculosis, dysentery, typhoid. Lowers blood pressure.

Ginger
For colds, coughs, sore throats, flu, digestive problems. Has heating and drying properties. Applied topically, stimulates circulation. A bath in ginger water soothes.

Hops
For flavoring and preserving (beer). Aids digestion. Stimulates the appetite.

Horehound
Ancient remedy for coughs and sore throats. Diaphoretic (breaks fever).

Kelp
Natural source of iodine. Good for pituitary and adrenal glands.

Lavender
For nervous tension and depression. Uplifting, purifying, soothing qualities. Good on insect bites. For indigestion and headaches.

Lemon Grass
Antiseptic. Revitalizing properties. For circulation, digestion, acne, oily skin.

Mint
Cool, stimulating, refreshing, clean, uplifting scent and taste. Also good for indigestion, flatulence, colds, flus. Name comes from Minthe, a nymph changed by Persephone into a plant to protect her from Hades, the god of the underworld.

Mugwort
Used as tea for nervous disorders. For moxibustion in Traditional Chinese Medicine.

Mullein
Its flowers and leaves relieve respiratory congestion and ear infections. The seeds contain poison and should never be used. Mullein protected Ulysses against the enchantress Circe. In India, mullein protects against evil spirits.

Mustard Seed
Strong preservative. Used as poultice to draw blood to lungs or arthritic, rheumatoid areas. Induces vomiting.

Nettle

Rich in iron, a traditional treatment for anemia. Relieves hay fever, inflammation from allergies. Clears chest and nasal congestion. Increases the milk supply in lactating women. Used for vaginal infections (yeast) and to control excessive menstrual flow.

Oregano

Name comes from Greek and means "Joy of the Mountains." Attracts bees and butterflies. For colds, headaches, coughs, irritability, exhaustion, menstrual pains.

Pa'akai (Hawaiian Sea Salt)

Cleanses and draws out infections. Colon cleanser. Preservative.

Pepper

Contains vitamin C and magnesium. Stimulates blood circulation. Aids digestion.

Peppermint

For indigestion, heartburn, gas, nausea, vomiting. Stimulates the gastric lining. Good for the nervous system.

Rose

Cleanses the blood, tones capillaries. Aids circulation (add to massage oil). Connected to the heart, as a symbol of love.

Rosemary

For memory and fidelity (sometimes found at either weddings or funerals). Dried stems stripped of the leaves can be used as smudging sticks for cleansing.

Sage

Estrogenic (for menstrual irregularities and to relieve symptoms of menopause). Aids digestion. Relieves colds. Tonifies the nervous system.

Sesame

Relieves constipation, hemorrhoids, and genito-urinary infections.

Senna

Laxative. Reduces fever. Eases sore throat.

Thyme

From *thymon* (Greek for courage). Used for courage, bravery, and vigor. Thymol oil extract is used as an antiseptic, for preserving biological specimens, and in embalming.

Yarrow

Botanical name *Achillea millefolium* from association with Achilles at the battle of Troy, who used yarrow to stop the flow of blood and heal warriors. The stems were used by the Chinese for throwing the I Ching and by the Celts for divination.

Chinese Herbs

Bai He (Lily Flower)
Clears heat and moistens the lungs (coughs, sore throat). Calms the spirit.

Bai Mu Er (Wood Ear, Black Fungus)
Nourishes the lungs and stomach. Moistens the lungs.

Bai Shao (Peony)
Nourishes blood and regulates menses. Nourishes and regulates the liver.

Bei Qi (Astragalus)
Major Qi tonic. Benefits lungs and spleen. Tonifies Qi and blood. Strengthens and stabilizes Wei Qi (guardian Qi). Stabilizes the exterior.

Bei Sha Shen (Sand Root, Ginseng for lungs)
Benefits lungs (moistens lungs, stops coughs). Nourishes stomach, clears heat, produces fluids. Relieves fever and constipation.

Dang Gui (Chinese Angelica Root)
Benefits heart, liver, spleen. Moistens intestines and frees the bowels. Tonifies, invigorates, and moves blood. Regulates menses. Disperses cold.

Dang Shen (Codonopsis)
Poor man's ginseng. Tonifies spleen (fatigue, diarrhea). Tonifies lungs (chronic cough from spleen Qi deficiency).

Deng Xin Cao (Juncus)
Clears heat out of the heart, small intestine channels. For insomnia and restless sleep.

Du Zhong (Eucommia Bark)
Tonifies liver, kidneys. Strengthens and nurtures bones, sinews, cartilage (weak, painful lower back, knees).

Fu Ling (China Root)
Benefits heart, spleen, lungs. Clears excess moisture; diuretic (difficult urination); for digestive and stomach problems (dampness, edema, diarrhea). Strengthens the spleen, harmonizes middle jiao (burner), transforms and transports fluids.

Gou Gi Zi (Wolfberry)
Nourishes and tonifies liver and kidneys (deficiency, impotence, back pain). Nourishes Essence and eyes.

Gou Ji (Dog Spine)
Tonifies the liver and kidneys. Strengthens sinews, bones, spine, lower back, and extremities.

Gu Zhi (Cinnamon Twig)

Regulates nutritive and protective Qi. Brings warmth and disperses cold. Helps to move Yang Qi in chest. Improves blood circulation.

Hai Long (Pipe Fish)

Tonifies kidneys (yin and yang). For debility in the elderly and impotence. Disperses stagnant blood.

Hai Ma (Sea Horse)

Benefits kidneys, liver. Tonifies kidneys (impotence, incontinence). Invigorates blood.

Hong Hua (Safflower)

Invigorates and moves blood (pain in chest or abdomen from blood stasis).

Hong Zao (Chinese Date)

Tonifies spleen (loose stools, spleen Qi deficiency, shortness of breath). Nourishes the blood (paleness, anemia) and calms the spirit (anxiety).

Ji Xue Teng (Chicken Blood Bark)

Benefits heart, liver, spleen. Tonifies and moves blood. Alleviates weakness in extremities in elderly, vertigo, irregular menstruation, dysmenorrhea.

Kelp

Benefits kidney, liver, lung, stomach. Clears heat. Helps reduce edema and urination.

Ou Jie (Lotus Root)

Stops bleeding. Clears heat in lungs and stomach.

Sheng Jiang (Ginger Root)

Benefits middle jiao (aids digestion, brings warmth, disperses cold, relieves nausea and vomiting). Regulates nutritive and protective Qi.

Star Anise

Benefits spleen, stomach, lungs. Warms, promotes digestion, appetite. Alleviates coughs, bronchitis.

Tu Fu Ling (Smilax)

Clears damp heat. Used for joint pain, hot skin lesions, painful urination.

Xuan Shen (Scrophularia)

Benefits kidneys, lungs, stomach. Reduces fevers, clears heat, nourishes yin (sore throat, constipation, swollen red eyes).

Zhu Ru (Bamboo Shavings)

Benefits gall bladder, lungs, stomach. Clears heat, congestion (phlegm-heat) in lungs.

Zhu Ye (Bamboo Leaf)

Benefits heart, small intestine, stomach. Clears heat (mouth sores, painful gums). Relieves irritability.

Glossary

The following definitions are not comprehensive but illuminate usage in this book.

'a'ā (Hawaiian)
> crusty, chunky lava

ahi (Hawaiian)
> fire, flame

acrylic medium
> in art, fast-drying clear, transparent to translucent substance that acts as glue, or when tinted, as the base for paint

Aesculapius (Greek)
> tutored by Chiron; became a gifted physician

'āina (Hawaiian)
> land, earth

akua (Hawaiian)
> spirit, god, supernatural being

aloha (Hawaiian)
> in the presence of divine breath, to share breath, compassion, love, kindness, mercy

amulet
> protective charm

ancestor
> in this book, one's predecessor genetically, ethnically, geographically, or spiritually

ānuenue (Hawaiian)
> rainbow

ao (Hawaiian)
> light, day, dawn, the world of daily experience; enlightened

archetype

primordial, recurrent symbol or image

'aumakua (Hawaiian)

ancestral guardian spirit; may assume the shape of certain animals

aura

energy generated by and enveloping the body of a person, being, or object

body totem

a ritualistic artistic creation formed by molding, painting, and decorating a plaster gauze sculpture of a part of one's body

centaur (Greek)

half-man, half-horse, usually savage creatures

chakra (Sanskrit)

one of (usually) seven wheels of energy or spiritual power in the human body, located at: base of the spine, lower abdomen, solar plexus, heart area, throat, third eye, and crown

Chiron (Greek)

a wise, respected, and immortal centaur gifted in healing and martial arts and mentor to many

craniosacral therapy

gentle form of bodywork focusing on the sacrum, spine, and skull and their movements and attunement to the cranio-rhythmic impulse

dan tian (Chinese)

"field of elixir"; reservoir of Qi; may refer to one of three dan tians: upper (mind/ head), middle (heart/chest), lower (body/lower abdomen); when not specified, refers to the lower dan tian, just below and inside the body from the navel

DNA

deoxyribonucleic acid, blueprint of genetic information

ethereal thread

energetic current passing through the axis of the body and connecting it to the energy of heaven and of earth

five elements

in Traditional Chinese Medicine, metal, water, wood, fire, and earth, the five alchemical influences on the body's organs, meridians, systems, and processes

guided imagery

a technique combining principles of hypnotherapy and shamanic journeying to access wisdom, images, and messages from subconscious and meta-conscious realms

hā (Hawaiian)
  breath, to breathe

hō'ailona (Hawaiian)
  omen, sign from the heavens

ho'omākaukau (Hawaiian)
  command: get ready!

kāhea (Hawaiian)
  invocation, summons

kai (Hawaiian)
  ocean, sea, seawater

Kali (Sanskrit)
  Hindu goddess and wife of Shiva; represents the destructive feminine aspect of Divinity

Kamapua'a (Hawaiian)
  a pig-man *kupua,* at one time Pele's lover

Kanaka Maoli (Hawaiian)
  Native Hawaiian; a person of Polynesian descent, having one or more ancestors who lived in the Hawaiian Archipelago before the arrival of Captain James Cook in 1778

Ke Akua (Hawaiian)
  God, Divinity, Universal Spirit

kōkua (Hawaiian)
  help, assistance

kumu (Hawaiian)
  teacher, source

kupua (Hawaiian)
  protean entity that can assume the form of man or beast

kupuna (Hawaiian)
  grandparent, ancestor, elder

la'a kea (Hawaiian)
  sacred light

lomilomi (Hawaiian)
  deep kneading massage, infused with the power of nature, *pule,* and *aloha,* that affects physical, emotional, and spiritual levels of the recipient's being

lotus posture (Sanskrit: *Padmasana*)
in yoga, an erect sitting meditation position in which the dorsum of each foot is placed in the hip crease of the opposite thigh

Macrocosmic Orbit
in Qigong the "large circulation" of energy; follows the path of the Microcosmic Orbit and includes paths along the legs and arms

***mahalo* (Hawaiian)**
expression of gratitude

***makani* (Hawaiian)**
wind, breeze

***mālama* (Hawaiian)**
to care for, preserve, protect

***mālamalama* (Hawaiian)**
reduplication of *mālama;* shining, radiant, clear; enlightenment

***mana* (Hawaiian)**
spiritual power

medulla oblongata
the lowest part of the brain where it connects with the spinal cord

***mele* (Hawaiian)**
song, chant

meridians
in Traditional Chinese Medicine, rivers of energy that travel in the body; acu-points are accessed where meridians flow near the skin

Microcosmic Orbit
in Qigong the "small circulation" of energy, following the path along the midline of the body, starting at the dan tian and traveling down the front of the torso, up the back of the torso and head, and back down the front to return to the dan tian

Nāmakaokahaʻi (Hawaiian)
goddess of the sea; Pele's sister

***namaste* (Sanskrit)**
greeting and gesture meaning, "the sacred in me bows to the sacred in you"

occiput
base of the back of the skull

***ʻohana* (Hawaiian)**
family, relative, clan, a community of individuals who care for and support each other

ola (Hawaiian)
life, health

oracle
medium of divine response to inquiry

pāhoehoe (Hawaiian)
smooth, ropy, undulating lava

Pele (Hawaiian)
goddess of the volcano

perineum
center of the body at the base of the torso between the anus and genitals

pī kai (Hawaiian)
to purify by sprinkling seawater or salted fresh water

piko (Hawaiian)
navel, umbilical cord, energy center

pō (Hawaiian)
night, darkness, the realm of the gods and the mysterious

pōhaku (Hawaiian)
rock, stone

Prometheus (Greek)
immortal who brought fire to mortals; Zeus punished him by having him chained to a peak where an eagle repeatedly ripped out his liver

pule (Hawaiian)
prayer

Qi (Chinese)
bioelectric current of energy, vital life force

Qigong (Chinese)
"energy work" affecting the physical, emotional, spiritual, and energetic bodies; a healing arts practice for cultivating, directing, storing, and transmitting Qi

Quan Yin (Chinese)
goddess of compassion

Sagittarius (Greek)
zodiacal embodiment of Chiron

savasana (Sanskrit)
corpse pose; supine lying meditation posture

spirit guide

in general, any helper from the spirit world; or more specifically, one's primary helper from the spirit world, who manifests one's deepest resources of inner wisdom and compassion; although its form may change over time, its essence remains constant

Taiji (Chinese)

internal martial art form that cultivates and directs the flow of Qi

talisman

an amulet engraved with sacred words or symbols

totem animal

also animal ally or power animal; embodies the power of the whole animal species; acts as a personal helper and guide and embodies qualities important to the individual with whom it connects

wai (Hawaiian)

fresh water; any liquid other than seawater

yang (Chinese)

one of the pair of opposing, complementary, and interdependent opposites; yang qualities are active, masculine, light, aggressive, hollow, positive, solar, rising, expanding, etc.

yin (Chinese)

the other of the pair of opposing, complementary, and interdependent opposites; yin qualities are still, feminine, dark, surrendering, solid, negative, lunar, descending, contracting, etc.

Zeus (Greek)

the supreme immortal

Zhan Zhuang (Chinese)

to stand like a staff or a stake, as in Qigong standing meditation

Selected Bibliography

Art/Maskmaking

Audette, Anna Held. *The Blank Canvas: Inviting the Muse*. Boston: Shambala Publications, Inc., 1993.

Barbier, Jean Paul, and Newton, Douglas. *Islands and Ancestors: Indigenous Styles of Southeast Asia*. New York: Metropolitan Museum of Art, 1988.

Bellingham, David. *Celtic Mythology: An Introduction*. Secaucus, NJ: Chartwell Books, Inc., 1990.

Boston, John. *Ikenga*. London: Ethnographica Limited, 1977.

Bremness, Lesley. *The Complete Book of Herbs*. New York: Viking Studio Books, 1988.

Burland, C., and Forman, W. *The Aztecs: Gods and Fate in Ancient Mexico*. London: Orbis Publishing, 1975.

Castleton, Kenneth B., MD. *Petroglyphs and Pictographs of Utah*. Salt Lake City: Utah Museum of Natural History, 1987.

Cox, J. Halley, with Davenport, William H. *Hawaiian Sculpture*. Honolulu: University of Hawai'i Press, 1988.

Edinger, Edward. *Anatomy of the Psyche*. La Salle, IL: Open Court, 1985.

Feller, Ron and Marsha. *Fanciful Faces and Handbound Books: Fairy Tales*. Seattle: The Arts Factory, 1989.

Feller, Ron and Marsha. *Paper Masks and Puppets for Stories, Songs, and Plays*. Seattle: The Arts Factory, 1985.

Fellman, Sandi. *The Japanese Tattoo*. New York: Abbeville Press, 1986.

Holm, Bill. *Spirit and Ancestor: A Century of Northwest Coast Indian Art at the Burke Museum*. Seattle: University of Washington Press, 1987.

Jonaitis, Aldona. *From the Land of the Totem Poles: The Northwest Coast Indian Art Collection at the American Museum of Natural History*. Seattle: University of Washington Press, 1988.

Kaeppler, Adrienne L. *Artificial Curiosities*. Honolulu: Bishop Museum Press, 1978.

Kirk, Malcolm. *Man as Art*. Berlin: Taco Verlagsgesellschaft, 1987.

Lincoln, Louise. *Assemblage of Spirits: Idea and Image in New Ireland*. New York: George Braziller, Inc., 1987.

Lommel, Andreas. *Masks: Their Meaning and Function*. New York: McGraw-Hill, 1972.

Martineau, LaVan. *When the Rocks Begin to Speak*. Las Vegas, NV: KC Publications, 1973.

Meyer, Laure. *Black Africa: Masks, Sculpture, Jewelry*. Paris: Editions Pierre Terrail, 1992.

Mindell, Earl. *Earl Mindell's Herb Bible*. New York: Simon and Schuster, 1992.

Penney, David W. *Art of the American Indian Frontier*. Seattle: University of Washington Press, 1992.

Segy, Ladislas. *Masks of Black Africa*. New York: Dover Publications, 1976.

Slattum, Judy. *Masks of Bali: Spirits of an Ancient Drama*. San Francisco: Chronicle Books, 1992.

Sivin, Carol. *Maskmaking*. Worcester, MA: Davis Publications, Inc., 1986.

Teuten, Timothy. *A Collector's Guide to Masks*. Secaucus, NJ: Wellfleet Books, 1990.

Tilford, Gregory L. *Edible and Medicinal Plants of the West*. Missoula, MT: Mountain Press, 1997.

Weiss, Gaea and Shandor. *Growing and Using the Healing Herbs*. New York: Wings Books, 1992.

Writing/Guided Imagery

Andrews, Ted. *Animal Speak: The Spiritual and Magical Powers of Creatures Great and Small*. St. Paul, MN: Llewellyn Publications, 1995.

Boyne, Gil. *Transforming Therapy: A New Approach to Hypnotherapy*. Glendale, CA: Westwood Publishing Co., Inc., 1989.

Brown, Joseph Epes. *Animals of the Soul*. Rockport, MA: Element, Inc., 1992.

Bugeja, Michael J. *The Art and Craft of Poetry*. Cincinnati, OH: Writer's Digest Books, 1994.

Churchill, Randal. *Become the Dream: The Transforming Power of Hypnotic Dreamwork*. Santa Rosa, CA: Transforming Press, 1997.

Churchill, Randal. *Regression Hypnotherapy: Transcripts of Transformation, Volume I*. Santa Rosa, CA: Transforming Press, 2002.

Cirlot, J. E. *A Dictionary of Symbols*. New York: Philosophical Library, 1971.

Cooper, J. C. *Symbolic and Mythological Animals*. London: The Aquarian Press, 1992.

de Mello, Anthony. *Wellsprings: A Book of Spiritual Exercises*. New York: Doubleday & Co., 1986.

Fox, Matthew. *Original Blessing*. Santa Fe, NM: Bear and Company, 1983.

Fox, Matthew. *The Reinvention of Work*. San Francisco: HarperCollins, 1994.

Fox, Matthew, and Sheldrake, Rupert. *The Physics of Angels: Exploring the Realm Where Science and Spirit Meet*. San Francisco: HarperSanFrancisco, 1996.

Goldberg, Natalie. *Long Quiet Highway*. New York: Bantam Books, 1993.

Goldberg, Natalie. *Wild Mind*. New York: Bantam Books, 1990.

Goldberg, Natalie. *Writing Down the Bones*. Boston: Shambala, 1986.

Hammond, D. Corydon, Ph.D., editor. *Handbook of Hypnotic Suggestions and Metaphors*. New York: W. W. Norton & Company, Inc., 1990.

Harner, Michael. *The Way of the Shaman: A Guide to Power and Healing*. New York: Bantam Books, 1980.

Hausman, Gerald. *Turtle Island Alphabet*. New York: St. Martin's Press, 1992.

Hunter, Marlene E. *Creative Scripts for Hypnotherapy*. New York: Brunner-Routledge, 1994.

Kowit, Steve. *In the Palm of Your Hand*. Gardiner, ME: Tilbury House, 1995.

Levine, Stephen. *Healing into Life and Death*. Garden City, NY: Anchor Press/Doubleday, 1987.

Lozoff, Bo. *It's a Meaningful Life*. New York: Penguin Putnam Inc., 2000.

McGill, Ormond. *Seeing the Unseen: A Past Life Revealed Through Hypnotic Regression*. Williston, VT: Crown House Publishing Limited, 1997.

Metzger, Deena. *Writing for Your Life: A Guide and Companion to the Inner Worlds.* San Francisco: HarperCollins, 1992.

Nelson, Richard. *The Island Within.* San Francisco: North Point Press, 1989.

Nelson, Richard. *Make Prayers to the Raven.* Chicago: University of Chicago Press, 1983.

Oliver, Mary. *A Poetry Handbook.* San Diego, CA: Harcourt Brace and Company, 1994.

Packard, William. *The Art of Poetry Writing.* New York: St. Martin's Press, 1992.

Pukui, Mary Kawena, and Elbert, Samuel H. *Hawaiian Dictionary.* Honolulu: University of Hawai'i Press, 1986.

Rainer, Tristine. *The New Diary.* Los Angeles: Jeremy P. Tarcher, Inc., 1978.

The Random House Dictionary of the English Language. New York: Random House, 1987.

Rezendes, Paul. *Tracking and the Art of Seeing: How to Read Animal Tracks and Sign.* Charlotte, VT: Camden House Publishing, Inc., 1992.

Acupressure/Traditional Chinese Medicine

Beinfeld, Harriet, and Korngold, Efrem. *Between Heaven and Earth: A Guide to Chinese Medicine.* New York: The Ballentine Publishing Group, 1991.

Calais-Germain, Blandine. *Anatomy of Movement.* Seattle: Eastland Press, 1993.

Carter, Joseph J. *Touching Spirit.* Berkeley, CA: self-published, 2000.

Ellis, Andrew, Wiseman, Nigel, and Boss, Ken. *Fundamentals of Chinese Acupuncture.* Brookline, MA: Paradigm Publications, 1991.

Ellis, Andrew, Wiseman, Nigel, and Boss, Ken. *Grasping the Wind.* Brookline, MA: Paradigm Publications, 1989.

Gach, Michael Reed. *Acupressure's Potent Points: A Guide to Self-Care for Common Ailments.* New York: Bantam Books, 1990.

Gach, Michael Reed. *Basic Acupressure: The Extraordinary Channels and Points.* Berkeley, CA: Acupressure Institute, 1995.

Gach, Michael Reed. *Intermediate and Advanced Acupressure Course Booklet.* Berkeley, CA: Acupressure Institute, 1984.

Gach, Michael Reed, with Marco, Carolyn. *Acu-Yoga.* New York: Japan Publications, Inc., 1981.

Kaptchuk, Ted J. *The Web That Has No Weaver.* New York: Congdon and Weed, 1983.

Larre, Claude, and Rochat de la Vallee, Elisabeth; transcribed and edited by Hill, Sarah. *The Eight Extraordinary Meridians.* Cambridge, England: Monkey Press, 1997.

Larre, Claude, and Rochat de la Vallee, Elisabeth; translated by Stang, Sarah. *Rooted in Spirit.* Barrytown, NY: Station Hill Press, 1995.

Larre, Claude, Rochat de la Vallee, Elisabeth, Schatz, Jean; translated by Stang, Sarah. *Survey of Traditional Chinese Medicine.* Columbia, MD: Traditional Acupuncture Institute, 1986.

Maciocia, Giovani. *The Foundations of Chinese Medicine.* Edinburgh: Churchill Livingstone, 1989.

Maciocia, Giovani. *The Practice of Chinese Medicine.* Edinburgh: Churchill Livingstone, 1994.

Mariel, Elaine N. *Essentials of Human Anatomy and Physiology, 5th ed.* Menlo Park, CA: Benjamin/Cummings Publishing Company, Inc., 1997.

Marin, Gilles. *Healing from Within with Chi Nei Tsang: Applied Chi Kung in Internal Organs Treatment.* Berkeley, CA: North Atlantic Books, 1999.

Mole, Peter. *Acupuncture: Energy Balancing for Body, Mind and Spirit.* Rockport, MA: Element Books, Inc., 1992.

Palmer, Martin, O'Brien, Joanne, and Ho, Kwok Man. *The Fortune Teller's I Ching.* New York: Ballantine Books, 1986.

Reid, Daniel. *The Complete Book of Chinese Health and Healing.* Boston: Shambala Publications, Inc., 1994.

Teegarden, Iona Marsaa. *Acupressure Way of Health: Jin Shin Do.* New York: Japan Publications, Inc., 1978.

Tobias, Maxine, and Sullivan, John Patrick. *Complete Stretching.* New York: Alfred A. Knopf, 1994.

Veith, Ilza, translation and introduction. *The Yellow Emperor's Classic of Internal Medicine.* Berkeley, CA: University of California Press, 1966.

Worsley, J. R. *Traditional Chinese Acupuncture, Vol. One: Meridians and Points, 2nd ed.* Rockport, MA: Element Books, Inc., 1993.

Ziyin, Shen, and Zelin, Chen. *The Basis of Traditional Chinese Medicine.* Boston: Shambala Publications, Inc., 1996.

About the Authors

Charlie Lucke

ELISE DIRLAM CHING, RN; M.A. Transpersonal Psychology; M.A. English; CAMT (Certified Acupressure Massage Therapist); CHT (Certified Hypnotherapist); Qigong teacher.

Elise is a published and award-winning poet. She is a Registered Nurse at the San Francisco County Jail.

KALEO CHING, M.A. Art; Certified Lithographer, Tamarind Institute; CAMT (Certified Acupressure Massage Therapist); CHT (Certified Hypnotherapist); Qigong teacher.

Kaleo is an exhibiting and award-winning artist. He teaches bodywork and Qigong classes at the Acupressure Institute in Berkeley, as well as elsewhere in the Bay Area. His private bodywork practice includes acupressure, Hawaiian *lomilomi* massage, Chi Nei Tsang, and hypnotherapy.

Elise and Kaleo's creative collaboration began seventeen years ago with poetry and maskmaking. Now through teaching they share with others this shamanic journey of self-discovery through the macrocosmic and microcosmic, the outer and inner, the upper and lower worlds. Their process of Qigong, guided imagery, art, and maskmaking engages the body/mind/spirit in a tactile, emotional, and ritual experience, involving Qi fields, internal alchemy, creative self-expression, the subconscious mind, and awareness of spirit. Presently they co-teach Spirit Guide, Totem Animal, Ancestor, Faces of Your Soul (maskmaking), and Qigong classes and workshops in the San Francisco Bay Area and beyond.

Their extensive teaching experience includes the Arts and Consciousness Program at John F. Kennedy University (since 1991), California Institute of Integral Studies, Desarrollo Transpersonal Instituto Universitario A.C. (Puebla, Mexico), Haight Ashbury Free Clinic's Jail Psychiatric Services, Idyllwild School of Music and the Arts, Institute of Transpersonal Psychology, Naropa University-Oakland, New College of California, San Francisco State University, University of Creation Spirituality, and various national and international conferences, workshops, and retreats.

Visit **kaleoching.com** for calendar of classes and gallery of masks with poetry.